THE BEST OF **Woodworker's Journal**

Workshop Projects

Fixtures & Tools for a Successful Shop

THE BEST OF **W**OODWORKER'S **J**OURNAL

Workshop Projects

Fixtures & Tools for a Successful Shop

from the editors of *Woodworker's Journal*

Fox Chapel Publishing

1970 Broad Street • East Petersburg, PA 17520

www.FoxChapelPublishing.com

Workshop Projects: Fixtures & Tools for a Successful Shop is a compilation first published in 2007 by Fox Chapel Publishing Company, Inc. The patterns contained herein are copyrighted by *Woodworker's Journal*.

Our friends at Rockler Woodworking and Hardware supplied us with most of the hardware used in this book. Visit *rockler.com*. For subscription information to *Woodworker's Journal* magazine, call toll-free 1-800-765-4119 or visit *www.woodworkersjournal.com*.

Fox Chapel Publishing Company, Inc.

President: Alan Giagnocavo
Publisher: J. McCrary
Acquisition Editor: Peg Couch
Editor: Gretchen Bacon
Associate Editor: Patty Sinnott
Series Editor: John Kelsey
Creative Direction: Troy Thorne
Cover Design: Lindsay Hess

Woodworker's Journal

Publisher: Ann Rockler Jackson
Editor-in-Chief: Larry N. Stoiaken
Editor: Rob Johnstone
Art Director: Jeff Jacobson
Senior Editor: Joanna Werch Takes
Field Editor: Chris Marshall
Illustrators: Jeff Jacobson, John Kelliher

ISBN 978-1-56523-345-4

Publisher's Cataloging-in-Publication Data

Workshop projects : fixtures & tools for a successful shop / from the editors of Woodworker's journal. -- East Petersburg, PA : Fox Chapel Publishing, c2007.

    p. ; cm.

    (The best of Woodworker's journal)

    ISBN: 978-1-56523-345-4

    1. Workshops. 2. Workshops--Equipment and supplies.
3. Workbenches. 4. Woodwork. I. Woodworker's journal.

TT152 .W67 2007
684/.08--dc22   0710

To learn more about the other great books from Fox Chapel Publishing, or to find a retailer near you, call toll-free 1-800-457-9112 or visit us at *www.FoxChapelPublishing.com*.

Printed in China
10 9 8 7 6 5 4 3 2 1

Note to Authors: We are always looking for talented authors to write new books in our area of woodworking, design, and related crafts. Please send a brief letter describing your idea to Peg Couch, Acquisition Editor, Fox Chapel Publishing, 1970 Broad Street, East Petersburg, PA 17520.

Introduction

The best shops I've seen are filled with more things built than bought. Even if you enjoy designing shop accessories, proven plans can be golden, too. That's where this book comes in. Here are more than two dozen of the best workshop projects we've published over the years to save you time, frustration, and even some sweat equity.

A workbench is the heart and soul of any workshop, so we're offering two classics to get things started. Rick White's budget bench was extremely well received by our readers, and John English's no-nonsense maple offering will last for many generations. Further into this book, you'll find another offering from Rick that combines a solid bench with dust collection (the "Downdraft Workbench").

Storage is a common shop conundrum, but a sturdy lumber and sheet goods rack can keep your floor from becoming a maze. John English shares some stationary options, or you could build Chris Marshall's clever rolling rack. If you have too many clamps and no good way to stow them, our mobile clamping cart or Rick White's clamping station may be just the fix.

Dedicated workstations improve efficiency, and we have some dandies to share. Rick White's sharpening station and Peter

Walsh's portable lathe station will keep your turning tools both sharp and easy to reach. If a disc sander is what you need, try making your own with a design from our own art director, Jeff Jacobson. And let's not forget, no shop is complete without a router table. Bruce Kieffer's version in this book is, hands down, the best I've ever seen.

But big shop projects are just the tip of the iceberg. This book is also packed with sensible, affordable jigs, caddies, and tools you can build—from Kerry Pierce's custom bench plane to John Premo's circle-cutting band saw jig…and nearly everything in between.

So, consider yourself fully loaded for weekends of satisfying workshop projects. You want the hardest-working shop on the block, and this book will help you make it a reality.

Larry N. Stoiaken, Editor-in-Chief

Acknowledgments

Woodworker's Journal recently celebrated its 30th anniversary—a benchmark few magazines ever reach. I would like to acknowledge both the 300,000 woodworkers who make up our readership and Rockler Woodworking and Hardware (*rockler.com*), which provided most of the hardware, wood, and other products used to build the projects in this book. Our publishing partner, Fox Chapel, did a terrific job re-presenting our material, and I am especially grateful to Alan Giagnocavo, Gretchen Bacon, John Kelsey, and Troy Thorne for their commitment to our content.

Larry N. Stoiaken, Editor-in-Chief

CONTENTS

132

Building a Workbench on a Budget

There are a number of woodworking fixtures you can get by without for a long while, but a sturdy workbench isn't one of them. The trouble is, those solid-hardwood benches we all lust after can completely blow a modest woodworking budget. Here's a bench that splits the difference. You'll get a top that can stand up to significant abuse, a sturdy, heavy base that keeps the bench planted where you put it, and an end vise and T-track system for holding workpieces and a variety of unique jigs. It may not look quite like a European bench, but it works just as hard as one for a lot less money.

by Rick White

Every woodworker dreams of owning a classic European workbench. The beautiful maple top and elaborate shoulder vise symbolize the essence of fine craftsmanship. But how many of us look at these benches and end up saying, "It's just too nice to use in my shop"? And when we see the cost of building such a bench, we pass on the project altogether.

On the other hand, settling for a barely adequate bench is frustrating.

Without a vise, you can't hold your workpiece, and without a heavy, solid surface, you can't expect to strike a chisel without having it bounce around and damage your wood.

Being caught between a rock and a hard place over a workbench is no fun. The workbench is, after all, the heart and soul of a shop. With this dilemma in mind, I set out to build a completely functional workstation for about $300. About half of that cost was for two essential products: The first is a Veritas vise with two screws connected by a bicycle chain that overcomes the racking problem commonly experienced with traditional vises. The chain drive can be quickly released to operate the screws independently, making it possible to cant the jaws a little when holding stock out near the edge of the bench. The second must-have is a T-slot system (see Figure 1). It offers great flexibility and, as you'll see, lends itself to dozens of homemade accessories.

The first thing a bench should offer is a sturdy surface, and this one fills the bill. You can surface an oak board with a hand plane, and the bench won't budge an inch. The hardboard top makes a sound work surface, and since it's

screwed down, it's easy to replace when it becomes worn or damaged. There's plenty of room for handling large panels, and you can clamp wood for sanding, surface and edge planing, edge and panel routing, joint cutting, and up to this point, any operation you can think of. The completed bench is heavy, which is perfect for deadening the blows of a pounding mallet.

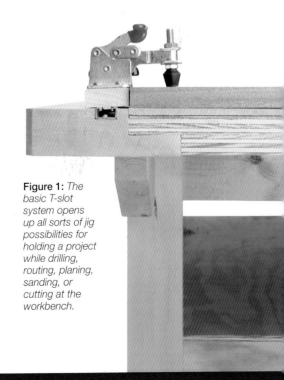

Figure 1: *The basic T-slot system opens up all sorts of jig possibilities for holding a project while drilling, routing, planing, sanding, or cutting at the workbench.*

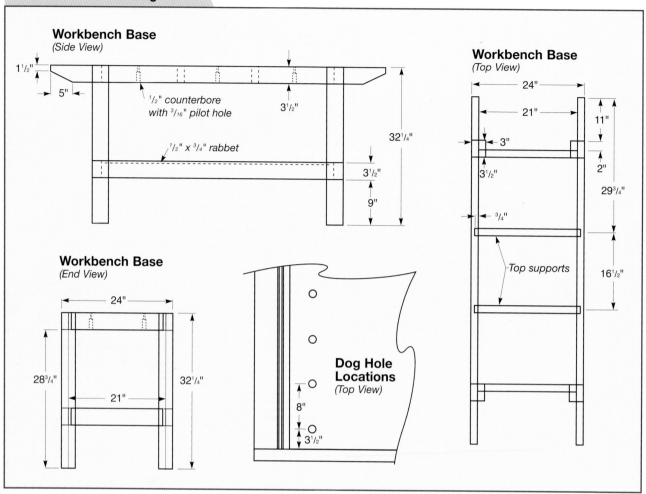

Workbench Base
(Side View)

1¹/₂"

5"

¹/₂" counterbore
with ³/₁₆" pilot hole

3¹/₂"

¹/₂" x ³/₄" rabbet

32¹/₄"

3¹/₂"

9"

Workbench Base
(Top View)

24"

21"

11"

3"

3¹/₂"

2"

29³/₄"

³/₄"

Top supports

16¹/₂"

Workbench Base
(End View)

24"

28³/₄"

32¹/₄"

21"

Dog Hole Locations
(Top View)

8"

3¹/₂"

In addition to the basic bench design, you may also want to add a cabinet to the leg structure. Although this isn't part of the original project, spending an additional $50 for one more sheet of plywood and three pairs of drawer slides makes better use of this otherwise empty space. The exploded view on page 7 will guide you through this addition.

Building the Base

The base of the workbench is made with standard 2" x 4" stock, and most of the joints are made with lap joints and screws. All the cutting was done with a table saw, and for this phase of the project, the only other tool you'll need quite a bit is a drill.

Begin by gluing up 2" x 4" stock for the legs (pieces 1), after cutting the pieces a couple inches longer than the lengths given in the Material List on page 4. Use two pieces of lumber for each leg, spreading yellow glue on both mating surfaces to get a perfect bond, and then clamp the pieces together. Clean off the excess glue from each lamination before it hardens.

Once the legs are removed from the clamps, go ahead and cut all the base pieces to length. The side aprons (pieces 2) and top supports (pieces 3) give the top much of its rigidity and help keep the base from racking. The side stretchers (pieces 4), end aprons (pieces 5), and end stretchers (pieces 6) complete the base, creating great stability and adding substantial weight to the bench.

Lay out the lap joint locations on the legs, as shown above and in the lap joint detail on page 5. Keep in mind that all the leg joint positions are essentially the same, but as with all table legs, each one has to mirror the leg across from it. To cut the laps, install a ¾" dado blade in your table saw, raise the blade 1½", and then, with the aid of your miter gauge, take several passes to remove the wood in each joint area.

Now, lower the dado blade to ¾", and lay out the dadoes on the side aprons for joining with the top supports. Cut each dado with a couple of passes over the blade. Next, cut a ¾"-wide x ½"-deep rabbet along the top inside edge of each side stretcher. Stop the rabbets 1" from each end of the pieces. To protect your fence during these rabbeting cuts, be sure to clamp on a wood face.

The clamp-holding jig steadies bar clamps on the bench top while you adjust boards in a panel assembly. That way, you can work at a comfortable height without tipping clamps over during an assembly.

Clamp Support Jig

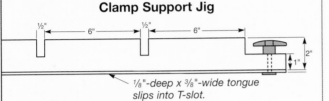

1/8"-deep x 3/8"-wide tongue slips into T-slot.

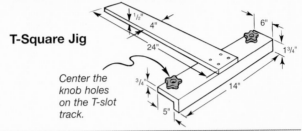

This T-square jig is a sweet invention. When routing multiple dadoes across a panel, it is unsurpassed for speed, and since everything references off the edge of the bench, it's super-accurate.

T-Square Jig

Center the knob holes on the T-slot track.

A pair of toggle clamps makes a nice combination for clamping: One set clamps in line with the T-slots, and the other set is at right angles to the slots. Between them, you can hold projects across or parallel to the bench length.

Toggle Clamp Jig

When sanding panels, you'll probably find that regular clamps often get in the way. To avoid this problem, make a set of cam dogs and a T-slot bar. Since the bar is adjustable, it can fill in between the dog holes for a midbench anchoring point.

Cam Clamp Jig

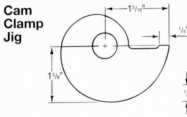
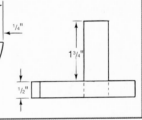

Before assembling the base, take care of two more small details that are easy to do now while other frame parts aren't in the way. First, drill 1/2" counterbores with 3/16" pilot holes in the bottom edge of the four aprons and two top supports (see the technical drawings on page 2). These holes will be used later for screwing down the bench top. The second detail is trimming the angles on the ends of the side aprons. The best tool for cutting the angles is a handheld circular saw, but a jigsaw with a stiff blade will work

almost as well. After making the cuts, belt sand the edges smooth.

Assemble the workbench base in two stages. First, glue and screw the side aprons and stretchers to the legs, and then join these structures with the end aprons, end stretchers, and top supports. Make sure that the two side stretcher rabbets face each other on the base assembly. Clean up any glue squeeze-out, and sand the base to remove the sharp edges.

If your shop floor is anything but level, add a leveling glide (pieces 7) to

the bottom of each leg. To install these optional glides, flip the base upside down, and drill a 1/2"-diameter x 2"-deep hole in the center of each leg bottom. Then, secure the threaded plates included in the package, and screw in the levelers.

Moving Up to the Top

The top is basically a three-layer sandwich that's banded with thick maple rails. First, two panels of fir plywood (pieces 8 and 9) are laminated together to make the top stable and

1/8"

Figure 2: *Batten boards, which have a curve of about 1/8" on the bottom edge, are used to apply pressure at the middle of a wide panel assembly.*

heavy, and then, above the plywood, a layer of removable hardboard (piece 10) is added to take the dings and dents suffered by any workbench. When the hardboard becomes too scarred from working at the bench, remove it and use it as a template for making a new one. To complete the top assembly, maple rails (pieces 11) are attached to the plywood, giving the top an attractive edge and a durable surface for anchoring the T-slot tracks (pieces 15).

Start building your top by cutting the two plywood panels to size and gluing them together. Use a brush or roller to spread yellow glue over both mating surfaces, and then center the smaller panel on top of the larger one. Next, to keep the panels from slipping out of position, drive a brad into the assembly at each corner of the smaller panel. Clamping the plywood requires consistent pressure throughout the lamination, so make sure you've precut a bunch of curved batten boards to apply pressure in the middle of the panels (see Figure 2).

Rip and crosscut your maple to size for the rails, and then drill 1½"-deep holes in one edge of each piece, as shown in the dog hole locations drawing on page 2. After drilling the 1" holes, install a ¾" dado blade in your table saw to cut a 1"-deep x 2"-wide rabbet in the other edge of each rail (see the drawing at right). Make several passes to complete each rabbet, making sure to clamp your protective wood face to the saw fence.

The maple rails should now be glued and screwed to the upper plywood panel. I recommend first clamping the rails without glue to the plywood and then drilling countersunk pilot holes through the plywood into the rail (drill seven evenly spaced holes along each rail). When you've finished drilling, release the clamps, spread glue in the rail rabbets, and reclamp the assembly. With everything in place, drive the screws, and then clean up any glue squeeze-out, especially along the inside edge of the rail.

The final piece to fit into the top is the tempered hardboard. Cut the sheet to fit between the rails as snugly

Workbench Exploded View

Material List – Workbench

		T x W x L
1	Legs (4)	3" x 3½" x 32¼"
2	Side Aprons (2)	1½" x 3½" x 76"
3	Top Supports (2)	1½" x 3½" x 22½"
4	Side Stretchers (2)	1½" x 3½" x 54"
5	End Aprons (2)	1½" x 3½" x 21"
6	End Stretchers (2)	1½" x 3½" x 21"
7	Leveling Glides (1 Set)	Heavy Duty
8	Top Panel (1)	¾" x 22" x 80"
9	Bottom Panel (1)	¾" x 18" x 80"
10	Hardboard (1)	¼" x 22" x 80"
11	Maple Rails (2)	1¾" x 6" x 80"
12	Endcap (1)	1¾" x 1¾" x 30"
13	Inside Vise Jaw (1)	1¾" x 5¾" x 30"
14	Outside Vise Jaw (1)	2" x 5¾" x 30"
15	T-Slot Tracks (4)	13/32" x 13/16" x 40"
16	Screws (30)	#6-1" Panhead
17	Lag Bolts/Washers (3)	3/8" x 2½"
18	Screws (15)	#12-2½"
19	Dog Heads (4)	½" x 2" x 2"
20	Dog Dowels (4)	1" Dia. x 1½" Long

End View Detail

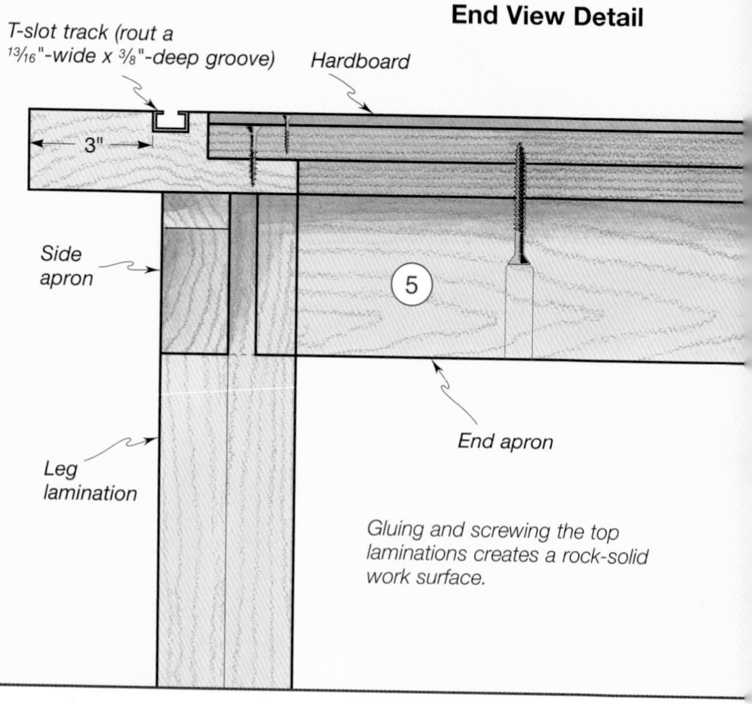
T-slot track (rout a 13/16"-wide x 3/8"-deep groove)
Hardboard
3"
Side apron
5
End apron
Leg lamination

Gluing and screwing the top laminations creates a rock-solid work surface.

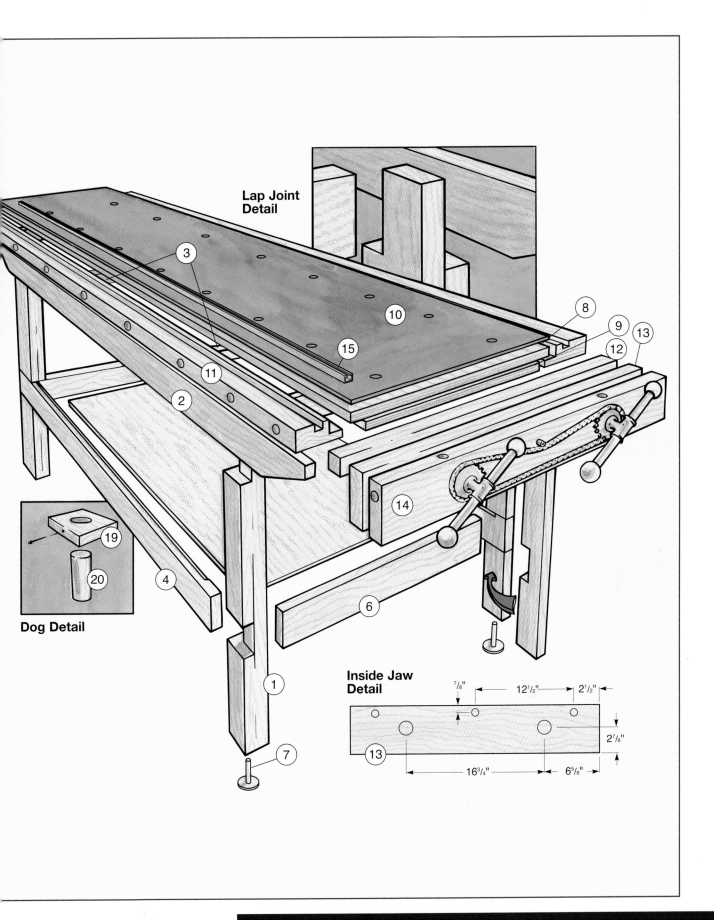

Lap Joint Detail

Dog Detail

Inside Jaw Detail

$7/8"$

$12^1/_2"$ $2^1/_2"$

$2^7/_8"$

$16^3/_4"$ $6^5/_8"$

as possible, and then drill countersunk pilot holes along its edges for the screws that will secure it to the plywood. Fasten it down.

Now, for the T-slot system. The efficient use of this bench really revolves around jigs made with a T-bolt and a knob clamp. The T-bolt slides in a metal track that's secured to the bench with screws, and then the knob on the bolt is tightened to hold the jig in place. The track will last through a lifetime of use.

Installing the metal track requires a simple ¹³⁄₁₆"-wide x ⅜"-deep groove. Make sure the groove depth is accurate: If it's too shallow, the track will stick up into the work surface, and if it's too deep, the accessories will pull the track out of the groove. Lay out the track grooves on the maple rails, as shown in the end view detail on page 4. Then, chuck a ½" straight bit in your router, and attach a straightedge guide. Now, rout one ⅜"-deep pass for each track, and then reset the edge guide to make a second pass, widening the grooves to ¹³⁄₁₆".

Since the track comes in 40" lengths, this bench requires four pieces to make up the two parallel slots. To secure the tracks, set them into the grooves, and drill ⁵⁄₃₂"-diameter holes every 6". Next, drive a #6-1"

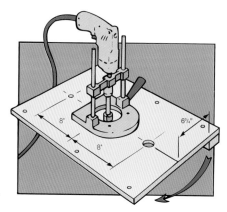

Figure 3: *A drilling jig ensures accurate dog holes; just be sure to switch the fence for each row.*

panhead screw (pieces 16) into each hole. If the track overhangs the end of the bench, cut the excess off with a hacksaw.

Bench Top Details

Drilling dog holes in the bench top requires a great deal of accuracy, so it helps to use a jig for this operation (see Figure 3). The idea behind the jig is to use one dog hole to establish the position of the next hole. To ensure accuracy, I incorporated a portable drilling guide into my jig. Since the jig is guided by the maple rails, you'll have two fence positions: one for the right-hand row of holes and one for the left-hand row.

Build the jig, and then set it against the bench top to drill the first hole, referring to the dog hole locations drawing on page 2. Drill the hole, and then use a center punch and the forward hole on the jig to locate the

next hole. Now, move the jig forward until you can slip a 1" dowel through the rear jig hole and into the first bench hole. Lower the drill bit to the second hole location to make sure the bit spur goes right into the punch mark. Drill the second hole, and use the center punch to mark the third hole. Continue this procedure for the rest of the dog holes. When you're done with the right-hand row, switch the fence, and then drill the left-hand row of holes. The more accurate your dog holes are, the better off you'll be when using your bench jigs.

On the back end of the bench top, the T-slots are left exposed so you can slip your fixtures and jigs in and out. On the front end, however, you must install an endcap. Cut the endcap (piece 12) and the vise jaws (pieces 13 and 14) to size, and then follow the exploded view detail on page 5 to drill their mounting and vise screw holes. Clamp the endcap into position against the bench top, and extend the pilot holes into the maple rails and the plywood lamination. Now, secure the endcap to the bench with glue and screws (pieces 18), extend the pilot holes for the inside vise jaw, and secure it with lag bolts and washers (pieces 17).

At this point, the bench top and the base are ready for assembly. Square the

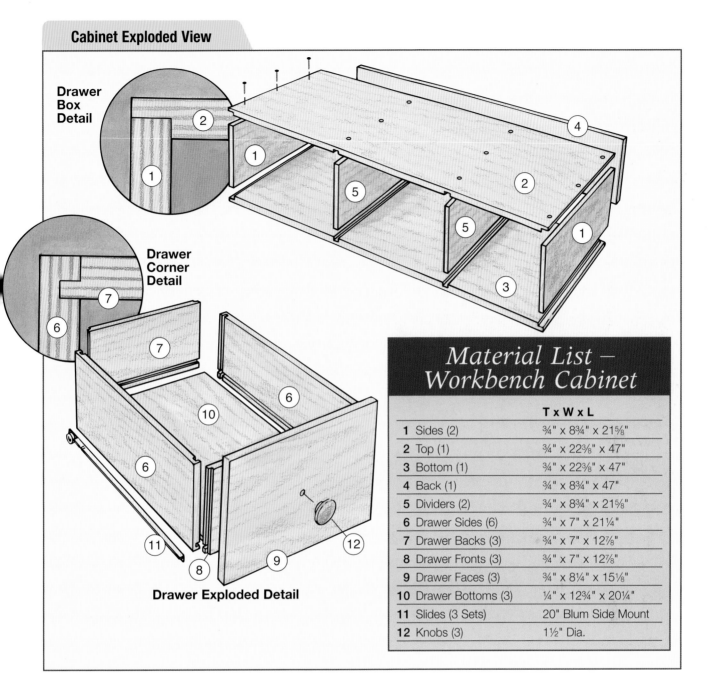

Cabinet Exploded View

Drawer Box Detail

Drawer Corner Detail

Drawer Exploded Detail

Material List – Workbench Cabinet

		T x W x L
1	Sides (2)	¾" x 8¾" x 21⅝"
2	Top (1)	¾" x 22⅜" x 47"
3	Bottom (1)	¾" x 22⅜" x 47"
4	Back (1)	¾" x 8¾" x 47"
5	Dividers (2)	¾" x 8¾" x 21⅝"
6	Drawer Sides (6)	¾" x 7" x 21¼"
7	Drawer Backs (3)	¾" x 7" x 12⅞"
8	Drawer Fronts (3)	¾" x 7" x 12⅞"
9	Drawer Faces (3)	¾" x 8¼" x 15⅛"
10	Drawer Bottoms (3)	¼" x 12¾" x 20¼"
11	Slides (3 Sets)	20" Blum Side Mount
12	Knobs (3)	1½" Dia.

top on the base, and then clamp the two together. Now, reach under the bench to extend the pilot holes in the aprons and supports. Use #12-2½" screws (pieces 18) to secure the assembly.

Some Final Thoughts

Next, make the bench dogs (pieces 19 and 20), as shown in the dog detail drawing on page 5. If you don't plan to build the drawer cabinet, cut a plywood panel to fit between the side stretchers in the base for a storage shelf. If you

plan to build the drawer cabinet, follow the drawings shown above.

The vise comes with instructions, so follow them for installation. However, you do need to make handles for the vise. Make them from a length of dowel. Then, flatten one side on four 1½"-diameter wood balls, and secure them to both ends of the dowels with dowel screws.

The jigs I developed for the T-slot system are shown in T-Slot Jigs on page 3. These are a small sampling of what's

possible with this system, and with time, you'll probably invent many more.

I sprayed my bench with lacquer to protect it from spills and then put the bench to good use. At the end of this project, you, too, will have a sturdy bench, a checkbook that isn't as light as it would have been if you had built a European-type bench, and a lot more flexibility for holding your work.

Workshop Classic: A Bench You Can Rely On

A family tradition of matching the workbench to the worker continues with this no-nonsense maple workbench. Granddad would likely have approved.

by John English

The worktop on my grandfather's bench consisted of a pair of railroad ties with an 8" gap down the middle. Granddad, who lived in Ireland, was a skilled artisan who built coaches and wagons.

My father is pretty good with his hands, too. The bench in his Dublin workshop is better suited to the work he does—refinishing antique furniture and tuning small engines—than Granddad's would have been. The 3"-thick hardwood top rests on an iron frame, but the vise is a metalworker's, and the top shows scars of butane torches, solder, and even a few hammer blows.

The point is that a workbench is personal—it must match both the work and the worker. Neither of the benches described above would be suitable for fine woodworking, but the model shown here is ideal for building furniture and casework. And it's easily modified to suit an individual craftsman's needs.

Design Basics

I built this workbench to fit my 6'-tall body. The rule of thumb is to locate the worktop at half the height of the user (in this case, 35⅜"). If you need to build it higher or lower, simply adjust the length of the legs (see the leg subassembly drawings on page 14).

The top of the bench features two parallel rows of bench dog holes. The front row is close to the edge, but the back row is set in a few inches to

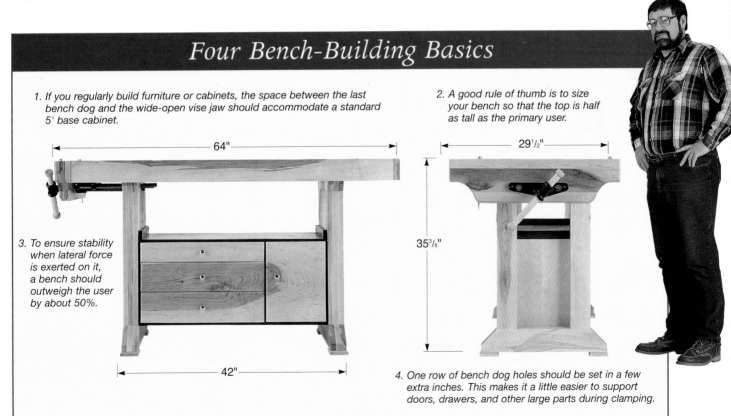

Four Bench-Building Basics

1. If you regularly build furniture or cabinets, the space between the last bench dog and the wide-open vise jaw should accommodate a standard 5' base cabinet.

2. A good rule of thumb is to size your bench so that the top is half as tall as the primary user.

3. To ensure stability when lateral force is exerted on it, a bench should outweigh the user by about 50%.

64"

42"

29½"

35³/₈"

4. One row of bench dog holes should be set in a few extra inches. This makes it a little easier to support doors, drawers, and other large parts during clamping.

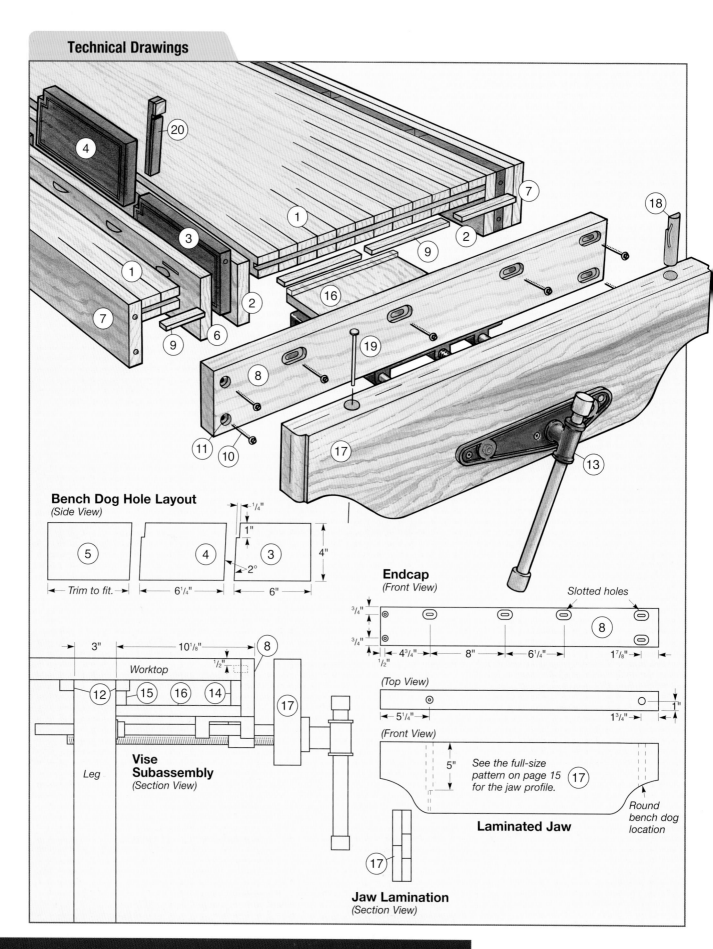

Bench Dog Hole Layout
(Side View)

⑤   ④   ③

1/4"
1"
4"
2°

← Trim to fit. →   ← 6¹/₄" →   ← 6" →

Endcap
(Front View)

Slotted holes

⑧

3/4"
3/4"
1/2"
← 4³/₄" →   ← 8" →   ← 6¹/₄" →   ← 1⁷/₈" →

(Top View)

← 5¹/₄" →   ← 1³/₄" →   1"

(Front View)

5"

See the full-size pattern on page 15 for the jaw profile.   ⑰

Round bench dog location

Laminated Jaw

3"   10¹/₈"   ⑧

Worktop   1/2"

⑫   ⑮   ⑯   ⑭   ⑰

Leg

Vise Subassembly
(Section View)

⑰

Jaw Lamination
(Section View)

help support wide subassemblies such as drawers or cabinet doors. The top is large enough to clamp a standard 5'-long kitchen base cabinet, with a few inches left to set down tools or hardware.

Before even sharpening a pencil for this project, make sure you have your vise and bench dogs on hand. Open the vise fully, measure the opening, and then subtract the thickness of the jaw (see the Material List below). This is the maximum spacing that you can allow between the dog holes in the bench top, but you may want to downsize that spacing a little; traditional bench builders have discovered that a space of 6" or 7" works best for most projects.

A Butcher-Block Top

While designing this bench, I recalled something from my days in the kitchen cabinet business: One of the most common kitchen renovations is countertop replacement, and more and more homeowners are discarding their gorgeous old solid-maple butcher-block tops. I got lucky on my third phone call and found a shop in the city's historical district that sold me an 8'-long section of 1½"-thick butcher block for just $10.

It took only a few minutes of trimming to make the butcher-block worktop (piece 1). I rough cut the blank a bit oversize with a circular saw, after first scoring with a utility knife to avoid tearout.

Then, I clamped on a straightedge and trimmed the top to final dimensions with a straight bit chucked in my router. During this process, I cut across the grain first and then with the grain—which virtually eliminates blowout on the corners.

If you prefer to build a top from scratch, make sure the quarter-sawn (tight) grain is visible, and the more open, wavy plain-sawn grain becomes the gluing surface. Glue and clamp three or four overly long pieces of ripped and jointed stock together at a time. When they're dry, glue and clamp these subassemblies together to form the completed piece. Biscuits help to line up all these edges as you clamp. After the glue dries, take the entire piece to a cabinet shop, and ask them to run it through their wide drum sander to reduce it to final thickness. Another option is to

Figure 2: *Dry fit the bench dogs and spacers, leaving gaps that are the size recommended by the dogs' manufacturer. When everything fits, trim the final spacer to length.*

Figure 1: *The spline grooves on the endcap are stopped, while those on the ends of the top are through cuts. After routing the grooves in the top, a 3"-wide strip is ripped off. This piece sits outside the liners and spacers.*

order your top glued-up and made to order at a local home center. This is a little more expensive but often results in a more secure and stable top.

The Bench Dog Holes

After trimming the top to size, chuck a ½" rabbeting bit in your portable router to cut the spline groove in each end of the worktop (see the exploded view on page 10 and Figure 1).

Rip a 3"-wide strip off one side of the top, and set it aside. Then, biscuit, glue, and clamp the inside liners (pieces 2) in place. Place the worktop on a couple of saw horses while attaching these liners, so your clamps have room to operate.

The liners need to be flush with the top of the butcher block when it's

Material List

		T x W x L			T x W x L
1	Worktop (1)	1½" x 24⅛" x 60"	**11**	Washers (14)	⅜" I.D.
2	Inside Liners (2)	¾" x 4" x 60"	**12**	Leg Cleats (4)	¾" x ¾" x 20"
3	First Spacers (2)	¾" x 4" x 6"	**13**	Large End Vise (1)	
4	Common Spacers (14)	¾" x 4" x 6¼"	**14**	Vise Support Endcap Cleat (1)	¾" x 1¾" x 12"
5	Last Spacers (2)	¾" x 4" x 5½"	**15**	Vise Support Leg Cleat (1)	¾" x 1" x 12"
6	Outside Liners (2)	¾" x 4" x 60"	**16**	Vise Support (1)	¾" x 10" x 9"
7	Worktop Sides (2)	¾" x 4" x 60"	**17**	Laminated Jaw (1)	2" x 7⅜" x 30"
8	Endcaps (2)	1" x 4" x 30"	**18**	Round Dogs (2)	Brass
9	Spline (1)	½" x 1" x 30"	**19**	Round Dog Button (1)	3½" Brass Hinge Pin
10	Lag Screws (14)	⅜" Dia. x 3½" Long	**20**	Square Dogs (2)	Steel

Getting Started

You should have the vise and bench dogs on hand before construction begins, in case you have to adjust the plan to fit the hardware. Beech and hard maple are the traditional species of choice for the frame and top, and walnut makes an excellent accent. During the course of construction, you'll use a table saw, a biscuit joiner, a band saw, a drill press, portable and table-mounted routers, and a belt sander.

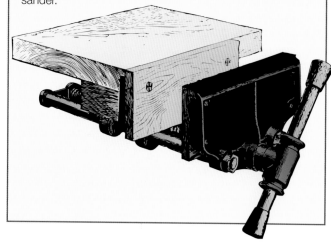

finished, so it's a good idea to set them in place a hair proud of the top rather than shy of it.

The bench dog holes are formed when a series of spacers (pieces 3 through 5) are attached to the liners. The business edges of these spacers are cut at a 2° angle (verify this angle by reading the bench dog manufacturer's instructions), and they're notched to allow the bench dogs to be stored below the worktop surface. All of these dimensions are shown in the elevation drawings, and the cuts can be made on a band saw. Dry fit and mark the spacer locations on the inside liners, verifying each placement with a bench dog (see Figure 2 on page 11). Score a shallow line about a ¼" in from the edge on both sides of each spacer—use a sharp knife or a rotary tool— to create a glue well; this will limit excessive squeeze-out.

Attach the spacers to the inside liners with glue and clamps. When they're dry, you can glue and clamp the outside

Figure 3: *Use your drill press to bore two-step slotted holes in the endcaps. These will allow the benchtop to adjust to various levels of moisture in the workshop.*

Technical Drawings

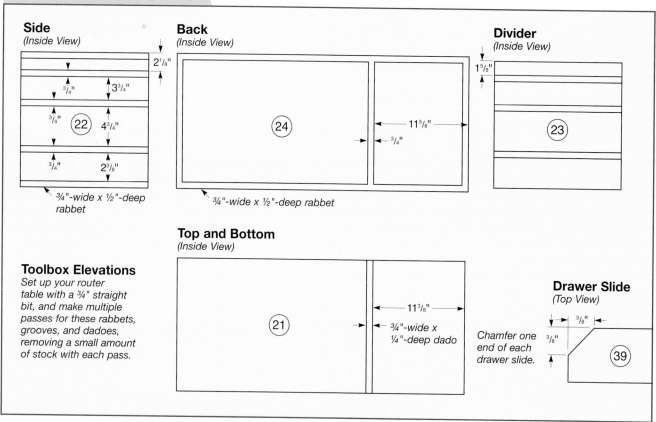

Side
(Inside View)

2¹/₈"

³/₄"   3³/₄"

³/₄"   (22)   4³/₄"

³/₄"   2³/₈"

¾"-wide x ½"-deep rabbet

Back
(Inside View)

(24)

11⁵/₈"

³/₄"

¾"-wide x ½"-deep rabbet

Divider
(Inside View)

1⁵/₈"

(23)

Top and Bottom
(Inside View)

(21)

11³/₈"

¾"-wide x ¼"-deep dado

Toolbox Elevations
Set up your router table with a ¾" straight bit, and make multiple passes for these rabbets, grooves, and dadoes, removing a small amount of stock with each pass.

Drawer Slide
(Top View)

³/₈"

³/₈"

(39)

Chamfer one end of each drawer slide.

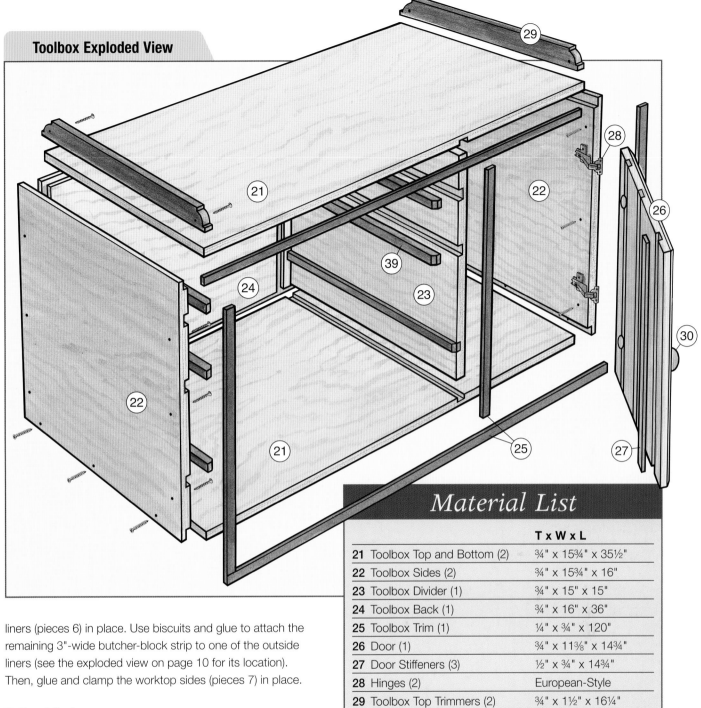

Material List

		T x W x L
21	Toolbox Top and Bottom (2)	¾" x 15¾" x 35½"
22	Toolbox Sides (2)	¾" x 15¾" x 16"
23	Toolbox Divider (1)	¾" x 15" x 15"
24	Toolbox Back (1)	¾" x 16" x 36"
25	Toolbox Trim (1)	¼" x ¾" x 120"
26	Door (1)	¾" x 11⅜" x 14¾"
27	Door Stiffeners (3)	½" x ¾" x 14¾"
28	Hinges (2)	European-Style
29	Toolbox Top Trimmers (2)	¾" x 1½" x 16¼"
30	Knobs (4)	Brass

liners (pieces 6) in place. Use biscuits and glue to attach the remaining 3"-wide butcher-block strip to one of the outside liners (see the exploded view on page 10 for its location). Then, glue and clamp the worktop sides (pieces 7) in place.

Splined Endcaps

As woodworkers well know, wood has an annoying habit of shrinking and swelling across the grain. To cope with this tendency in a large assembly such as the worktop, the endcaps (pieces 8) are splined and attached with lag screws driven through oversize, slotted holes (see the elevations on page 10 for marking the slotted hole locations).

Chuck the rabbeting bit (the one you used earlier to create grooves in the worktop ends) in your portable router, and with the workpieces held securely, create a stopped groove in each endcap. Then, mark the locations of the lag screw holes in each groove.

Trim splines (pieces 9) to fit around the lag screws, and then move to the drill press to bore the two-step elongated and round lag screw holes, as shown in Figure 3. Note that the endcaps are not identical but are mirror images of one another. Use the drilled endcaps to locate pilot holes in the worktop, drill these holes, insert the splines, and attach the endcaps with lag screws and washers (pieces 10 and 11). Don't glue the splines in; otherwise, the worktop will buckle or crack if it's not allowed to move.

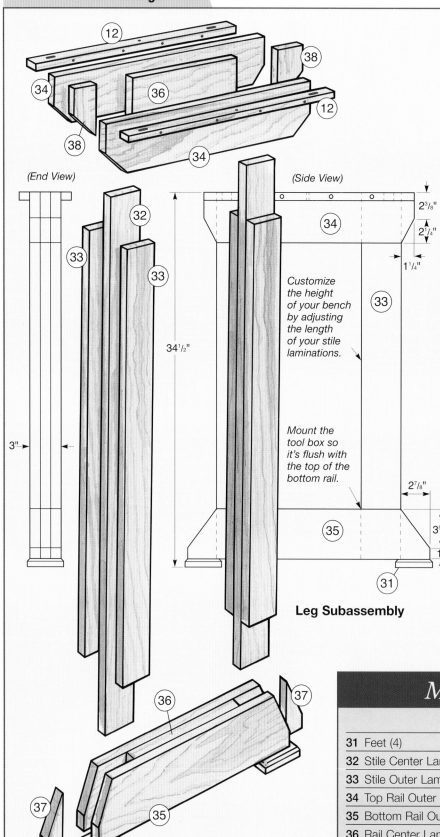

(End View)

(Side View)

34½"

2³⁄₈"

2¼"

1¼"

Customize
the height
of your bench
by adjusting
the length
of your stile
laminations.

3"

Mount the
tool box so
it's flush with
the top of the
bottom rail.

2⁷⁄₈"

3⁵⁄₈"

1"

Leg Subassembly

Brace-Up for Some Brackets

Turn the benchtop upside down, and mark locations for the leg cleats (pieces 12), using the dimensions in the section view on page 10. You'll use these locations as a reference as you build up a support structure for the large end vise (piece 13). Begin by screwing and gluing a vise support cleat (piece 14) to the endcap, located ¾" up from the bottom (see the elevation and detail drawings on page 10). Drill pilot holes, and screw a second cleat (piece 15) to the vise support (piece 16) at the location shown on the elevation drawings. Then, dry fit the vise support to the endcap cleat, and finish drilling your pilot holes. When all the screw holes have been established, remove the screws until the legs and the laminated jaw (piece 17) are installed. At that time, you'll also address the bench dogs (pieces 18 through 20).

The Toolbox

Stability is perhaps the number-one requirement in a workbench, so the storage area on this bench is designed to add weight and lateral stability to the legs, while also providing three drawers, a cupboard, and a large shelf for tool storage.

The toolbox top, bottom, sides, divider, and back (pieces 21 through 24) are cut from one sheet of ¾" hardwood-veneered plywood (see the

Material List

	T x W x L
31 Feet (4)	¾" x 3½" x 3½"
32 Stile Center Laminations (4)	1" x 3¾" x 33¼"
33 Stile Outer Laminations (8)	1" x 3¾" x 24½"
34 Top Rail Outer Laminations (4)	1" x 4⅝" x 20"
35 Bottom Rail Outer Laminations (4)	1" x 4⅝" x 23¼"
36 Rail Center Laminations (4)	1" x 4⅝" x 10"
37 Foot Inserts (4)	1" x 4⅝" x 2⅞"
38 Top Inserts (4)	1" x 4⅝" x 2⅞"

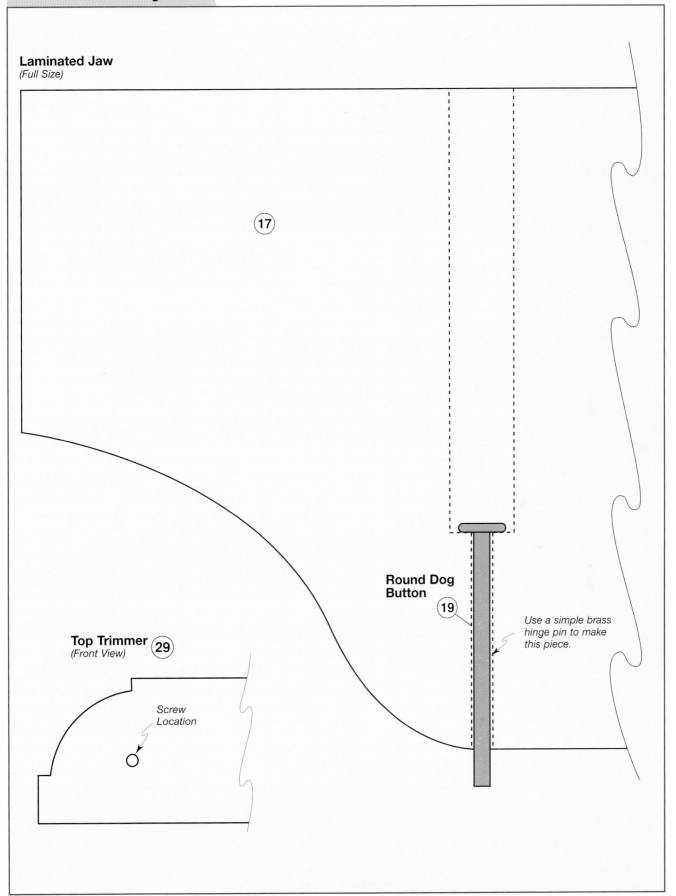

Laminated Jaw
(Full Size)

17

Round Dog Button

19

Use a simple brass hinge pin to make this piece.

Top Trimmer 29
(Front View)

Screw Location

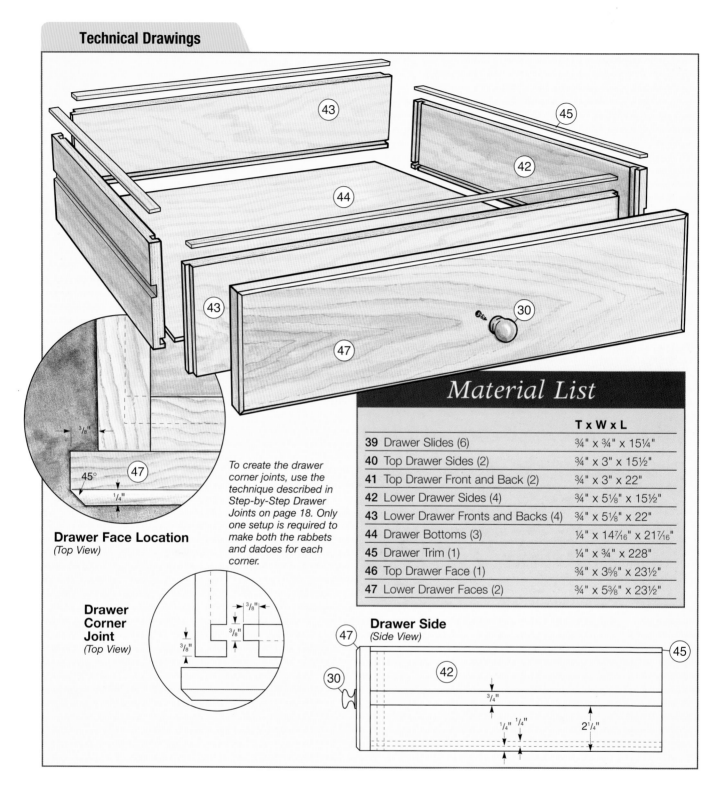

Drawer Face Location
(Top View)

To create the drawer corner joints, use the technique described in Step-by-Step Drawer Joints on page 18. Only one setup is required to make both the rabbets and dadoes for each corner.

Drawer Corner Joint
(Top View)

Drawer Side
(Side View)

Material List

	T x W x L
39 Drawer Slides (6)	¾" x ¾" x 15¼"
40 Top Drawer Sides (2)	¾" x 3" x 15½"
41 Top Drawer Front and Back (2)	¾" x 3" x 22"
42 Lower Drawer Sides (4)	¾" x 5⅛" x 15½"
43 Lower Drawer Fronts and Backs (4)	¾" x 5⅛" x 22"
44 Drawer Bottoms (3)	¼" x 14⁷⁄₁₆" x 21⁷⁄₁₆"
45 Drawer Trim (1)	¼" x ¾" x 228"
46 Top Drawer Face (1)	¾" x 3⅝" x 23½"
47 Lower Drawer Faces (2)	¾" x 5⅝" x 23½"

Material List on page 13). I used birch ply, a good color and grain match for the maple in the rest of the bench and far easier to find as a stock lumberyard item than maple ply. Use the elevation drawings to lay out rabbets on the appropriate edges of these pieces, and then mill them with a ¾" straight bit chucked in your router table. For clean and safe cuts, make several passes to mill each rabbet.

Use the same bit to plow dadoes for the drawer slides and divider. Glue and clamp the top and bottom

to the sides. Dry fit the back, check for squareness, and glue it in place.

The front edges of the case are trimmed with walnut (piece 25). Apply this with glue and 3d finish nails. Set the heads, fill them after the glue dries, and then scrape or plane the trim flush with the plywood. Now, you need to build and install the legs before coming back to finish the rest of the toolbox— the door, top trimmers, and knobs (pieces 26 through 30).

Stile and Rail Legsets

The bench's legs are standard stile-and-rail construction, with a twist: Both stiles and rails are built-up laminations. This allows you to assemble the leg sets with mortise-and-tenon joints without ever having to chop a single mortise.

Cut all the leg parts (including the feet, pieces 31) to the sizes on the Material List on page 14. Then, dry fit the stile center laminations (pieces 32) to the outside laminations (pieces 33); their dimensions are shown on the leg elevations on page 14. Face glue and clamp each set of three laminations together to create four individual legs, and then set them aside.

Don't be overly anxious about perfect matches or glue squeeze-out—after the glue dries, you can scrape off any excess and then joint the uneven edges.

Use the elevation drawings to lay out the top and bottom rails' outside laminations (pieces 34 and 35), and then cut these to shape on your band saw. Dry fit these and the rail center laminations (pieces 36) to the legs, and then temporarily clamp them in place. Use this setup as a template to lay out and mark the foot and top inserts (pieces 37 and 38), as shown in Figure 4. Trim the inserts to size on your band saw, glue and clamp each legset together, and set them aside to dry.

Attaching the Legs to the Top

Sand the worktop thoroughly, and then turn it upside down. Use your drill press to create slots in one face of the leg cleats (pieces 12) and pilot holes in the other face of the piece. Attach the cleats flush to the top of the legs with glue and screws driven through the holes—not the slots. When the glue dries, attach the legs to the toolbox (flush with the top of the bottom rail) by temporarily clamping everything in place. Predrill the inside of the toolbox for 2" screws, and when everything is lined up, drive them home.

Round up some strong help, and set the leg assembly upside down on the underside of the worktop. Complete the assembly, driving screws through the cleat slots into your predrilled holes in the underside of the worktop. This secures the legs and toolbox to the top.

Installing the Vise

You have already made all the parts for the vise support assembly. Now, begin the vise installation by positioning the vise on its support at the location shown on the elevation drawings. Next, use the vise as a template to mark mounting holes on the support. Predrill these holes (see the manufacturer's

Figure 4: *Dry fit the legset parts together, and then use this as a template to determine the shape of the foot and top inserts.*

instructions), and then install the cleat subassembly you made earlier with screws (see the section view on page 10). You can now begin to mount the vise to the bench.

Again using the vise as a template, gently wind in the jaw until the two guide rods just touch the leg rail. Mark the rod locations, as well as the locations of the screw holes in the guide rod bushings that come with the vise, as shown in Figure 5.

Remove the vise and platform, and use a Forstner bit to drill slightly oversize holes in the leg's rail assembly for the rods and screw to pass through. You may want to remove the legs and perform this step on your drill press to ensure truly vertical bores. Then, screw the bushings in place.

Figure 5: *The vise attaches to both the endcap and vise support. With two screws holding the unit in place, establish the locations for the guide rod and center screw holes in the legs.*

The Laminated Jaw

There are two good reasons to use five separate boards to laminate a blank for the movable vise jaw (piece 17): It will be more stable than a single board, and it will be far stronger. Follow the jaw lamination layout on page 10 to face glue and clamp the blank together.

Using the pattern drawing on page 15, cut the jaw to shape on your band saw, and then sand out the saw marks with a 2" drum sander. Shape the outside bottom and side edges with a ½"-radius guided beading bit chucked in your portable router.

Step-by-Step Drawer Joints

Step 1: *Install a ⅜" dado head and a zero-clearance insert in the saw, and cut a rabbet at the end of each drawer front and back.*

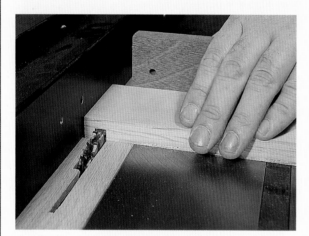

Step 2: *Without moving the rip fence, switch to the miter fence to form matching dadoes in the drawer sides.*

Step 3: *Dry fit the joints, and then switch to a ¼" dado head to cut the grooves for the bottoms.*

To locate the holes in the jaw for the guide rods and screw, remove the screw and guide rods, clamp the jaw in place, and use the vise mounting plate as a guide to locate the three holes. Drill these holes ⅛" oversize.

Slip the laminated jaw over the guide rods and the screw, and then gently wind the vise closed. Position the wooden jaw flush with the top and sides of the worktop's endcap, drill pilot holes for the mounting screws, and drive them home.

Building the Drawers

Chamfer the leading edges of the drawer slides (pieces 39), as shown in the elevation drawings on page 12, and then glue them in their dadoes.

Cut the drawer sides, fronts, and backs (pieces 40 through 43) to size (see the Material List on page 16). Then, use the dimensions shown in the drawer corner joint drawing on page 16 to create the locking joints on their corners (see Step-by-Step Drawer Joints at left). These joints are cut on the table saw. It's a good idea to make a practice joint on scrap wood to establish the saw settings before milling the actual workpieces.

Stay at the table saw to cut grooves in the inside faces of these pieces for the drawer bottoms (pieces 44), as shown in the exploded view on page 16. Glue and clamp the drawers together, checking that they're square and flat before setting them aside. When the glue is dry, trim the top edges of the plywood drawers with solid hardwood (piece 45), gluing and nailing at 6" intervals. Fill the nail holes, and sand the filler flush. Then, install a dado head in your table saw to mill grooves in the drawer sides for the slides. Test your setup with scrap, using three pieces to represent the three drawer sizes, and make any minor adjustments needed to ensure that the drawers will slide properly. After milling, test fit the sides in the case to be sure they move easily on the slides.

The Drawer Fronts and Door

I cut the drawer fronts and the door for my bench from a single wide board, to take advantage of a very attractive grain pattern. You may have to glue up stock for this process. Cut the faces (pieces 46 and 47) to size, and then shape their front edges on the router table with a chamfering bit (see the elevation drawings for dimensions).

You can now return to the door and finish machining it. The grain pattern on the door (piece 26) ran horizontally. To prevent cupping, I plowed three dadoes from top to bottom in its back and glued in three stiffeners (pieces 27). After sanding, I chamfered the door's front edges to match the look of the drawer faces.

European-style hinges with a ¼" overlay (pieces 28) are completely hidden when the door is closed. Follow the included instructions for mounting these hinges.

On your band saw, shape the walnut toolbox trimmers (pieces 29) to the profile shown in the pattern drawing on page 15, and then sand them smooth. Screw one to the legs at each end of the toolbox top, to stop tools from falling off the shelf. Finally, chamfer the top and bottom edges of the feet, and screw them to the bottoms of the legs.

Finishing Up

Disassemble the entire bench, and sand all surfaces with 120-grit, 180-grit, and finally 220-grit sandpaper. Wipe it down with a tack cloth, and apply four coats of natural Danish oil to the legset and toolbox and an additional couple of coats to the worktop. Sand each coat except the last with 400-grit sandpaper, wiping it clean before and after sanding. When the finish is dry, reassemble the bench, and mount the knobs on the drawers and door.

Install a pair of bench dogs (pieces 18) by using the elevation drawings to locate their holes in the top of the vise jaw. Drill the right-hand hole vertically all the way through the jaw (back up the exit area with some scrap to avoid tearout). Drill the left hole to a depth of 4½", and then use a bit extender or a long twist bit to drill a second hole in the bottom of this boring (see the elevation drawings for dimensions). This hole is for a brass pin that's actually a door hinge pin, available at most hardware stores. This pin is used as a button to push the top of the bench dog up above the surface of the jaw when needed.

Pop the square dogs into their holes at this time, and then fill the top drawer in the toolbox with all those project plans you'll need over the next few decades. After all, once people see the great job you did on building your workbench, they're bound to have all sorts of great ideas that will help you use it!

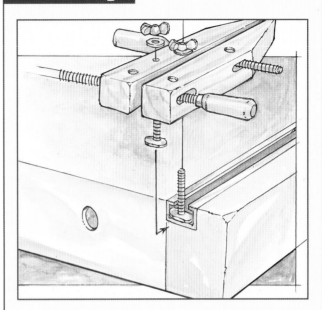

*Quick*Tip

Instant Workbench Vise

Most workbenches have more than one vise so the user can work either along an edge or at the end of the bench. If your workbench has only one vise, you can provide a second means of clamping using a length of metal T-track, T-bolts, wing nuts, and a few hand-screw clamps. Rout a dado in your benchtop to recess the T-track, bore a hole through the thickness of the hand-screw clamp, and assemble the parts. Install a second hand screw for holding long work when necessary.

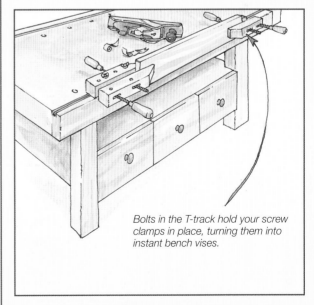

Bolts in the T-track hold your screw clamps in place, turning them into instant bench vises.

Lumber and Plywood Storage

Lumber storage is an issue for any size workshop. What starts out long or wide ends up as much shorter offcuts that are too valuable to throw away. A good lumber rack needs to stow the big stuff so it's easy to load and unload, while also storing shorter pieces so they're easy to sort and see. Here are two good plans for full-duty lumber racks and a couple of options for simpler bracket systems. One of these styles is sure to suit your shop.

by John English

The Mobile Rack

The mobile rack shown in the center drawing is designed to store all the essentials: full sheets of plywood and composites, partial sheets, long lengths of lumber, and short lengths. The rack is mounted on casters so it can be moved out of the way for cars.

The key to the design is a wide and stable base platform, upon which the rack is built. The platform is a 2" x 4" frame topped off with a ½"-thick oriented strand board (OSB) skin. Four large, 4"-diameter heavy-duty casters are attached to the bottom of the frame: two fixed casters at one end and a pair

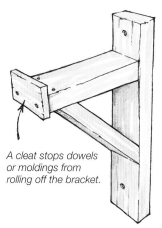

A cleat stops dowels or moldings from rolling off the bracket.

If you don't have room for a freestanding lumber rack, simple wall-mounted brackets are a good alternative.

of swivel casters at the other. The rack steers somewhat like a car.

A 2" x 4" is attached vertically to the platform about halfway across each end. In front of these posts, a couple of bins with angled tops provide storage for short lengths of lumber and partial sheets. Behind the posts is a space for full sheets of plywood and other sheet goods. On top of this rear compartment is a rack for long lengths of lumber, pipe, and the like.

The Stationary Rack

The key to the second lumber storage system for a basement is standard 1" I.D. black gas pipe. As designed, there are three lengths of pipe that run from floor to ceiling, each positioned 42" away from its neighbor.

These are not continuous lengths: Install T-shaped connectors at various intervals along the pipe (see the top drawing on page 21), including one at floor level. Tie these three uprights together with ¾" I.D. pipe, running it about 16" off the floor and the same distance from the ceiling. Anchor the rack using circular metal pipe flanges, screwing them to cleats between the joists in your basement ceiling.

To convert this skeleton into a rack, screw a 21"-long piece of threaded pipe

into each of the Ts in each upright. Then, to provide a stable base for the rack, use short elbows to cap off the lowest piece of pipe, which creates feet for the unit. With the pipes all in place, you're ready to start building the rest of the system with AC plywood.

Two ½" plywood boxes (9" x 30" x 40" long) roll in under the rack, each mounted on a set of four 1½"-diameter casters. These boxes hold hardwood and

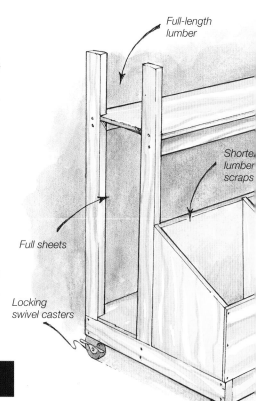

Full-length lumber

Shorter lumber scraps

Full sheets

Locking swivel casters

softwood shorts (pieces of stock under 40" long). Above them, two pairs of pipe arms support 8'-long lengths of thick (over 4/4) lumber.

The next three sets of arms each support an 8'-long tray. These 8"-high x 24"-wide trays hold stock that measures from 3' to 7' long. The two spaces above these trays are reserved for stock that is over 8' long.

Three trays should be sufficient to manage all the medium-length stock in a serious hobby shop. These are made of ½" AC plywood, glued and screwed together. Round over a radius on the top front corner of each end piece to avoid catching yourself on a sharp corner or splintering the plywood.

Insert dividers in the trays if you wish to further organize wood by species, thickness, or other characteristics pertinent to your work.

Simpler Solutions

If both of these storage racks are a bit ambitious for your needs, maybe a simpler rack will do. See the drawing on page 20 for a sturdy wall bracket design, or see the L-bracket system in A Wall-Mounted Lumber Rack at right.

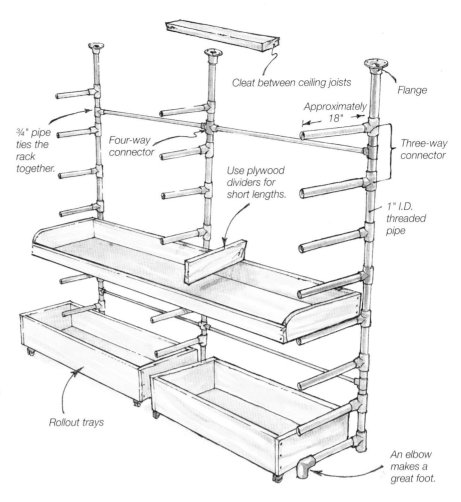

Cleat between ceiling joists

Flange

Approximately 18"

¾" pipe ties the rack together.

Four-way connector

Three-way connector

Use plywood dividers for short lengths.

1" I.D. threaded pipe

Rollout trays

An elbow makes a great foot.

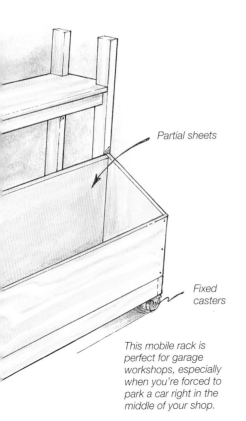

Partial sheets

Fixed casters

This mobile rack is perfect for garage workshops, especially when you're forced to park a car right in the middle of your shop.

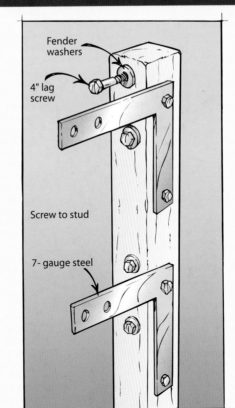

A Wall-Mounted Lumber Rack

Fender washers

4" lag screw

Screw to stud

7- gauge steel

Here's an option for a space-saving, low-tech lumber rack that you can easily build in an afternoon. Metal L-brackets serve as shelf brackets here. You can also use them as connection points for continuous wood shelving.

Look for brackets that are at least 7-gauge steel for maximum strength. Mount these brackets directly to the wall studs with lag screws if your shop walls have exposed studs. For drywall-sheathed walls, screw the brackets onto lengths of 2" x 2" lumber, and bolt these to the wall studs instead. Make sure the lag screws are driven at least 2" into the studs, and use fender washers to help distribute the weight.

Rolling Lumber Cart

In a small garage or basement shop, floor space isn't the only real estate that can be in short supply—walls get filled up, too. If there isn't room for a wall-mounted lumber rack in your shop, here's a rolling lumber cart that offers more than 70 square feet of shelf space, a separate compartment for storing sheet goods, and a roomy bin on top for cutoffs. Heavy-duty shelf standards and brackets keep it all high and dry.

by Chris Marshall

Starting with the Base

Get this project rolling by cutting the base parts (pieces 1 through 5) to size (see the Material List on page 26). Five cross-brace assemblies reinforce the base and serve as attachment points for the uprights. Notice in the drawings on pages 24 through 26 that the end and center cross-brace assemblies are sandwiches of two 2" x 6"s and blocking; the other two cross braces are just pairs of 2" x 6"s. Build the thicker cross braces by gluing and screwing each base end (piece 1) to a cross brace (piece 3), with two sections of short blocking (pieces 4) in between. Make the thick center cross brace the same way,

using two cross braces instead of a base end. Leave the center cavities of these assemblies open for now.

To make the other two, narrower cross-brace assemblies, first plow a pair of ¾" x 3½"-wide dadoes across the face of each cross brace to form bridle joints for housing the uprights (see Figure 1). Follow the drawings on page 24 to locate these cuts. Fasten pairs of cross braces together with glue and screws, and then rout a shallow recess along the top edge of each to install plastic slides (pieces 15). Make the recesses ⅛" deep and 1½" wide so they span the distance between the upright cutouts.

Figure 1: *After machining your stock to overall size, use your table saw to form the dadoes on the uprights and the half laps on the cross braces.*

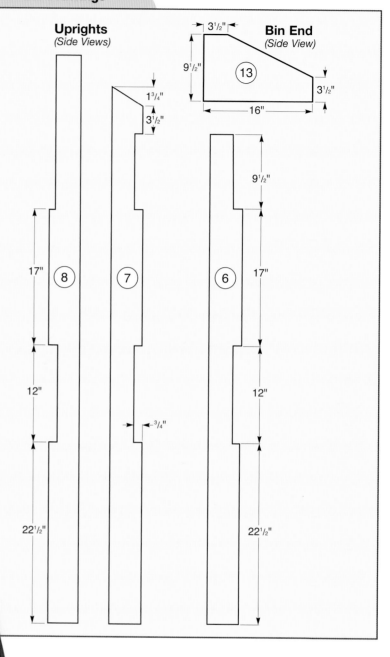

Figure 2: *Drill counterbores to recess the lag bolt heads and washers that fasten the base sides and ends to the cross braces. Clamp a straightedge to the table to keep the counterbores aligned.*

Assemble the base framework by attaching the five cross-brace assemblies to the base sides (pieces 2) with 5⁄16" x 4" countersunk lag bolts and washers (see Figure 2). Space the cross braces evenly along the base.

Making the Rack

When you get this rack all filled up, there's going to be some substantial weight involved. That's why I turned to cross braces and blocks—this is one project you don't want to be guilty of underbuilding.

Refer to the drawings to lay out the 10 uprights (pieces 6 through 8). Cut them to size and shape (see Figure 3). Cut the top cross braces (pieces 9) to length now, too. Use a dado blade for milling the long, 3⁄4"-deep recesses in the uprights, as well as the tongues on the

Figure 3: *The tops of the outer uprights are angled, as shown in the drawing above. After cutting the angle, sand it flush.*

Technical Drawings

Uprights (Side Views)

Bin End (Side View)

ends of the top cross braces. When you're through dadoing, slide the uprights into their cutouts in the base to test the fit. If needed, use a small block plane to refine the fit.

With the uprights in place, fill the voids in the center and end base cross braces with long

blocking (pieces 5). Tap the blocking down below flush to form 1⁄8"-deep recesses between the uprights for more plastic slides. Glue and screw the blocking into place.

Install the top cross braces, including the pair that wraps around the center uprights. Attach all the cross braces to the uprights with carriage bolts. Cut the wide and narrow upright braces (pieces 10 and 11) to size (I used plywood for these pieces), and attach them to the uprights with deck screws.

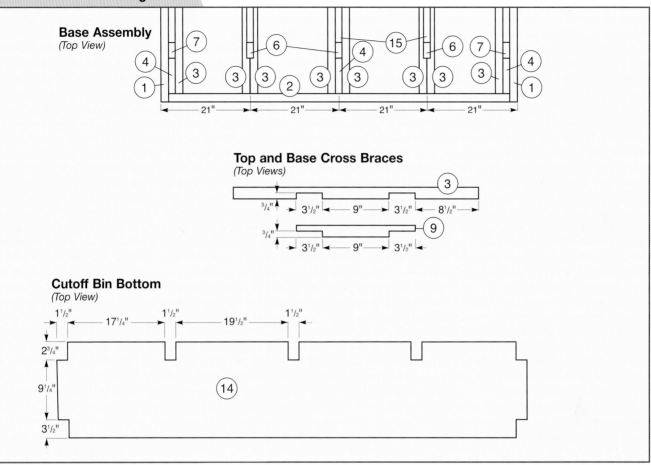

Base Assembly
(Top View)

Top and Base Cross Braces
(Top Views)

Cutoff Bin Bottom
(Top View)

QuickTip

Shop-Made Hold-Downs
Hold-downs provide a good means of keeping lumber pressed tightly to a machine fence while cutting or routing. Here are a couple of options for making inexpensive but effective hold-downs.

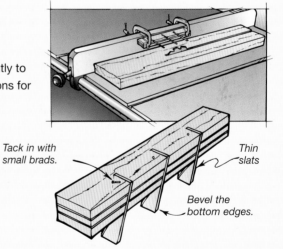

Tack in with small brads.

Thin slats

Bevel the bottom edges.

1. Simply slice a piece of ¾" plywood with a band saw kerf at about a 30° angle. Then, install a flexible-blade putty knife in the kerf with a dab of quick-setting epoxy. Clamp the hold-down to the table saw's rip fence at the desired height. Set the hold-down just low enough so the putty knife blade flexes against your workpiece to hold it securely.

2. Another option is to cut kerfs in a piece of ¾" plywood wide enough to hold wooden slats about the thickness of paint-stirring paddles. Make the slats project a few inches beyond the plywood so they'll flex reasonably easily. (Bevel the bottom edges of the slats so they make better contact with the wood.) Glue and tack the slats in the kerfs. This hold-down style can be made any length or width you need. Long hold-downs are especially useful for ripping longer boards on a table saw.

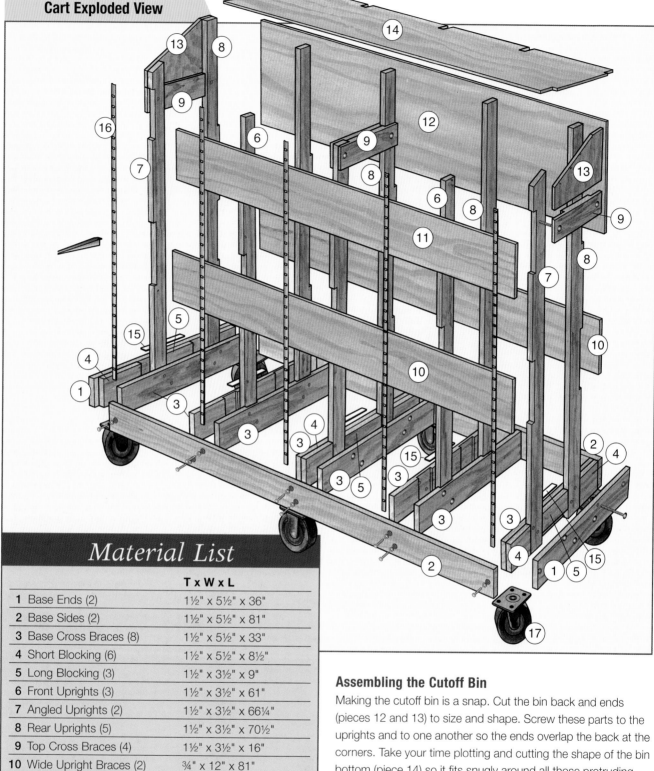

Material List

		T x W x L
1	Base Ends (2)	1½" x 5½" x 36"
2	Base Sides (2)	1½" x 5½" x 81"
3	Base Cross Braces (8)	1½" x 5½" x 33"
4	Short Blocking (6)	1½" x 5½" x 8½"
5	Long Blocking (3)	1½" x 3½" x 9"
6	Front Uprights (3)	1½" x 3½" x 61"
7	Angled Uprights (2)	1½" x 3½" x 66¼"
8	Rear Uprights (5)	1½" x 3½" x 70½"
9	Top Cross Braces (4)	1½" x 3½" x 16"
10	Wide Upright Braces (2)	¾" x 12" x 81"
11	Narrow Upright Brace (1)	¾" x 9½" x 81"
12	Cutoff Bin Back (1)	¾" x 19" x 81"
13	Cutoff Bin Ends (2)	¾" x 9½" x 16"
14	Cutoff Bin Bottom (1)	¾" x 15½" x 81"
15	Slides (5)	¼" x 1½" x 9" UHMW
16	Shelf Standards (10)	1½" x 55" Steel
17	Casters (6)	4 Swivel, 2 Fixed

Assembling the Cutoff Bin

Making the cutoff bin is a snap. Cut the bin back and ends (pieces 12 and 13) to size and shape. Screw these parts to the uprights and to one another so the ends overlap the back at the corners. Take your time plotting and cutting the shape of the bin bottom (piece 14) so it fits snugly around all those protruding uprights. Chamfer the front edge to keep it from splintering later. Drop it into place, and screw it to the ends, back, and braces.

Wrapping Things Up

Time to install some hardware. Bolt shelf standards to the uprights. I used heavy-duty standards and brackets available from Hartville Tool (*www.hartvilletool.com*). Use four ⁵⁄₁₆" x 3½" lag bolts and 1½"-diameter (O.D.) fender washers to attach each standard. Cut pieces of Ultra High Molecular Weight (UHMW) plastic into slides (pieces 15), and chamfer the top edges. You can buy sheets of this super-slippery plastic from many woodworking suppliers. These slides make it much easier to load and unload heavy sheet goods by yourself.

Slip the slides into their recesses in the base cross braces, and attach with countersunk screws. Arrange six heavy-duty casters around the base. Choose fixed wheels for the center pair and swiveling casters for the corners. Make sure that the casters you buy are rated to support at least 500 pounds each.

*Quick*Tip

Options for Displaying Those Project Plans and Notes

Keeping blueprints and notes handy when you're in the middle of a project can be a real challenge, especially if you're working on a small bench.

One solution is to mount an ordinary roll-up window shade above your workbench. Tape your drawings and plans right on the shade. When you need whatever is behind the shade, simply roll it up out of the way. While it's rolled up, everything stays neat, protected, and right where you can find it.

If you have some open wall space near the bench, consider mounting an inexpensive bulletin board or a dry-erase board there. Tack or tape up your drawings to keep them accessible while you work.

Calendar of Shop Maintenance Tips

Every Day (of Use):
- Empty shop garbage cans and any open dust bins.
- Clean out rag storage cans; hang rags soaked with oil finish out to dry.
- Lubricate air-powered tools (nail guns, random-orbit sanders, and the like), and/or refill reservoirs on automatic oilers.

Every Week:
- Clean sawdust from shop floors and benches.
- Drain moisture from compressor's air storage tank, pipes, and manifold and filter/moisture trap(s).
- Shake dust collector filter bags to remove excess dust cake (more often if necessary).
- Empty sawdust from dust collector bags or bins (more often if necessary).
- Empty shop vacuum, and clean filter (more often if necessary).

Every Month:
- Vacuum fine dust from tops of light fixtures and out of electrical outlets, switches, and junction boxes.
- Vacuum prefilters on air filtration devices.
- Clean out sanding tables and machines not connected to dust collection.
- Clean off built-up finish on spray guns, spray booth walls, and the like.
- Check the condition of the air filter and the oil level in your compressor's pump (latter not required for oil-less models).
- Test and reset ground-fault interrupt (GFI) outlets and circuits.

Twice a Year:
- Inspect condition of machines and portable power tools; service as needed.
- Check fire extinguishers; recharge or replace as necessary.
- Change oil in air compressor pump (oil-less compressors exempt).
- Treat metal surfaces on tools with rust-preventative spray or wax.
- Check compressed air system (tank, hoses, and fittings) for leaks.
- Check condition of filter bags or cartridges on dust collectors, air cleaners, and shop vacuums; replace as necessary.
- Inspect central dust collection system's ductwork and flexible hoses for air leaks or clogs.
- Check first-aid kit for completeness; refresh supplies as necessary.
- Check condition of glues and finishes; properly discard products that are past their expiration dates, dried out, or partially cured in the can or bottle.
- Check shop for leaks or moisture that may ruin tools and stored lumber and supplies.

Easy-Access Storage Bins

Tired of searching for fasteners or piling boxes of them on a shelf? Still using baby-food jars to store nails and screws? Here's an easy-to-build wall system that keeps fasteners and shop sundries organized, visible, and at the ready.

by Barry Chatell

I'm an organized fellow and prefer to keep my fasteners and small hardware tidy. But I've never liked the usual options for storage containers. Little glass jars are prone to break, and other types of plastic containers are hard to see into or difficult to open. Then, a lightbulb came on when I noticed bulk-food bins at the grocery store. I employed the same basic container shape for this wall-mounted storage bin system. It features open, forward-slanting bins with clear plastic fronts. You can use my dimensions or modify the bin sizes to suit your needs.

Cutting the Back and Bottom Strips

You can build this project from any ⅝"-thick sheet material (see the Material List on page 30). Start by cutting a workpiece large enough for the back panel (piece 1) and the four bottom strips (pieces 2). Use a table saw and dado blade to plow six parallel dadoes into this workpiece, following the locations and dimensions shown in the drawings on page 30. These dadoes form tracks for the bin sides. Rip the four bottom strips off one end, as shown in Figure 1.

Making the Bin Sides

Make the bin sides from lengths of 4"-wide material. To begin, swivel your miter saw's blade to 45°, and fix a wide stop block to the saw table with double-sided tape. Index the stop block off the blade so you can clip the corners off the ends of the 4" strips and form a point in the middle. The stop block will be cut partially off with the first miter cut, so make it at least 4" wide to preserve some bearing support. To cut the points, set the strip against the stop block, clip the first corner off, flip the strip over, and trim the second corner off the same end (see Figure 2 on page 31). Turn the strip end-for-end, and trim off the corners on the other end.

Use your table saw and miter gauge to crosscut the pointed ends off the strips, forming two bin sides per strip. Set up these crosscuts so the distance from the tip of the point to the crosscut is 3³⁄₁₆". Now, simply repeat the mitering and crosscutting procedure to make all 24 bins.

Figure 1: *First, cut six dadoes into your oversize panel. Then, rip the four bottom strips off one end, and trim the panel to its final size.*

Material List

		T x W x L
1	Back* (1)	⅝" x 18½" x 24¾"
2	Bottom Strips* (4)	⅝" x 1" x 24¾"
3	Plexiglas Bin Fronts (4)	⅛" x 2⅞" x 23¾"
4	Bin Sides (24)	⅝" x 3³⁄₁₆" x 4"
5	French Cleats** (2)	¾" x 2⅜" x 23¾"
6	Spacer Strip (1)	¾" x 1" x 23¾"

Cut pieces 1 and 2 to size from one larger piece after cutting grooves.

**Both pieces are cut from one piece of material.*

French Cleat Detail

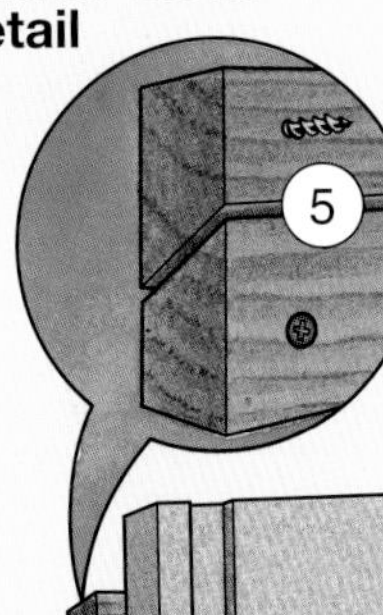

French cleats are a great way to securely hang something on a wall while allowing for easy removal.

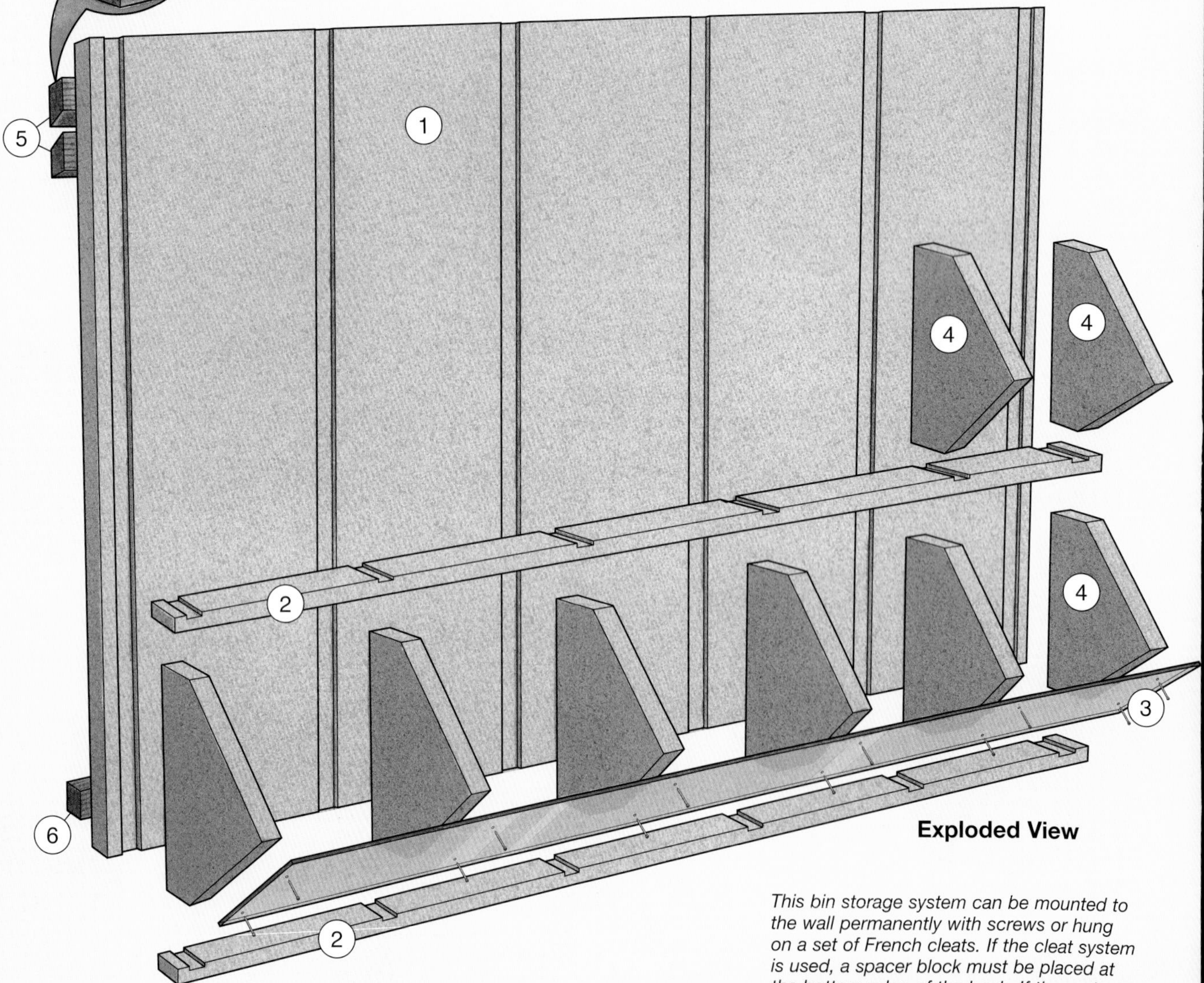

Exploded View

This bin storage system can be mounted to the wall permanently with screws or hung on a set of French cleats. If the cleat system is used, a spacer block must be placed at the bottom edge of the back. If the project is screwed to the wall, omit the cleats and spacer (pieces 5 and 6).

Back and Bottom Strip Groove Layout
(Top View)

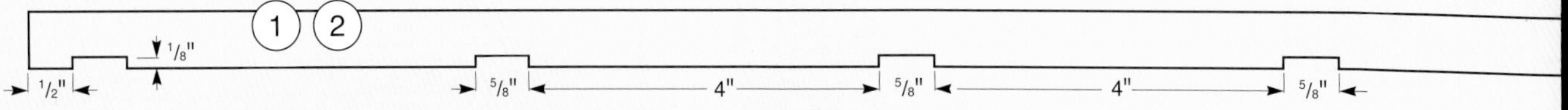

⅛"   ½"   ⅝"   4"   ⅝"   4"   ⅝"

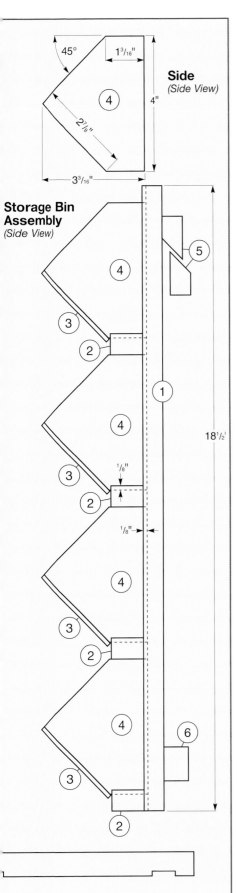

Side
(Side View)

45° 1³/₁₆"

4

4"

2⁷/₈"

3³/₁₆"

Storage Bin Assembly
(Side View)

4

5

3

2

1

4

18¹/₂"

3

¹/₈"

2

¹/₈"

4

3

2

4

3

6

4

3

2

Time for Assembly

Assembly is as simple as gluing the first bottom strip flush with the lower edge of the back and then gluing six bin sides in the dadoes. Add another bottom strip and six more bin sides on top of the first. Build up four rows of bins this way.

Use a triple-chip tooth or a plywood-cutting blade in your table saw to cut strips of ⅛"-thick acrylic plastic for the bin fronts (see Figure 3). I nailed these front strips to the bin sides, but first, I drilled pilot holes through the plastic to keep it from cracking.

I simply screwed my storage bins to the wall. Alternatively, you can mount the unit on French cleats (pieces 5) for easy removal. To make French cleats, bevel rip a 4"-wide piece of wood along its centerline with the blade tilted to 45°. Screw one cleat to the back of the bin system at the top with the beveled edge pointing down, and attach the other cleat to the wall with its bevel up (see the drawings). This allows the two beveled cleats to interlock. Then, attach a spacer strip (piece 6) along the bottom edge of the back panel. Now, hang the bins, and fill 'em up.

Figure 3: *Keep the paper facing on the plastic during drilling and cutting to minimize chipping and make it easier to mark your layout lines and centerpoints. Cut it with a fine-toothed saw blade.*

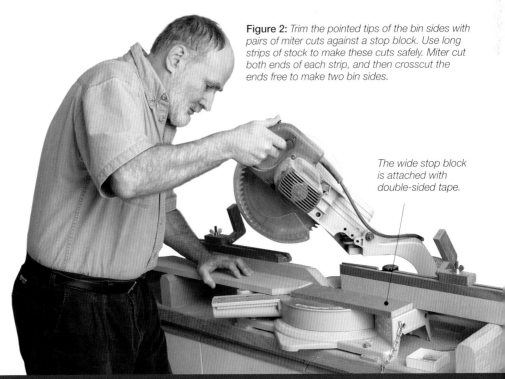

Figure 2: *Trim the pointed tips of the bin sides with pairs of miter cuts against a stop block. Use long strips of stock to make these cuts safely. Miter cut both ends of each strip, and then crosscut the ends free to make two bin sides.*

The wide stop block is attached with double-sided tape.

Battery Charger Cabinet

If you have more cordless tool chargers than outlets, keeping all your batteries charged and organized can be a problem. This compact charging cabinet stows multiple chargers and batteries neatly, and the contents hide away behind a tambour door that's easy to build. A weekend of shop time is all it takes to turn charger clutter into an efficient charging system—and it's a fitting way to learn tambour door construction, too.

by Sandor Nagyszalanczy

If you're one of those woodworkers who wholeheartedly believes that "he who dies with the most tools wins," then chances are, your shop has more portable power tools in it than you can count on both your hands…and feet. And if you're a thoroughly modern woodworker, chances are good that an ever-growing number of those portables are of the cordless variety.

The downside to having all this high-tech hardware on hand is that you're likely to have tools made by three or four different manufacturers, each of which requires separate, dedicated batteries—and battery chargers.

It's all too easy to end up with a half-dozen chargers and extra batteries sprawled out across your benchtop.

My solution to keeping a gaggle of different battery chargers organized, neatly stored, and plugged in is to build a wall-hung cabinet especially for them. This charger cabinet has four trays that accommodate six or more battery chargers, as well as a handful of spare batteries and accessories. Each tray is wide enough to handle any of the battery chargers currently on the U.S. market and is angled forward, to make it easier to plug in or remove batteries. Charger cords run neatly through the bottom of the trays along the sides of the cabinet to a multi-outlet power strip, which is screwed to the bottom of the cabinet. A tambour-style door encloses the entire interior of the cabinet to keep dust and chips from fouling battery contacts or sensitive charger electronics.

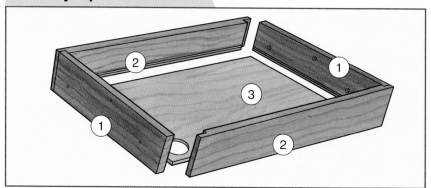

Tray Exploded View

The cabinet is designed to mount directly to your shop's 16" on-center wall studs. It's slender and tall, to fit the narrowest spot and save on wall space.

The intent from the start was to create a good-looking cabinet from hardwood but to keep the design easy to build. I assembled the trays using simple but strong rabbet joints and a captured bottom and then screwed the trays to the cabinet sides using wood screws. I also used an unorthodox shortcut method for making the tambour door and the grooved track it slides in without painstaking work or elaborate jigs. Although these construction methods may be called "quick and dirty," they are aimed at producing a strong, functional piece of shop cabinetry that looks terrific and doesn't take a week to build.

Relatively few parts are needed for the charger cabinet, as you can see from the Material List on page 36. There are two solid-wood cabinet sides, each with a grooved track for the tambour door (routed using a special router fence setup); four trays with solid-wood sides and plywood bottoms; a narrow bottom rail that joins the cabinet sides and supports a powerstrip; and a tambour door. The door consists of 59 narrow wood slats held together by a canvas backing glued and ironed into place as the tambour is held and aligned in a simple shop-made jig.

Start the cabinet project by cutting and assembling the parts for the four identical trays (pieces 1 through 3). The trays serve as the major structural elements that support and align the sides of the cabinet. Cut the solid-wood components to size, making sure all the long sides are exactly the same length, as any variation will negatively affect the way the tambour door slides.

To capture the plywood bottom of each tray, cut a groove along the inside of each side, positioned as shown in the drawing on the top of page 36. Next, cut out the four plywood bottoms. Take the bottoms to the drill press,

Figure 1: Use your drill press to drill and counterbore holes in the tray sides. Placement isn't critical, but use your first side as a template for drilling the others for a uniform appearance.

Figure 2: Setting up for repeatable cuts is critical for the trays in this project (above), as they also serve as structural elements in the cabinet. You can add a little strength to the glued-up corners with several thin brads (right).

Figure 3: *Use a sharp carpenter's pencil and a bevel gauge set to 70° to mark out where the tray bottoms meet the cabinet sides.*

and using a Forstner bit or hole saw, bore two 1¼"-diameter holes in each bottom, positioned as shown in the drawings on page 36; these holes accommodate the plugs on the charger cords. As long as you're at the drill press, bore three holes in each of the tray's short sides (see the drawings) for the flathead screws that attach the trays to the sides. Since placement isn't critical, mark out hole positions on one side, and then use it as a template to drill the other sides, as shown in Figure 1. Countersink the holes (on the inside-facing surfaces) for the screws.

To create a strong, simple joint that joins the tray sides, cut a rabbet on each end of each long side piece, using a dado blade in the table saw. A miter fence with a built-in stop helps to keep the work dependably square and in position as it's cut, as shown in Figure 2. You could also use your miter saw for these cuts.

After sanding the inside surfaces of the tray sides and plywood bottoms, glue and clamp them together. It is important to make sure at this stage that none of the tray pieces are twisted. After clamping, check each tray for square by measuring diagonally from corner to corner.

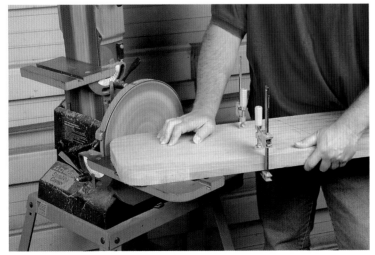

Figure 4: *Use a disc sander to smooth the corners of the sides to the marked radii. The goal is to end up with three quarter-round corners on each cabinet side.*

Precision Tracking

Make a runoff block with ¾" x 1½" x 8"-wide scrap wood, and screw on a 2" x 4"-long cross piece at 90°, as shown above. When you've routed the track, use a chisel to create a bit more relief space at the corners.

This tambour-track-routing method doesn't require a routing template or a rub collar. Instead, I used MicroFence's two-point-contact router fence, which rides against the edge of the cabinet side. The contact points guide the cut at a fixed distance from the edge, even around rounded corners. The trick is that the shape of the side's edge determines the shape of the routed track.

As such, the cabinet must have two rounded top corners and another at the bottom rear. This provides the curved track for the tambour when the door is opened all the way. It takes some skill to guide a two-point fence around a corner, so practice on scrap first.

You could make your own fence for this job, but MicroFence's router fence makes this sort of groove routing very easy (*www.microfence.com*). This is because the MicroFence comes with two semicircular guides that mount in place of its normal straight fence bar, making it just right for this track-routing method. If you decide to make or adapt your own two-point fence, be sure the two rounded lobes have 1" radii and are set on center, 2" apart.

Cabinet Exploded View

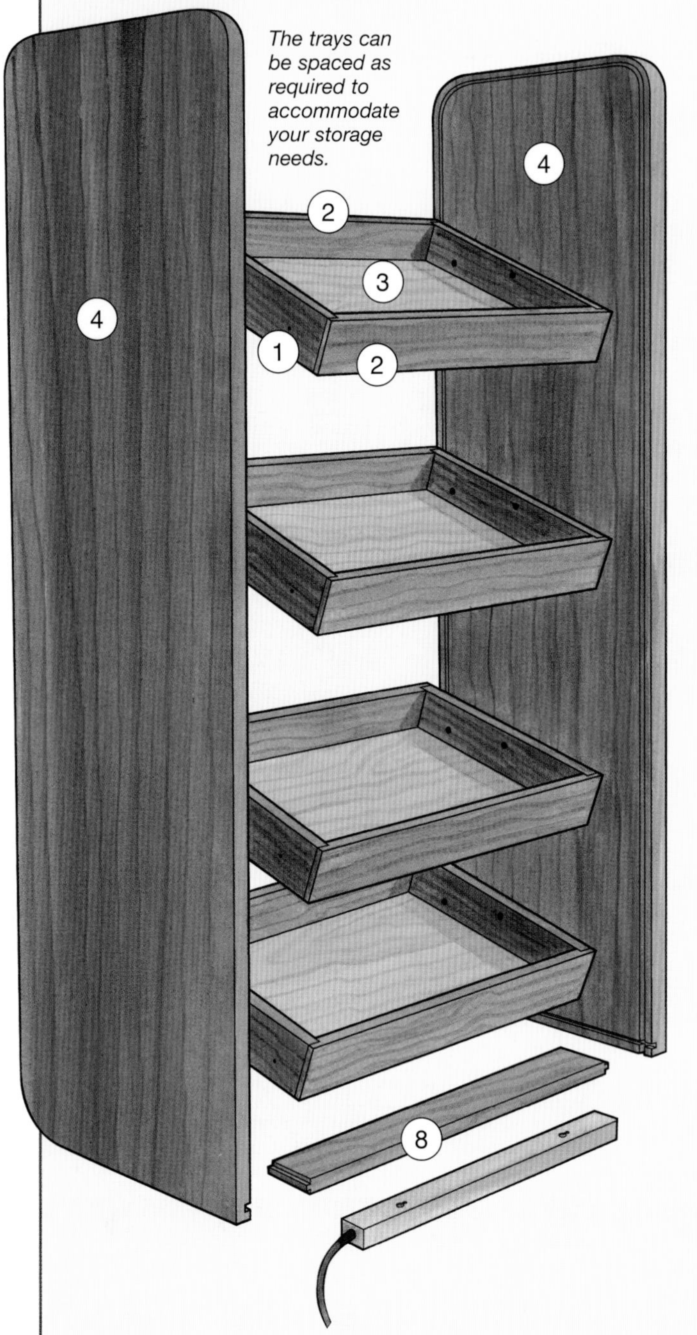

The trays can be spaced as required to accommodate your storage needs.
4
4
2
3
1
2
8

Material List – Cabinet

		T x W x L
1	Tray Sides (8)	½" x 2¼" x 8"
2	Tray Fronts and Backs (8)	½" x 2¼" x 17"
3	Tray Bottoms (4)	¼" x 7¹⁵⁄₁₆" x 16⅜"
4	Cabinet Sides (2)	¾" x 11" x 40½"
5	Tambour Slat Blanks* (64)	⁵⁄₁₆" x ¹³⁄₁₆" x 17½"
6	Tambour Backing (1)	1 Yd. 10-oz. Cotton Duck
7	Door Pull (1)	¹³⁄₁₆" x 1⅛" x 16¾"
8	Bottom Rail (1)	¹³⁄₁₆" x 2½" x 17½"
9	Bumper Stops (2)	Screwed-On Rubber

Trim to fit after door is glued up; cut extra slats to select from.

Cabinet Side
(Side View)

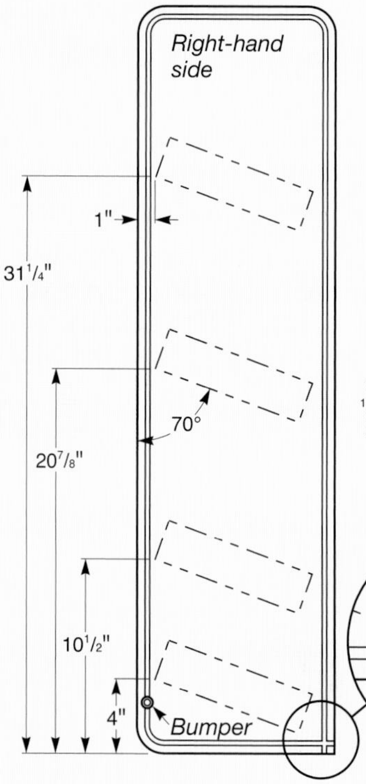

Right-hand side
1"
31¼"
20⅞"
70°
10½"
4"
Bumper

Bottom Rail
(Front View)

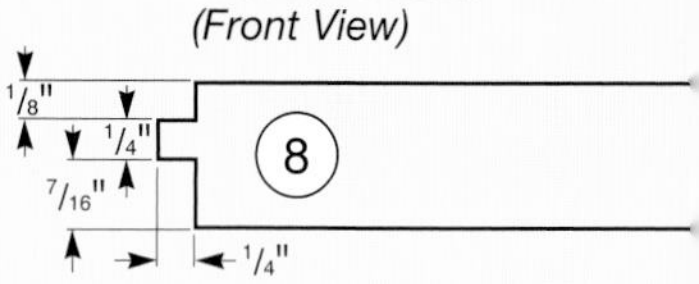

⅛"
¼"
⁷⁄₁₆"
¼"
8

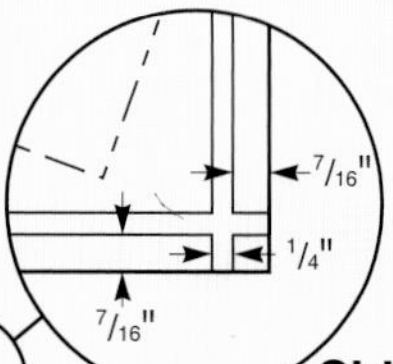

⁷⁄₁₆"
¼"
⁷⁄₁₆"

Side Corner Detail

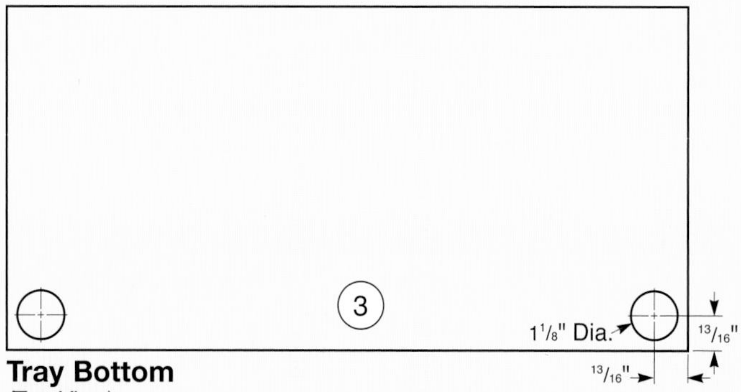

3
1⅛" Dia.
¹³⁄₁₆"
¹³⁄₁₆"

Tray Bottom
(Top View)

Tray Front Machining Detail
(End View)

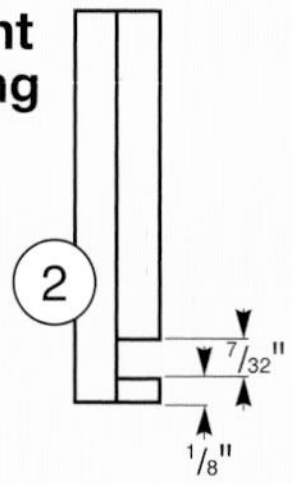

2
⁷⁄₃₂"
⅛"

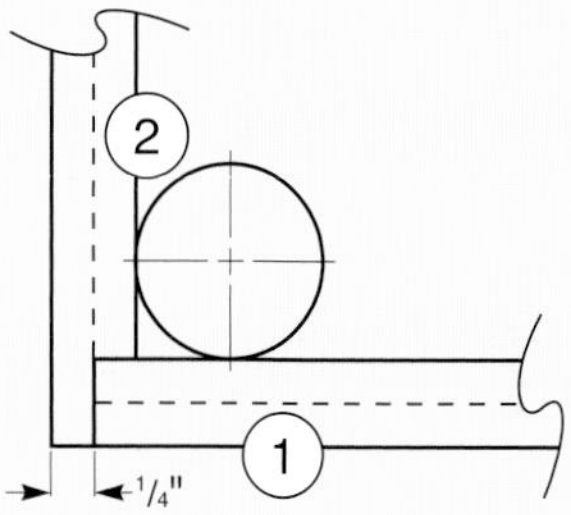

2
1
¼"

Tray Corner
(Top View)

Tambour Door
Exploded View

6

5

9/32"

3/16" 13/16"

Canvas Side

Tambour
Slat Detail

5

7

Door Pull
(End View)

1/2"

3/8"

13/16"

7

Tambour Slat
Glue-Up Jig

1/2" x 2½" x 22"

¾" x 24" x 58"

½" x 2½" x 51"

¾" construction-grade plywood

The jig rails must form perfectly square corners.

Use a band saw to rip the thin tambour slats from a thick blank. Choose the best-looking slats for your door.

Making this tambour door requires about 59 slats (pieces 5). Select wide, 13/16"-thick lumber with a clean, evenly planed surface. Crosscut your blanks 17½" long and perfectly square, with edges jointed square and parallel to one another. You'll need enough stock to yield about 64 slats (a few extra to choose from). It helps to cut the slats on a band saw, since the blade's thin kerf wastes less wood. Set the rip fence to cut strips 11/32" thick. Rip slats from the edges of the blanks you prepare.

When all your blanks have their edges cut once, clean up their edges on the jointer, and then rip another set of slats. After repeating this process a few times, check to make sure the edges of all blanks are still parallel.

Once all the slats are cut, it's time to run them through your thickness planer once (paying close attention to grain direction), shaving down the rough side. This should produce a big stack of slats each 5/16" thick, with two clean and parallel surfaces.

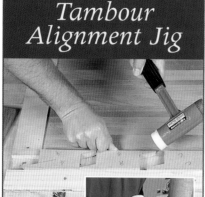

Tambour Alignment Jig

Use wedges to hold and align the slats in your jig (above). Tamp the slats flat with a hammer and block (right), and then retighten the wedges.

Once the slats are set in the jig good-side down, you're ready to apply the lightweight (10-oz.) canvas cotton duck (piece 6). Don't cut it to exact size yet; just trim one long edge straight with a razor blade and straightedge.

I used an iron to quick-cure the glue. Fully heat the iron to high before you start. Quickly apply a thin layer of PVA glue to one face of the canvas and slats (see Gluing the Slats to the Canvas on page 39).

Place the canvas on the slats, aligning the trimmed edge with the long stop of the jig (if the glue is starting to dry, don't worry; the iron's heat will reactivate it). Without dawdling, iron the entire surface of the canvas with large, back-and-forth sweeping passes. It will only take a minute or so to cure the glue. Remove the glued-up tambour from the jig right away, and flex it to be sure the joints between slats move freely. If adjacent slats are stuck together, clean them with a damp rag. Knock off the slats' sharp edges with some 120-grit sandpaper.

Trim the canvas using a sharp razor and straightedge. Cut it back ⅜" on each long side of the door and flush to the edges of the slats at each end.

After the glue has set and the clamps are off, reinforce the corners by driving a few 1"-long brads into each end, as shown in the inset photo in Figure 2 on page 34.

The two sides of the cabinet (pieces 4) are made from 4/4 wood thickness-planed down to ¾". Take care to make sure each end is square. After picking the good face of each cabinet side, lay them both good-face down on your bench, edges aligned. Draw a line 1" in from the back edge of each side, and, using the dimensions in the cabinet side view drawing on page 36, measure out and mark the bottom, back corner position of each tray. Then, using a bevel gauge set to 70°, mark a fine line with a carpenter's pencil where the bottom edge of each of the trays will go (see Figure 3 on page 35). The pencil indents the wood so you can still see lines after the sides are sanded. Label their front and top edges so you don't rout the wrong surfaces.

Clamp the two cabinet sides together with their inside faces facing in, using three or four clamps positioned well away from the ends. Set a pencil compass to a 3" radius, and mark a quarter-circle at the two top corners and at the single bottom rear corner. Now, rough cut the corners just shy of the pencil line. With the sides still clamped together, use a disc sander to smooth all three corners down to the marked radius (see Figure 4 on page 35).

Routing the Tambour Track

A narrow groove routed around the edges of both sides, as shown in the cabinet side view drawing, creates a track to guide the tambour door. The method I used to rout this track requires a special router fence setup, as described in Precision Tracking on

Figure 5: *To begin assembling the cabinet, align the trays on the marks you scribed earlier, and secure them with screws. The trays are the structural members that join the cabinet sides and hold them square.*

page 35. To provide a surface for the fence's guide to ride on where the groove enters and exits the end of each side, you'll need a runout block. This block is clamped to the end and front edge before routing at those locations.

The tambour track is routed with a ¼"-diameter straight bit. You can use a fixed-base or plunge router, but a laminate trimmer is easier to maneuver than a full-size router. Rout the track in three passes, each successively deeper. Move the router carefully around the corners, using constant and full pressure to keep the edge guide always against the edge of the work. Don't worry if you make a slight goof, because most of the length of the track itself is hidden by the tambour, and small divots won't affect its operation too much.

Once the track routing is complete, use a chisel to widen the inside radius of the grooves at each of the track corners. This adds a little relief and allows the tambour to negotiate the corners more easily. Sand the track grooves smooth along their entire length

Figure 6: *With the cabinet assembled, gently slide the tambour door into its track. This step will require a bit of patience and care, since even slight racking or one misaligned slat can hang things up. If the door sticks, slide it back a nudge and try again.*

using either a foam-backed sanding pad or a short strip of 120-grit sandpaper wrapped around a small piece of stiff foam. For areas that fuzzed up or splintered during routing, start with coarser, 80-grit sandpaper. All surfaces of the track groove should end up very smooth, with their top edges slightly rounded.

One result of this track-routing method that you may notice is that the radius of the routed track is slightly less than that of the corner itself. To make them match, clamp the cabinet sides together again as you did before, and sand the top corners down to a radius of 3¼". The bottom corner won't show, so you can leave it alone.

To complete the cabinet sides, round their top and front-facing outer edges with a ¼"-radius piloted roundover bit. Don't rout the straight portion of the back or the bottom edges, as these should stay square for attaching the bottom rail and mounting the cabinet to the wall. Finally, sand the routed edges and inside faces of the cabinet sides smooth.

Turn your attention to page 37 and the sidebars throughout this article to build the tambour door (pieces 5 and 6). Once you've completed all the steps, you'll still have to make and install a U-shaped pull (piece 7) from solid wood (see the door pull drawing on page 37). Cut the ⅜"-deep channel in the underside of the pull with a ½"-wide dado blade in the table saw. After rounding or beveling its ends with a rasp or stationary sander, glue the pull to the end slat at the bottom of the door. When the glue sets, nail through this slat to further secure the pull.

The next step is to assemble the cabinet and do a trial fitting of the tambour in its track. With one of the cabinet sides on the benchtop, carefully position the bottom edge and back corner of each tray, following the lines marked earlier. Drive in the three #8 x 1" screws that attach each end of each tray to the side, as shown in Figure 5. Once all the trays are attached, carefully flip the assembly over, set it atop the other cabinet side, and finish screwing on the trays to join the sides together.

Gluing the Slats to the Canvas

Quickly apply a thin layer of glue (yellow or white woodworking glues work equally well) to one side of the canvas and then the slats. This takes quite a bit of glue.

Place the canvas on the slats, aligning the trimmed long edge to the long stop of the jig. Don't worry if the glue starts to dry; ironing will reactivate it. Press the canvas flat using a round-edged block of wood.

Quick-set the glue with a hot iron. After the glue has cured, cut the canvas back ⅜" on each long side of the tambour. Cut it flush to the edges of the slats at each end. If the canvas starts to lift, apply a dab of glue and stick it back down, ironing it as necessary.

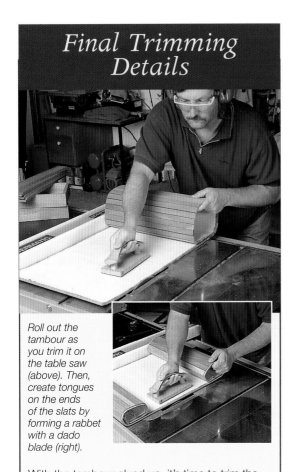

Final Trimming Details

Roll out the tambour as you trim it on the table saw (above). Then, create tongues on the ends of the slats by forming a rabbet with a dado blade (right).

With the tambour glued up, it's time to trim the door to its final 17⅜" width, using a table saw and crosscut blade. Start with the canvas side up, positioning the edge that was butted up to the long stop in the jig against the saw's rip fence. Next, rabbet the slats to create a wood tongue on each end; this makes it easier for the door to negotiate the corners of the track. Fit the table saw with a dado blade that's at least 5⁄16" wide, and set its height to produce a tongue that's just a skosh over 3⁄16" thick (see the tambour slat detail drawing on page 37). Set the rip fence to produce 9⁄32"-long tongues on each side of the tambour. With the canvas side up, carefully feed the tambour over the blade, using a push block to keep it flat and to ensure a full depth of cut. It's easiest to unroll the tambour as you feed it through the cut and then roll it back up again at the back of the saw. Sand all surfaces of the tongues to round their edges slightly, to help the door slide more easily. Roll the tambour up, and sand the slats with the outer corners of each tongue exposed.

With the cabinet lying on its back, gently insert the tambour into its groove at the bottom edge. Work it slowly up the front and all the way around the track to the back (see Figure 6 on page 39), pulling it back and forth to wear it in slightly. If the tambour hangs up in the corners, check to see if any of the tongues or sections of the groove need a little more trimming or sanding. Stay with it until the tambour slides all the way around the track without too much effort.

Finishing Up

When you're finally pleased with how the tambour fits into the cabinet, remove it from its track. You're just about ready for finishing. But first, make the bottom rail (piece 8) that joins the cabinet sides and provides a place to mount the electrical power strip (see the bottom rail drawing on page 36 for details). Using a dado blade in your table saw, cut the short tongues that fit into the track grooves. Check the rail for a snug fit, but don't install it just yet.

A wipe-on finish such as satin polyurethane gel makes a good finish for this project. Spread finish over the surfaces of the assembled cabinet, the good side of the tambour door, and the bottom rail, and then wipe the excess off. Wipe finish on and off the edges of all the tambour slats, and leave the wet tambour door rolled up on its edge to dry without adjacent slats sticking together. After a few hours, quickly touch sand with 320-grit sandpaper, and then apply a second coat of finish. The result is a serviceable finish that looks great on the outside of the cabinet and okay on the inside—perfect for a shop project.

When the finish dries, apply a bit of paraffin or candle wax to the slat tongues, as well as to the tambour track all the way around. Reinstall the tambour, and position the door pull at the top of the front track curve. Now, screw on two rubber bumper stops (pieces 9) against the edge of the last slat and directly over the track groove. These keep the door from sliding too far open.

Drive the cabinet's bottom rail flush with the front of the cabinet, as shown in Figure 7. Then, drive two #8 x 1½" screws into pilot holes drilled into each end to secure the rail. The screws let you remove the rail in the future, in case you need to adjust the tambour. Mount the power strip to the underside of the bottom rail with a pair of screws.

Mounting the Cabinet

Hang the cabinet by "toe-screwing" directly through each side into the wall studs. First, drill four holes spaced evenly along the straight portion of the back edge of each side, angling them at about 45°. Next, position the cabinet on the wall so that it straddles a pair of wall studs. Support and level the cabinet, and then drive the #8 x 2"-long bugle-head screws into the studs. If your walls lack properly spaced studs, screw a piece of plywood to the wall, and then mount your cabinet to it instead.

Now for the fun part: filling the cabinet's trays with your chargers and other gear. Feed each charger's electrical cord down through the holes in the bottom of the trays, and plug the cords into the power strip. Wind up the excess lengths of cord, and use wire or plastic ties to keep them neatly coiled. Plug the strip's cord into an outlet, and your tool batteries will always be juiced up and ready for action.

Figure 7: *One of the last steps is to drive home the cabinet's bottom rail. A power strip is mounted to the rail to provide electricity to all the battery chargers.*

QuickTip

Egg-cellent Solution

Egg cartons can form convenient bases to support knobs and such for painting or finishing. Punch a small hole in the base of each recess in one half of a carton, and screw the knobs in place. This way, the knobs stay put and separated for applying the finish, your hands end up cleaner, and the carton forms a handy drying rack.

Simple Veneer Press

Woodworkers have used all sorts of unorthodox ways to flatten veneer, but a veneer press still works best. Here's an effective design that you can build on the cheap.

by Tom Caspar

The best all-around solution for flattening veneer is to use a veneer press. Here's a simple one that's cheap and easy to build. In fact, the materials are readily available at any building center, and the technique is adaptable to any size workpiece. Like many other presses, the heart of the design is a set of curved, or cambered, bearers. These bearers distribute pressure onto

the veneer with the help of three cauls. The difference is that my design incorporates a method for curving the bearers so they provide continuous contact along their full length. An improperly curved bearer just presses down at a few points, creating irregular pressure.

All the measurements given here will create a press that accommodates

panels up to 24" wide. You can build yours any size you want; just be sure to make your bearers as long or as wide as the panels you intend to veneer, plus 4" for supporting the hardware.

To begin, select a 2" x 8" x 8' piece of Douglas fir that's as knot free as possible. Crosscut the board into three 24"-long sections. Select the best piece and rip it in half for making

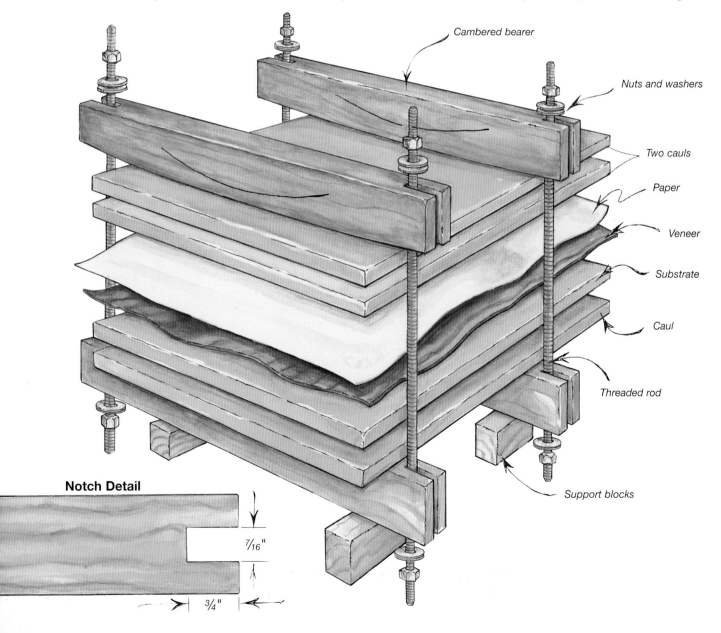

Cambered bearer

Nuts and washers

Two cauls

Paper

Veneer

Substrate

Caul

Threaded rod

Support blocks

Notch Detail

7/16"

3/4"

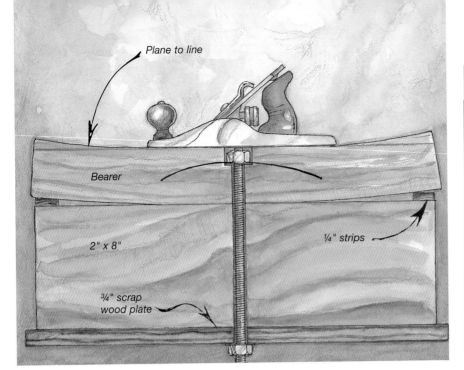

Plane to line

Bearer

2" x 8"

¼" strips

¾" scrap wood plate

Figure 1. *Make a stand out of the 2" x 8"s for bending the first bearer. Stand them on top of the plate, and then slip a threaded rod through the bearer, between the 2" x 8"s and through the plate hole. Place the ¼"-thick strips beneath the bearer, add the washers, and tighten the nuts until the bearer touches the 2" x 8"s.*

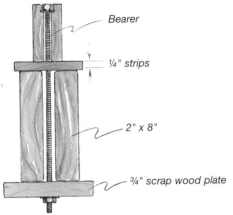

Bearer

¼" strips

2" x 8"

¾" scrap wood plate

your first bearer. Mill the halves down to 1¼" x 2½". Then, mark the edge on one piece at its center, and drill a 1"-diameter x ½"-deep counterbore and a ⅜" pilot hole.

Now, drill a ⅜"-diameter hole in the center of a ¾"-thick scrap wood plate, and set the other two sections of the 2" x 8" on the plate, as shown in Figure 1. Position two ¼"-thick sticks on the 2" x 8"s, and place the bearer on the sticks. Slip a 12" piece of threaded rod through the hole, between the 2" x 8"s and through the plate, and then tighten nuts on both ends of the threaded rod with a socket wrench. Stop tightening when the bearer touches the 2" x 8"s, and use a straightedge to draw a line near the top of the bearer showing the low point of the curve.

Release the bearer from the threaded rod, and band saw just outside the line. Then, return the bearer to the fixture, tighten the nut, and hand

plane the edge right to the line. Since the camber is so subtle, draw a large curved line on the side of the bearer to indicate the correct edge.

Take the assembly apart, and then rip and mill the other 2" x 8"s as you did the first one. Trace the shape of the first bearer onto each of the other pieces, and band saw them close to the finished profile. Now, screw the first bearer to the others, and rout identical curves using a long flush-cutting laminate bit. Cut ⁷⁄₁₆"-wide x ¾"-deep notches in both ends of each bearer, and nail support blocks to half of the bearers to raise the press off your workbench.

Generally, you'll want a pair of bearers pressing on your veneer every 4" to 6", so be sure to make enough for your anticipated needs.

Using Your Veneer Press

Before spreading any glue, try a dry run to familiarize yourself with the mechanics of the press. Set it up on a level surface, spacing the bottom bearers evenly. Now, lay down the cauls, substrate, veneer, and paper, as shown in the drawing on page 42. Add the top bearers and the hardware, and then begin tightening the bearer nearest to the center of the panel. Tighten one end about three-quarters of the way, and then completely tighten the other end. Return to the first end to finish tightening the nut. Work your way through the other bearers to the ends of the press.

Use a small roller to spread glue evenly on the substrate. To avoid excessive curling, don't put glue directly on the veneer.

Place the veneer on the substrate, and then lay newspaper down to keep excess glue from bonding the cauls to the veneer.

Tighten the nuts with a box wrench until you see a consistent bead of glue squeeze-out along the edges of the panel.

Handcrafted Joiner's Mallet

Every woodworker should have a personalized mallet for carving and chiseling tasks. Build your own so the handle fits your palm like a glove. It's a joy to make and to use.

by Chris Inman

A woodworker's mallet is a very personal tool. You learn its subtleties of weight and balance so that the slightest tap can accomplish just what you need from a chisel or a carving gouge. After many years of service, with a handle darkened by sweat and glue and the scars of time, your mallet begins to feel like an extension of your hand.

Mallets purchased from a store do everything you expect of them in a practical way, but they lack that undefinable quality that's so evident in a handmade tool. Given the years of service that a mallet provides, the time it takes to make one just for you is well worth the effort.

Among domestic wood species, maple is the best choice for a mallet. It's both hard and dense, so it withstands repeated blows against chisel handles. Many exotic species are even harder than maple, so they also work well for this application. Padauk, for example, is hard and stable and, because of its beauty, makes an excellent accent wood.

Look over the drawings and the Material List on page 45. Notice that the mallet's head (pieces 3 and 4) is built around the end of the handle (pieces 1 and 2). Laminating the mallet this way is much easier than trying to mortise a hole completely through the head, and it still results in a strong assembly.

To make the handle, glue the pieces of maple (pieces 1) to each side of the padauk strip (piece 2). (If you have a little bird's-eye maple around, use it to really make this a special piece.) Padauk, as with many exotics, is an oily wood and sometimes doesn't bond well with yellow glue or hide glue.

Figure 1. *A comfortable handle is the key to a successful mallet. To reduce tearout while spokeshaving (above), work from the high points to the low.*

Therefore, just to be on the safe side, use epoxy to prevent any possibility of delamination due to oil in the padauk. Another advantage of epoxy is that it remains somewhat flexible after it dries, giving the mallet more resiliency when delivering a heavy blow (glues that are brittle will crack with this kind of shock).

Once the glue dries, rip the handle to a width of 1¾", and then lay out the handle, as shown on page 45. Next, cut a shoulder 2¾" from the top end of the handle so you can positively position the two core pieces (pieces 3) of the head during the final glue-up. To do this, raise your table saw blade to ⅛", clamp a setup block to the rip fence, and position it 2¾" from the far side of the blade. Pass the handle over the blade a number of times to cut the shoulder and complete the tenon. Clean up the saw marks on the tenon with a sharp 1" chisel, and then use a band saw to cut the wedge kerf and shape the handle. Take a few strokes with a spokeshave to chamfer the grip until it fits comfortably in your hand (see Figure 1).

Now, from maple stock that's the same thickness as the handle, cut two 2¾"-wide x 2¼"-long pieces for the mallet head's core (pieces 3). Cut the outside edge of each piece (the striking faces of the mallet) at a 3° angle.

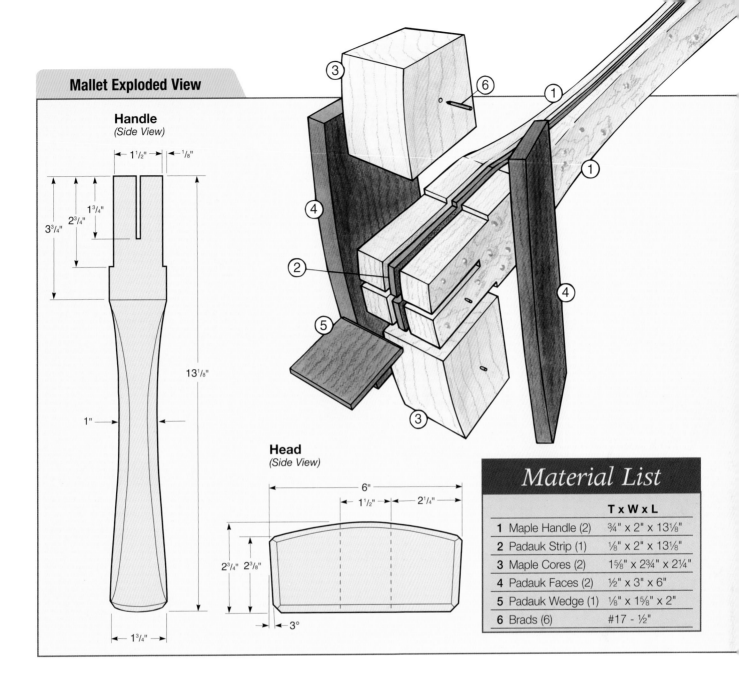

Handle
(Side View)

1¹⁄₂" · ¹⁄₈"

1³⁄₄"

2³⁄₄"

3³⁄₄"

13¹⁄₈"

1"

1³⁄₄"

Head
(Side View)

6"

1¹⁄₂" · 2¹⁄₄"

2³⁄₄" 2³⁄₈"

3°

Material List

		T x W x L
1	Maple Handle (2)	¾" x 2" x 13¹⁄₈"
2	Padauk Strip (1)	¹⁄₈" x 2" x 13¹⁄₈"
3	Maple Cores (2)	1⁵⁄₈" x 2¾" x 2¼"
4	Padauk Faces (2)	½" x 3" x 6"
5	Padauk Wedge (1)	¹⁄₈" x 1⁵⁄₈" x 2"
6	Brads (6)	#17 - ½"

The padauk faces (pieces 4) measure 2¾" wide x 6" long and have ends cut at a 3° angle to match the core. From padauk scrap, also cut a 2"-long x 1⁵⁄₈"-wide x ¹⁄₈"-thick piece for the wedge (piece 5). Belt sand one end of the wedge to a blunt point so it will enter the kerf easily.

Assembling the mallet is a sloppy task given all the glue that's involved, especially when the pieces begin sliding around. But you can prevent the sliding by driving three small brads just slightly into each padauk face and then, using a wire cutter, cutting off the brad ¹⁄₈" above the surface. Press the core pieces and the handle into position on

top of one padauk face, and then press the second face on the other side of the head. The nails will indent the wood, preventing the pieces from slipping around when the glue is added.

Now, disassemble the mallet, spread epoxy on all the joining surfaces, and clamp the pieces back together. Be sure to adjust one clamp to lightly hold the maple core sections against the handle— but be careful not to clamp too tightly, or you won't be able to insert the wedge. Put a little epoxy on the pointed end of the wedge, and drive the wedge into the top of the handle. You'll have plenty of squeeze-out, so have a few rags ready for cleaning up the excess glue.

The next day, belt sand the pieces in the head lamination flush, and scrape off any glue residue. Band saw the curved top on the head, and then sand this cut smooth. Now, use a block plane to chamfer all the long-grain edges of the head and a chisel to chamfer the cross-grain edges. Chamfer the end of the handle, too. Use a palm sander with 100-grit paper to remove any belt sander marks and to ease all the corners. Once you're satisfied with the feel of the tool, apply two coats of a penetrating oil finish, and you're ready to go to work.

Plane Making 101

Making your own plane teaches you much about this fundamental tool, and as a bonus, your woodworking will be more satisfying when it relies on a fine hand tool you made to suit yourself.

by Kerry Pierce

Despite the availability of good-quality new planes at reasonable prices and good-quality antique planes at even more reasonable prices, there are still compelling reasons to make your own.

First, the process of making, setting up, and tuning your own plane will teach you things about planes that you can't learn as quickly from a book or even from lessons taught by a first-rate instructor. But —at least for me—the very best reason for making a plane is the same as the very best reason for making the furniture I'll produce with that plane: The process gives me an opportunity to take material in my hands and, with it, fashion something that is both beautiful and useful.

Iron Choices
The irons in traditional wooden planes were tapered in thickness from approximately ³⁄₁₆" at the business end to ¹⁄₁₆" at the other end. I have a supply of these irons because of my practice of buying junk antique wooden planes with good irons at cheap prices. Typically, I'll pay $8 or $9 for the plane, pull out the iron/cap iron assembly, and toss the checked and beaten body in the trash. Modern irons only half the length of these antiques typically sell for $40 or more.

The tapered iron is reputed to be more resistant to slippage when wedged against a plane's bed than is an iron with parallel faces, such as the irons in a Stanley bench plane—but Ron Hock

at Hock Tools (who knows much more about plane irons than I do) told me this isn't so. To test the idea, I put a Stanley bench plane iron (a tapered iron) and cap iron into this little smoothing plane, and it worked just fine, although the mouth—opened for a ³⁄₁₆" traditional iron—was a little too spacious.

Ron Hock stocks a supply of iron/cap iron assemblies at *www.hocktools.com*.

Making the Body
Refer to the Material List on page 49. Then, begin by ripping, jointing, planing, and cutting to length the plane blank (piece 1). It should finish out 2¾" on a side, with every face exactly 90° from every adjacent face, as shown in Figure 1.

I recommend a hollow-ground planer blade for making the finish cuts because these blades leave behind surfaces that require very little effort to smooth. Set up your table saw to take a 2"-deep cut that removes ⅛" of material from the sides and ends of your blank, as shown in Figure 2. Form the shoulder at the top of the step by setting your table saw to take a ⅛"-deep cut that is ¾" from the fence. This will leave a step that is ⅛" thick and ¾" high all around your plane blank, as shown in Figure 3.

Next, locate the mouth on the sole of the plane. The mouth is typically placed about a third of the way back from the toe of the plane, although the exact location is a matter of personal choice.

Figure 1: *Prepare the plane blank by first cutting it to length. Use your jointer to mill the blank so that all six of its faces are 90° to their adjacent faces. A precision tool must be precisely made.*

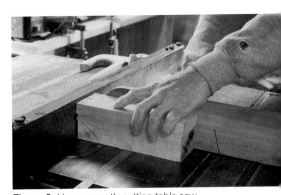

Figure 2: *Use a smooth-cutting table saw blade to begin forming the plane's distinctive step-out shoulder. A carbide-tipped 60- or 80-toothed blade is an acceptable choice.*

Figure 3: *Complete the stylish and practical step-out with a ⅛"-deep cut that is ¾" from the table saw's fence. In the steps shown in these photos, take note of the prudent use of push sticks and pads.*

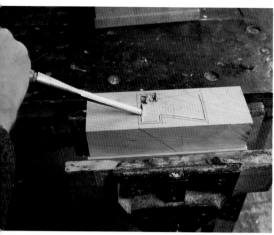

Figure 4: *After laying out the plane's mortise, secure the blank in your vise. Carefully begin chopping out the waste, cutting only the portion of the bedding slope between the abutment cheeks.*

Figure 5: *To begin the mouth, drill two holes in the center of its width with a ³⁄₁₆" bit. These act as references as you chop a hole on top of the blank, which will then become the mouth on the bottom of the plane.*

Figure 6: *Use a ³⁄₁₆" chisel to form the mouth of the plane. The holes you drilled in the previous step serve as guides for this process.*

The line designating the back edge of the mouth will be the terminus of the bedding slope. For the time being, mark the front of the mouth ¼" ahead of the back edge. Once you have an iron/cap iron installed, you'll more precisely locate the front of the mouth. Remember that the opening in the sole includes not just the distance from the cutting edge of the iron to the front of the mouth, but also enough room to accommodate the bevel on the end of the iron.

After you have located the mouth, use a bevel gauge as a guide to make lines on both sides of the plane blank that reach from the extended back edge of the mouth up to the top of the plane blank at a 45° angle. These lines mark the bedding slope you will cut on the inside of the plane. Then, follow the drawings on page 49 to lay out the rest of the plane's mortise. You will cut the groove for the cap iron screw head later on.

Secure the plane blank in your vise. Then, very carefully, begin chopping out the waste, as shown in Figure 4. At this stage, you should cut only that portion of the bedding slope that falls between the abutment cheeks.

When you have reached a maximum depth of approximately 2", invert the blank and resecure it with the sole facing up. It's now time to begin cutting the mouth.

Forming the Mouth

Although the mouth could be fully excavated with chisels, I begin the process by making a couple of holes with a ³⁄₁₆" drill bit in the center of the mouth's width, as shown in Figure 5. These holes constitute the first connection between the opening I'm chopping on the top of the plane and the mouth on the bottom of the plane, serving as references to let me know if my work is on track. Once the connection is completed, use a ³⁄₁₆" chisel to begin to actually form the mouth, as shown in Figure 6.

Once you've connected the excavation on the top of the plane and the mouth, clamp the plane blank in place so that the mouth just peeks over the edge of your bench top. The sole behind the mouth must be supported when you're chopping the bottom section of the throat, or your chisel work will break out sections of the sole. Positioning the mouth just over the edge of the bench top (see Figure 7 on page 50) provides the necessary support and also allows chips to fall to the floor through the mouth instead of clogging up your work.

At this point in the process, you'll probably want to work back and forth, chopping away from the top for a while and then shifting to the bottom. When the bedding slope extends from the back of the mouth to the top of the plane, you're ready to cut the wedge slots.

Because the tops of the wedge slots are cut at a steeper angle than the bedding slope, the slots taper from the point at which they enter the plane's top surface to the bottom of the abutments. Tapping the wedge into this taper allows you to create the pressure that keeps the iron from chattering when it's used.

Two saw cuts are necessary to define the wedge slots. The first is simply an extension of the bedding slope that reaches all the way to the outside of the wedge slot. The saw cut should actually be made a bit above the bedding slope. The surface is then pared down to the bedding slope. The second cut should be made above the first cut at a distance great enough to accommodate the thickness of the iron, the cap iron, and the wedge.

If you're working with an antique tapered iron (piece 2) like the one I'm using here, you can use my measurements and then make a wedge (piece 3) with a thickness that fits into the slots on your plane. If, however, you're using a parallel iron, such as those made by Ron Hock, take some thickness measurements of the iron and cap iron assembly, and then cut the wedge

Technical Drawings

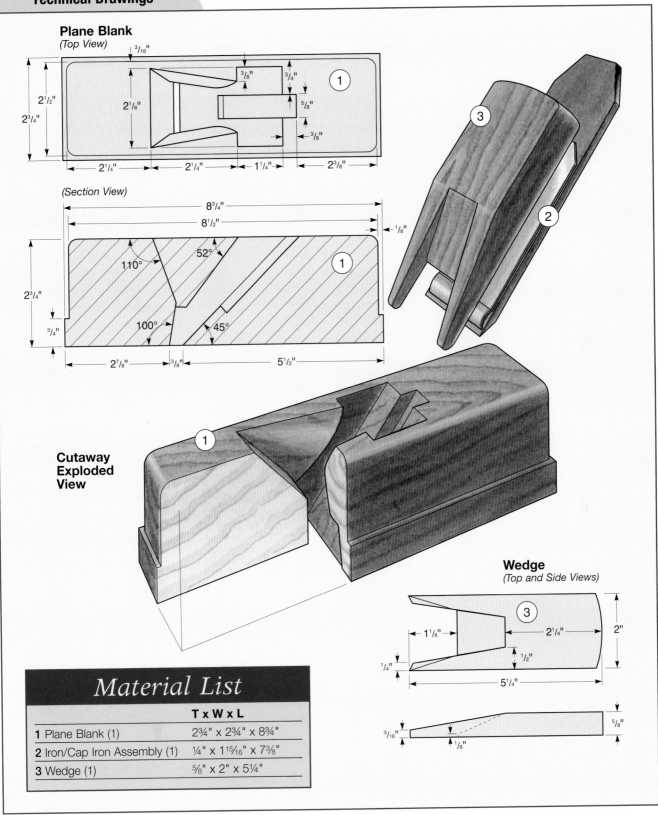

Plane Blank
(Top View)

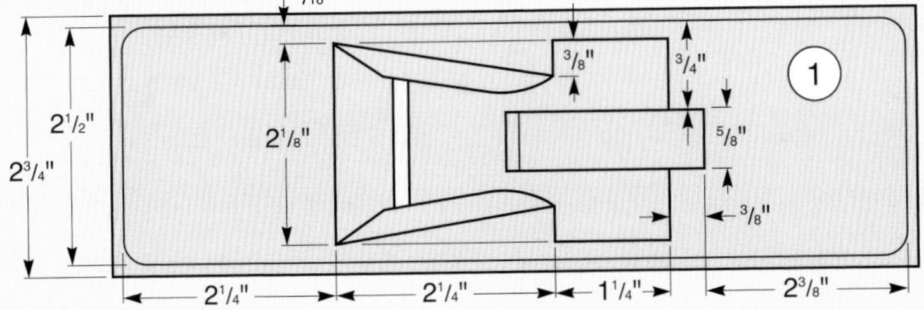
3/16"
3/8"
3/4"
1
5/8"
3/8"
2 1/2"
2 3/4"
2 1/8"
2 1/4"
2 1/4"
1 1/4"
2 3/8"

(Section View)

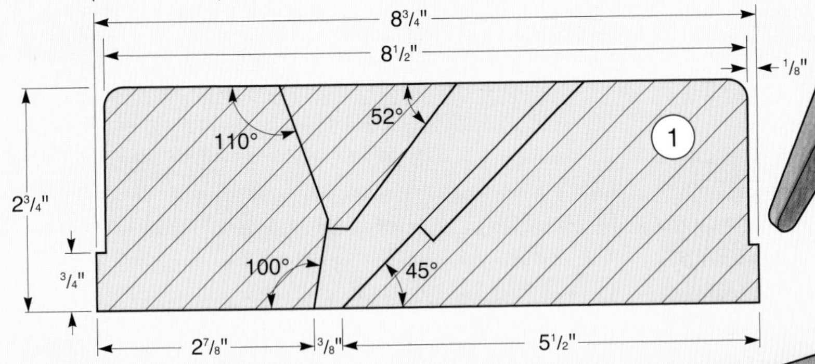
8 3/4"
8 1/2"
1/8"
52°
110°
1
2 3/4"
3/4"
100°
45°
2 7/8"
3/8"
5 1/2"

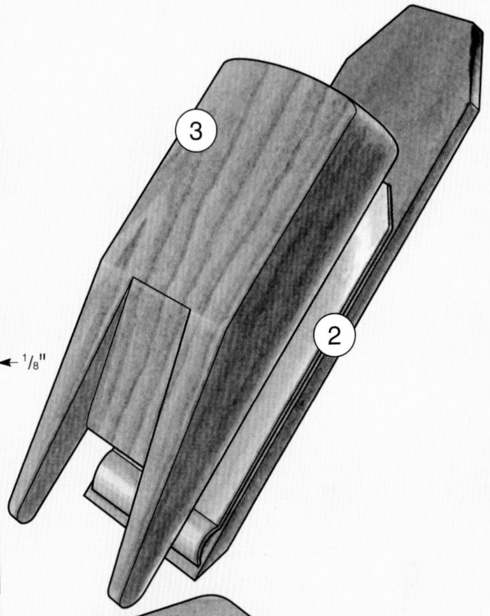
3
2

Cutaway Exploded View

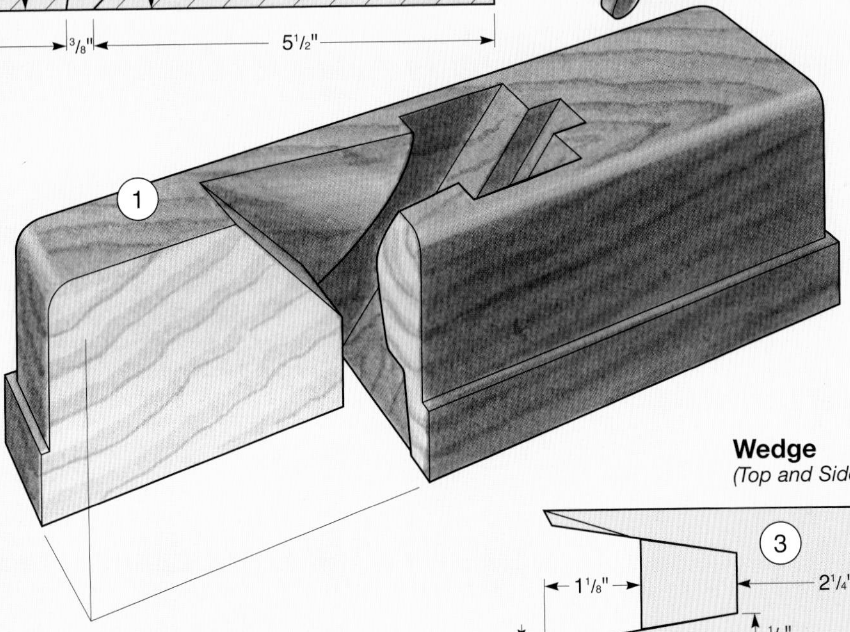
1

Wedge
(Top and Side Views)

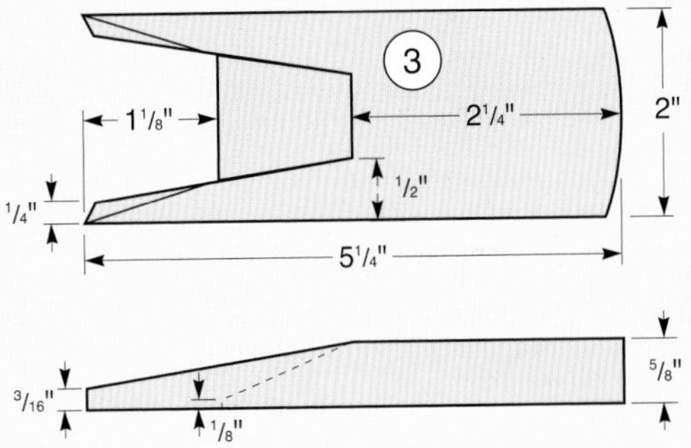
3
1 1/8"
2 1/4"
2"
1/2"
1/4"
5 1/4"
5/8"
3/16"
1/8"

Material List

	T x W x L
1 Plane Blank (1)	2¾" x 2¾" x 8¾"
2 Iron/Cap Iron Assembly (1)	¼" x 115/16" x 7⅜"
3 Wedge (1)	⅝" x 2" x 5¼"

Figure 7: *Position the mouth just over the edge of the benchtop to support the sole behind it when you're chopping the bottom section of the throat. Otherwise, you risk chopping out sections of the sole.*

Figure 8: *The detail saw used here to cut the top of a wedge slot can also be used to cut the floor of each wedge. Be careful not to cut too deep and go through the ¼" sidewall of the wedge—it's the only thing holding the plane body together at this point.*

Figure 9: *After getting the bedding slope as flat as you can with a wide paring chisel or a float, mark and cut the groove for the head of the machine screw that attaches the cap iron to the iron.*

slots to fit. You can try conventional Stanley-type irons in planes made this way, but I think they're a bit thin. In any case, you'll want to cut your wedge slots to a thickness that will accommodate the iron you're going to use in your plane. To cut the abutments, try a keyhole saw.

Before you make the cuts marking the bottom of the wedge slots, do a little fine-tuning with a paring chisel to make sure the bedding slope is reasonably flat. You can check this by sighting down the throat and comparing the line at the back of the mouth and the line on the top of the plane that marks the upper end of the bedding slope.

Then, cut the floor of each wedge slot with your little saw, as shown in Figure 8 (I'm actually cutting the top of a wedge slot in that photo). Take care not to cut too deep, because the only thing holding the plane body together is the thin sidewall of each wedge slot, which is only ¼" thick on the finished plane. Next, use a bevel square to mark the top of the wedge slot on the cheek of each abutment. Cut those with your small saw, and clear out the waste from each wedge slot.

The next step in the process is one that traditional plane makers performed either with a wide paring chisel or with a special tool called a float. In the hands of a master plane maker, the wide paring chisel could quickly create a flat bedding slope. A float—which looks a bit like a rasp with widely separated teeth that run across the full width of the tool—could also be used to remove any irregularities in a nearly finished bedding slope.

When the bedding slope is as flat as you can make it, mark and cut the groove that will accept the head of the machine screw holding the cap iron to the iron, as shown in Figure 9.

Fitting the Mouth and Wedge

I intended for this plane to be a smoother, so I cut a fairly tight mouth, one open a bit less than ¹⁄₁₆" from the cutting edge to the front of the mouth. Although, theoretically, you could mark the final limits of the mouth before you've bedded the iron, I prefer to finish the bedding slope, load the iron, and then move the front edge of the mouth forward a bit at a time until I reach the final placement. If you look closely at Figure 10, you can see scorings at either end of the mouth, indicating tentative locations of the mouth's front edge.

The final step is to equip your plane with a wedge that will keep the iron/cap iron assembly pressed firmly against the bedding slope, while, at the same time, offering no obstruction to the shavings that exit up through the throat and over the sides of the plane.

Begin by cutting out the distinctive two-pronged wedge shape from ⅝" material. Then, stand the wedge on its side, and use the band saw to cut the slope that runs from the tips of the wedge's prongs to that part of the wedge that will enter the top of the wedge slots. Cut the wedge a bit heavy so you can later fit it with a plane.

When the wedge is very nearly planed to its final shape, I rub a little pencil lead onto the top of the wedge slots. I then tap the wedge into place atop the iron/cap iron assembly. When I remove the wedge, smudges of pencil lead will indicate where I need to do the final paring to fit the wedge. If you look closely at Figure 11, you'll see one of those smudges. A little later, as shown in Figure 12, I'm paring away the smudged areas to achieve the final fit.

Take a Test Drive

To set the iron, place the plane—with the sole down—on a flat wood surface. Then, insert the iron/cap iron assembly with the cutting iron's bevel down. Allow the iron to slide down the bedding slope until the cutting edge strikes the level surface on which the plane is resting. Then, insert the wedge, and press it snugly into the wedge slots. It should be tight enough that you can lift the plane without the iron sliding out. Next, hold the plane up to your eye with the toe facing you, and sight along the length of the sole. When the iron is properly set, the cutting edge will be just barely visible.

If no iron is visible, tap the toe of the plane with your plane mallet. This should cause the iron to slide just a bit farther down the bedding slope, despite the wedge you've pushed into place. Since I'm left-handed, I do this while I'm holding the plane in my right hand with two fingers wrapped around the wedge and the iron. Those two fingers will catch the iron in case the tapping knocks it loose.

Now, sight along the length of the sole once again. If there is still not enough iron visible, tap the toe again. If there is too much iron showing, tap the heel of the plane with your mallet. Until you've applied the plane to your work, you won't really know if you've exposed the proper amount of cutting edge. The first few times you set your iron you'll be relying on guesswork.

As you work your way through this process, remember to confirm that the edge is exposed a consistent amount across the width of the plane. If it isn't, tap the sides of the iron to bring it into alignment. Once you've achieved what looks like the correct amount of exposure, give the top of the wedge one or two solid raps to set the wedge tightly enough so that you can use the plane without the iron coming loose.

Then, apply the plane to a work surface. If you're lucky, that first time out, your plane will produce a thin, translucent shaving. More likely, you'll have to reset the iron another time or two before it produces the kind of shaving you want.

Figure 10: *The scorings that can be seen here mark possible locations of the mouth's front edge. I adjust the location after loading the iron, moving the front edge of the mouth forward a bit at a time until it's correctly placed.*

Figure 11: *Cut a ⅝", two-pronged wedge, creating its slope on the band saw. Then, rub pencil lead on top of the wedge slots, tap the two-pronged wedge into place on the assembly, and remove it.*

Figure 12: *The pencil smudges from the previous step that can be seen here indicate the location where final paring is required to fit the wedge into the assembly.*

Trapped-Wedge Layout Gauge

This quick-set cutting gauge features a knife cutter that scribes razor-thin layout lines, either with or across the grain. It'll be a handsome and useful addition to your tool collection.

by Tom Caspar

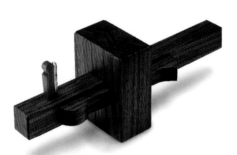

Half the challenge of cutting tight dovetail or mortise-and-tenon joints is getting them laid out precisely. A standard marking gauge featuring a sharp pin for a marker does a fine job scribing lines that follow the grain, but it tends to tear the wood when going across the grain. A knife tip makes a cleaner line than a pin on cross grain; it cleanly severs the wood fibers to establish a precise shoulder, which helps guide a chisel or saw during the joint-cutting process.

Besides the knife cutter, this gauge features a trapped wedge, which allows for quick, one-handed adjustments and eliminates the need for special hardware. Many hand tools constructed 150 years ago, when hardware was costly and more difficult to come by, utilized the trapped wedge.

Most of the machining for this project is completed on the table saw, and since many of the pieces are small,

it's important that you use holding devices to safeguard your fingers. I also recommend that you make a new plywood throat plate for your table saw to reduce the chance of cutoffs falling down beside the blade and shooting back out at you.

Traditionally, rosewood is the wood of choice for gauges of this type. It resists wear exceptionally well, any interlocking pieces operate smoothly, and it's very pleasing to hold. Just remember that when you glue rosewood, the surfaces must be fresh for a good bond to form, so always sand or plane the mating edges just before gluing up. This project requires less than 1 board foot of ¾" stock (see the Material List on page 53). Buy a ¼" spade bit for the knife stock, which you'll regrind to achieve the correct edge.

Start Your Cutting

It's always safer to cut smaller pieces from larger ones, so begin making your cutting gauge by ripping a slice of rosewood for the splines (pieces 1). These will eventually slip into a saw blade kerf, so cut a

saw groove in some scrap to test the fit. Next, rip a ¼"-thick x 8"-long strip to use later for the beam insert and small wedge (pieces 2 and 3). Then, slice a ½"-thick strip for the large wedge (piece 4). Sand off the saw marks, and cut the splines and large wedge to length.

Cut the beam (piece 8) so that its width and thickness are unequal. This may seem odd, but through experience—meaning goof-ups— I've learned to avoid the age-old headache of fitting parts together the wrong way. By cutting the beam in this manner, it will fit into the gauge head correctly every time. Rip the beam to size, and then rip a 1¼"-wide piece for the parts that make up the head assembly (pieces 5 through 7). Trim all the pieces ¼" longer than their finished sizes.

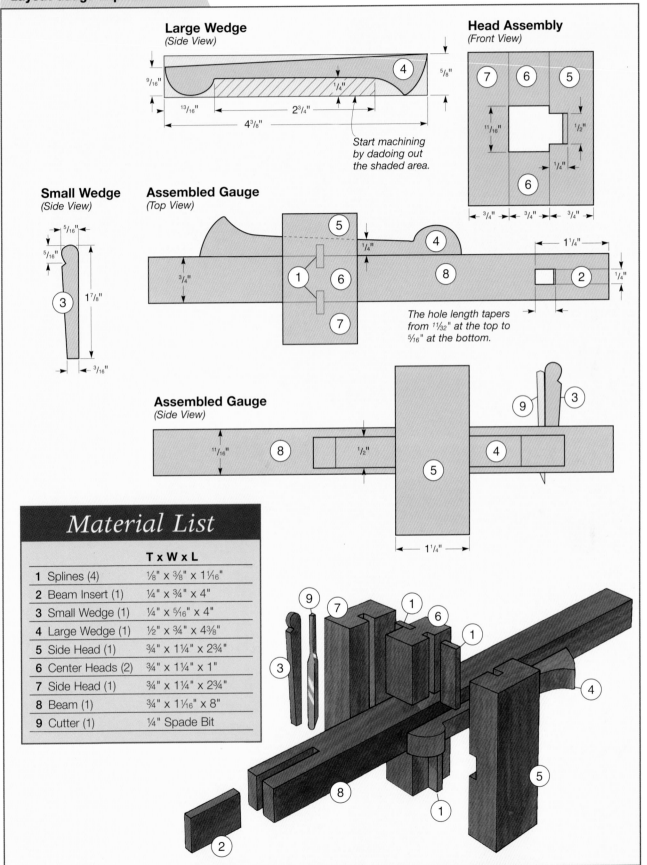

Large Wedge
(Side View)

4

$^9/_{16}$"

$^5/_8$"

$^1/_4$"

$^{13}/_{16}$"

$2^3/_4$"

$4^3/_8$"

Start machining
by dadoing out
the shaded area.

Head Assembly
(Front View)

7 6 5

$^{11}/_{16}$"

$^1/_2$"

$^1/_4$"

6

$^3/_4$" $^3/_4$" $^3/_4$"

Small Wedge
(Side View)

$^5/_{16}$"

$^5/_{16}$"

3

$1^7/_8$"

$^3/_{16}$"

Assembled Gauge
(Top View)

5

$^1/_4$"

$^3/_4$"

1

6

7

8

2

$1^1/_4$"

$^1/_4$"

The hole length tapers
from $^{11}/_{32}$" at the top to
$^5/_{16}$" at the bottom.

Assembled Gauge
(Side View)

$^{11}/_{16}$"

8

$^1/_2$"

4

5

9

3

$1^1/_4$"

Material List

	T x W x L
1 Splines (4)	$^1/_8$" x $^3/_8$" x $1^1/_{16}$"
2 Beam Insert (1)	$^1/_4$" x $^3/_4$" x 4"
3 Small Wedge (1)	$^1/_4$" x $^5/_{16}$" x 4"
4 Large Wedge (1)	$^1/_2$" x $^3/_4$" x $4^3/_8$"
5 Side Head (1)	$^3/_4$" x $1^1/_4$" x $2^3/_4$"
6 Center Heads (2)	$^3/_4$" x $1^1/_4$" x 1"
7 Side Head (1)	$^3/_4$" x $1^1/_4$" x $2^3/_4$"
8 Beam (1)	$^3/_4$" x $1^1/_{16}$" x 8"
9 Cutter (1)	$^1/_4$" Spade Bit

9 7 1 6 1

3

1

4

8 1 5

2

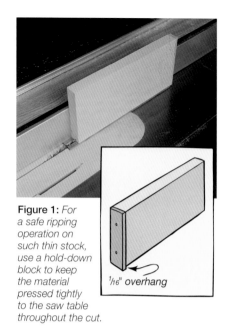

Figure 1: For a safe ripping operation on such thin stock, use a hold-down block to keep the material pressed tightly to the saw table throughout the cut.

$^1/_{16}$" overhang

Arrange the head pieces for assembly, matching their grain patterns so they appear to be one piece, and mark the front face of the assembly so you can reorder it again later. Next, separate the pieces, and rip a $^3/_{16}$"-deep groove in the center of each adjoining edge for inserting the splines. For perfect alignment, be sure to always run the front face of each piece against the saw fence during these cuts.

Ripping the splines to their final size requires a special hold-down block. Cut a block measuring $^3/_4$" x 4" x 9", and screw a thin, narrow piece to its back end, as shown in Figure 1. Set the blade height at $^3/_8$", and rip your spline, using the block to hold it tightly to the table. Next, crosscut the strip into four segments (pieces 1), and check their fit in the head piece grooves you just made.

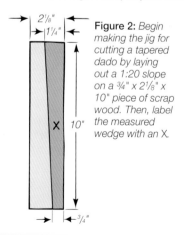

2$^1/_8$"
1$^1/_4$"

X 10"

$^3/_4$"

Figure 2: Begin making the jig for cutting a tapered dado by laying out a 1:20 slope on a $^3/_4$" x 2$^1/_8$" x 10" piece of scrap wood. Then, label the measured wedge with an X.

Cutting the Head Dado

The bottom of the dado in the side head (piece 5) is tapered to fit the large wedge. The tapered dado jig for making the cuts is built from softwood scraps. First, draw the pitch for the wedge taper, and then mark this measured wedge with an X (see Figure 2). Next, cut a $^1/_4$" x 1$^1/_2$" x 12" piece of plywood, and nail it to the wedge stock so it's aligned with the pitch line and covering the side marked with the X. With your fence set at 1$^1/_2$", rip the wedge stock while the plywood rides against the fence, as shown in Figure 3. Trim the wedge ends so they're identical. Complete the jig by nailing the wedges to a $^3/_4$" x 3$^1/_2$" x 14" board, and nail a fence block on top of the wedges (see Figure 4).

To use your tapered dado jig, just raise your table saw blade 1", and set the fence 1$^1/_4$" away. Push the jig into the blade until the center of the blade just passes under the front of the fence block. At this point, clamp a stop to the saw fence in front of the jig, as shown in Figure 4. Draw a line on the front edge of the fence block $^1/_4$" from its bottom, and raise the saw blade to hit the line.

Figure 3: With the plywood riding against the fence, rip the wedge stock for the jig.

Make your cut by placing the side head (piece 5) on the jig with its marked front facing the fence block and one end bearing against the saw fence. Make your first pass, and continue moving the saw fence to make several more passes until the dado is $^1/_2$" wide. Be sure to fine-tune the last pass so the dado fits the large wedge precisely, and then smooth the dado's angled bottom with a file.

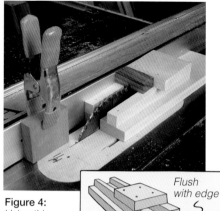

Figure 4: Using this jig, cut the tapered dado in several passes, moving the fence a little for each pass.

Flush with edge

1$^1/_4$"

Assembling the Head Pieces

Sand any saw marks off the beam, and dry assemble the head pieces and splines around it, sanding the $^3/_4$" dimension of the beam, if necessary, so it slides through the opening.

To prevent the beam from bonding to the head, coat its first 2" with paraffin wax. Now, glue the head and spline pieces together, and while pinching the assembly with your fingers, quickly clean out the excess glue in the opening. Slip the waxed end of the beam into the head assembly, and clamp everything tight in both directions (top to bottom and side to side). Later, when the glue has dried, you can sand the beam's 1$^1/_{16}$" dimension so it slides in the opening easily, trim the head to final size, and chamfer all its edges and corners.

Making the Trapped Wedge

Begin making the trapped wedge (piece 4) by ripping the stock you cut earlier to $^5/_8$" wide and cutting a dado, as shown in the large wedge drawing on page 53. Once the dado is cut, remove one of the wedges from the tapered dado jig, and nail a stop to its wide end to make a tapering jig for the large wedge (see Figure 5). Set the wedge against the

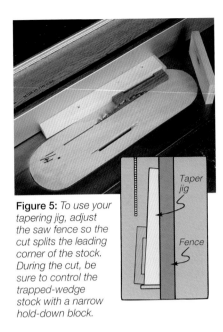

Figure 5: *To use your tapering jig, adjust the saw fence so the cut splits the leading corner of the stock. During the cut, be sure to control the trapped-wedge stock with a narrow hold-down block.*

taper jig, and rip the piece, splitting the lead corner with the blade. For safety, use scrap wood to press down on the wedge as you cut. Now, center the wedge in the dado to see if its back edge is flush with the shoulder of the larger hole. If the fit isn't right, continue trimming the wedge in very small increments. Then, shape the ends of the wedge with a coping saw and a file.

Cutting the Beam Slot

The hole in the beam that holds the knife and small wedge is tapered on its forward edge. It sounds unorthodox, but this is easily done on the table saw. Make the jig shown in Figure 6, and then use it to cut a ¼"-wide x 1¼"-deep

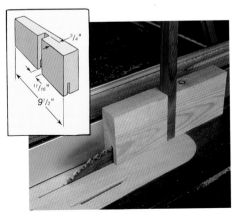

Figure 6: *Cutting a 1¼"-deep slot for the beam insert is safe and easy using this jig.*

slot in the end of the beam (remember, the beam isn't square, so be sure to cut into its wider edge).

Earlier, you cut a ¼"-thick strip for making the small wedge and the beam insert. To cut the strip in half, set your tapering jig against the table saw's miter gauge, and place the strip against the jig. The resulting angled cut is just what you need for the end of the beam insert. Sand one of the pieces to fit into the slot in the beam, and glue it into place with the angled end pointing into the beam and leaving a ⁵⁄₁₆"-long hole on the bottom side for the cutter and the small wedge. Trim off the excess when it's dry, and chamfer the ends of the beam.

A stout knife blade (piece 9) is easy to resharpen, and I've found that regrinding a ¼" spade bit is ideal (see Four Easy Steps to Grind the Cutter at right). In use, the knife's bevel should always face the waste side of the work because this snugs the gauge against the board when you scribe the line, leaving a square shoulder on the proper side of the cut.

Use the remaining ¼"-thick piece for the small wedge (piece 3). First, taper one edge on the table saw with the tapering jig, and then plane the piece to width and cut it to length (see the small wedge drawing on page 53). Shape the top of the wedge with a file, and smooth any saw marks.

Final Assembly and Finishing

Slip the cutter into the beam hole, and install the small wedge. Trim the end of the wedge so it's flush with the bottom of the beam, and then pull it back out to chamfer the end with a file. Coat the gauge with a penetrating oil-type finish, and put a little more wax on the beam so it slides easily. You'll quickly find that the trapped wedge locks with slight hand pressure to maintain the exact position you set it at.

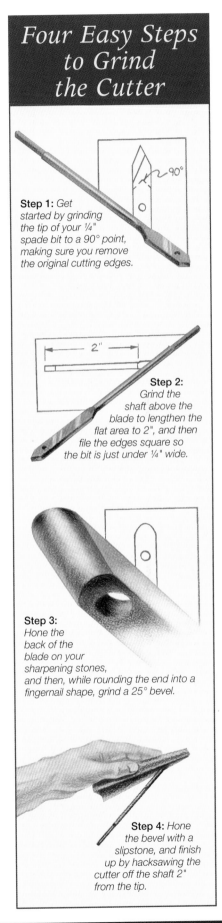

Four Easy Steps to Grind the Cutter

Step 1: *Get started by grinding the tip of your ¼" spade bit to a 90° point, making sure you remove the original cutting edges.*

Step 2: *Grind the shaft above the blade to lengthen the flat area to 2", and then file the edges square so the bit is just under ¼" wide.*

Step 3: *Hone the back of the blade on your sharpening stones, and then, while rounding the end into a fingernail shape, grind a 25° bevel.*

Step 4: *Hone the bevel with a slipstone, and finish up by hacksawing the cutter off the shaft 2" from the tip.*

Tabletop Downdraft Jig

A downdraft table for your day-to-day sanding doesn't have to be an intricate, time-consuming project with squirrel-cage fans and layers of filters. This little beauty comes together in one afternoon and will handle the lion's share of your shop dust.

by Rick White

Here's a helpful accessory for anyone who wants to breathe a little easier during sanding, especially with those wood species such as cedar, walnut, and cocobolo that can cause allergic reactions. And, given the recent research that suggests wood dust might be a carcinogen, anything we "lifer" woodworkers can do to manage dust is a good idea. Even with this jig, continue to use your sander's dust bag or canister for added dust control.

The jig is essentially an air box. Its thin profile keeps the volume of air to a minimum. This increases the airflow rate, which improves efficiency. Storing it is easy. The case is only the thickness of a 2" x 4", so it hangs neatly out of the way on the shop wall. (You can make the sidewalls higher if you need to accommodate a larger dust hose.) When it's on the workbench, that thin profile also means the top of the jig is low enough to work on without raising your arms too high—which is a prescription for fatigue.

It's a good idea to cover the empty portion of the table with paper or hardboard during use, to boost suction in the section of the top you are using. Start construction by cutting the ends, sides, and cleats (pieces 1 through 4) to size (see the Material List on page 57). Then, secure the corners with glued and nailed butt joints. Cut the bottoms (pieces 5) next, and install them in two halves to form a slight

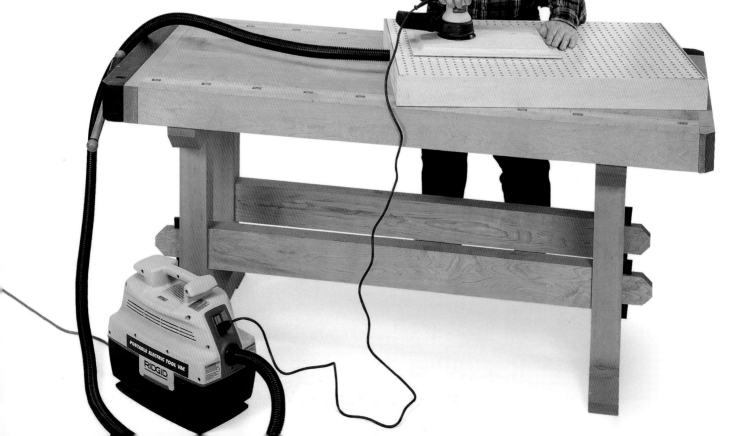

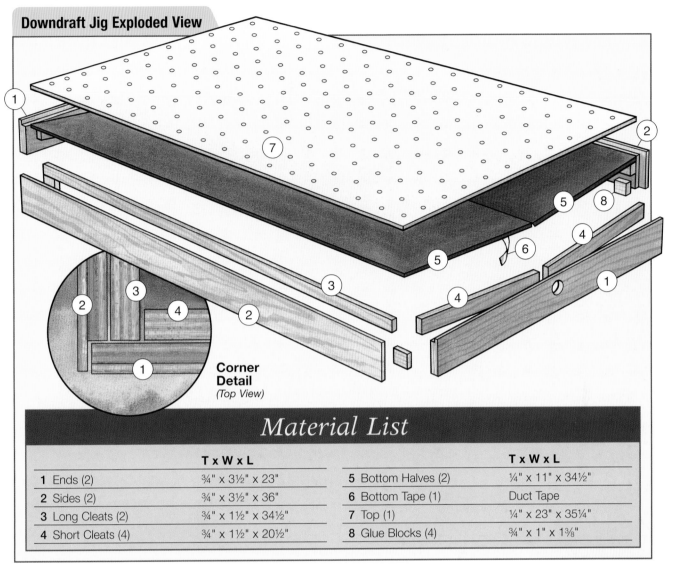

Corner Detail
(Top View)

Material List

	T x W x L			T x W x L
1 Ends (2)	¾" x 3½" x 23"		**5** Bottom Halves (2)	¼" x 11" x 34½"
2 Sides (2)	¾" x 3½" x 36"		**6** Bottom Tape (1)	Duct Tape
3 Long Cleats (2)	¾" x 1½" x 34½"		**7** Top (1)	¼" x 23" x 35¼"
4 Short Cleats (4)	¾" x 1½" x 20½"		**8** Glue Blocks (4)	¾" x 1" x 1⅜"

V-shape, as shown in the exploded view, above.

The V-shape creates a valley that catches dust and funnels it more efficiently toward the vacuum. To begin, glue and nail (or screw) all four cleats in place, at the locations shown in the detail drawing, above. Cut the bottom to size, and temporarily install the two halves.

Clamp a few scraps to the sides, just to hold the bottom in place for a minute. Then, turn the jig upside down, and apply duct tape (piece 6) along the joint. Turn the jig back upright, and secure the bottom to the cleats with small nails or brads, squaring the box as you go.

The top (piece 7) is nothing more than a piece of ¼" pegboard. I used a brand with a finished face to help prevent scratching. You can cut it to rest on the top and secure it with duct tape, or you can trim it to fit just inside the box and let it rest on the bottom. Either method allows for easy replacement when it gets worn. If the top flexes too much, add a couple of band-saw triangular cleats to the carcass ends.

Hooking It Up

Attaching a vacuum (see Figure 1) or dust collector is generally just a matter of drilling the right size hole for the hose end. Or you can buy a flange that screws to the box to connect your dust collector or vacuum

Figure 1: *Use a shop vacuum with a special switch designed to be used with dust-creating power tools. When you plug your sander into the vacuum, each time you start the tool the vacuum turns on, too. When you turn your tool off, the vacuum continues for a short time to catch the last bit of dust.*

hose. Bring your hose to a home center and spend a little time in the plumbing aisle to find the right connector. Virtually any size dust collector will work with this jig, but it goes without saying that bigger is better—just be sure to wear earplugs.

Downdraft Workbench

This big project gives you a large and robust work center, and it brings the huge benefit of getting the last of the dust out of the workshop and out of your lungs.

by Rick White

I admit that I dithered for a while before beginning this project, but I really did need a larger work center, and my goal of a dust-free workshop was close at hand. All I needed to do was bring myself to get rid of the trusty old workbench that was occupying the middle of my shop. Then, it came to me in a flash, and it was just too simple: I could make a new workbench that would be the size I needed, and I could build a dust-sucking downdraft table right into it.

My downdraft workbench features a power strip, full-extension pullout shelves, and room for sanders, drill drivers, and routers, in addition to an efficient, built-in downdraft unit. For durability and strength, it has a solid-maple top, and for good measure, I tossed in a vise and an interchangeable second top (see Figure 1). As you can see in the finished project, this workbench turned out great.

From the Bottom Up

Start this project with basic casework joinery on the carcass. The stiles and rails, as well as the end and back panels, (pieces 1 though 9) are made from solid-hardwood lumber. I used hard maple to match the top. Find the dimensions for all these pieces in the Material List on page 61. The machining details and the subassemblies you'll be creating are shown in the elevation drawings on the next few pages.

Make the front, back, and end subassemblies separately. Where the stiles and rails meet, I joined them with dowels so the joints would really stand up to a beating. Glue up the solid panels (pieces 7 and 8) a bit oversize, and then trim and sand them smooth after the glue cures. Form ¼" tongues on their edges, as shown in the drawings. Note that where the stiles and rails capture the end and back panels, you will need to rout stopped grooves (I used a handheld router and a slot cutter for this task) to accept the tongues on the panels' edges. Glue and clamp up the four separate subassemblies, checking to be sure they are square as the glue cures.

While you wait for the glue to dry, grab your plywood sheetstock and slice up the dividers and the bottom (pieces 10 and 11).

Grooves, Holes, and Rabbets

Now that the subassemblies have cured, you need to do a little more machining to each of them. With a handheld router and straight edge, plow matching grooves and dadoes for the bottom and dadoes for the dividers (there are dadoes in the bottom, too). Don't worry when the grooves and dadoes nip into the panels'

tongue-and-groove joints—it will work out fine. Using the same setup, form the rabbets at the edges of the front and back stiles (pieces 6).

Put the router aside, and grab your jigsaw to cut the six notches on the top edges of the two long rails. These will serve to capture the notched cross braces later on. The last bit of machining before you put together the subassemblies is to drill the safety vent holes in the upper rails. If all the holes on the draft vent happened to get covered, these holes would prevent the motor from overheating. These safety holes are best bored on the drill press, so either you'll need a buddy to help you hold up the frames as you drill or you'll have to use a couple of roller stands.

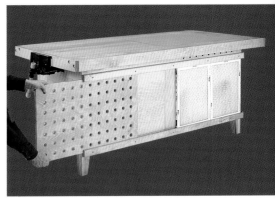

Figure 1: *The worktop of this bench has two inserts that fit into a rabbeted opening over the downdraft unit. When not in use, either insert can easily be stored on the back face of the bench.*

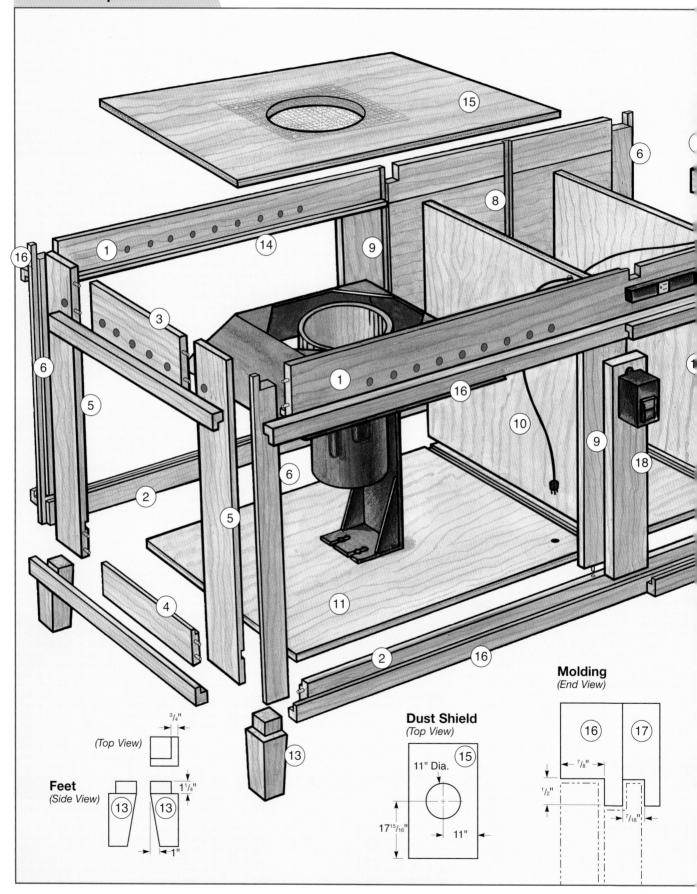

Feet
(Side View)

(Top View)

3/4"

1 1/4"

1"

13

13

13

Dust Shield
(Top View)

11" Dia.

11"

17 15/16"

15

Molding
(End View)

16

17

7/8"

1/2"

7/16"

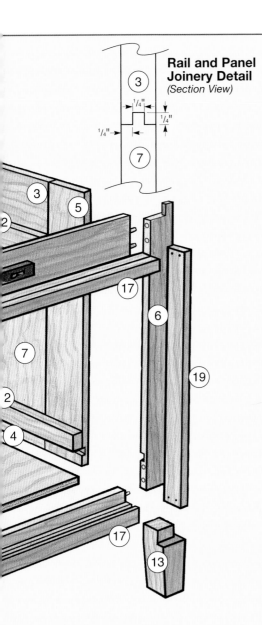

Rail and Panel Joinery Detail
(Section View)

③

¹/₄" ¹/₄"

¹/₄"

⑦

③ ⑤ ② ⑰ ⑥ ⑦ ② ④ ⑲ ⑰ ⑬

Material List — Carcass

		T x W x L
1	Upper Long Rails (2)	¾" x 5⅝" x 66"
2	Lower Long Rails (2)	¾" x 2" x 66"
3	Upper Short Rails (2)	¾" x 5⅝" x 14½"
4	Lower Short Rails (2)	¾" x 2" x 14½"
5	End Stiles (4)	¾" x 3⅞" x 26¼"
6	Front and Back Stiles (4)	¾" x 2" x 26¼"
7	End Panel (1)	¾" x 19" x 15"
8	Back Panel (1)	¾" x 19" x 31"
9	Center Stiles (2)	¾" x 5" x 18½"
10	Dividers (2)	¾" x 22½" x 24½"
11	Bottom (1)	¾" x 22½" x 69"
12	Spacers (2)	1¼" x 2¼" x 22"
13	Feet (4)	2¾" x 2¾" x 6¾"
14	Cleats (2)	¾" x ¾" x 36"
15	Dust Shield (1)	¾" x 22" x 35⅞"
16	Large Molding (1)	1¼" x 2" x 328"
17	Small Molding (1)	¾" x 2" x 72"
18	Door Cap (1)	¾" x 2" x 23"
19	Door Stop (1)	1¼" x 3⅛" x 19"
20	Sliding Doors (2)	¾" x 16½" x 19⅞"

Door
(Front View)

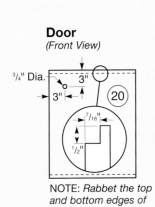

¾" Dia.

3"

3"

⑳

⁷/₁₆"

½"

NOTE: *Rabbet the top and bottom edges of one of the doors.*

Back Long Wall Subassembly
(Inside View)

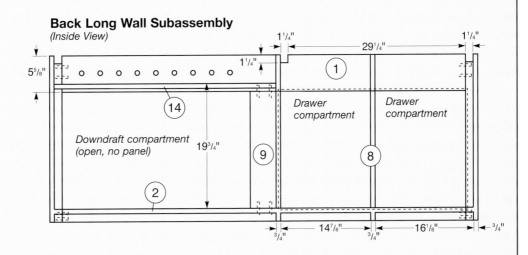

1¼" 29¼" 1¼"

5⅝" 1¼"

①

⑭

Drawer compartment

Drawer compartment

Downdraft compartment (open, no panel)

19¾"

⑨ ⑧

②

¾" 14⅞" ¾" 16⅛" ¾"

Technical Drawings

Bottom
(Top View)

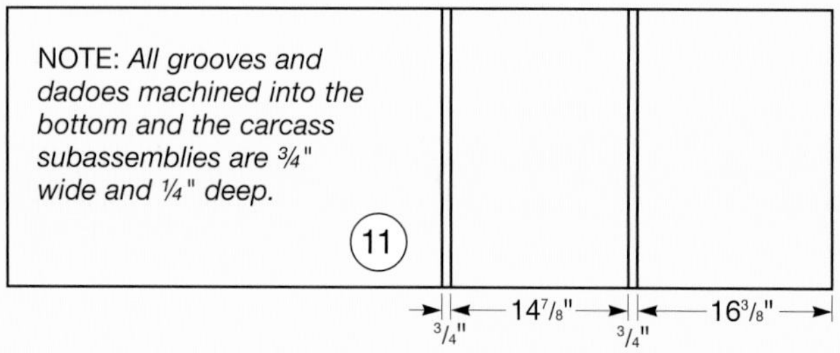

NOTE: All grooves and dadoes machined into the bottom and the carcass subassemblies are ¾" wide and ¼" deep.
11
3/4"
14 7/8"
3/4"
16 3/8"

End Wall Subassembly Downdraft Compartment
(Inside View)

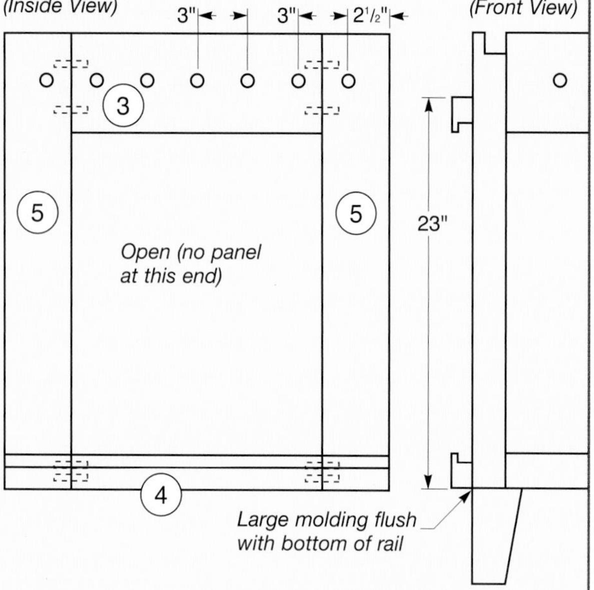

3"
3"
2 1/2"
(Front View)
3
5
5
Open (no panel at this end)
23"
4
Large molding flush with bottom of rail

End Wall Subassembly Drawer Compartment
(Inside View)

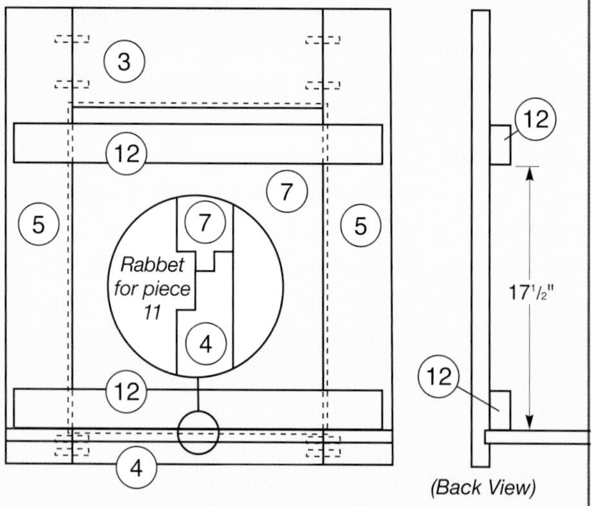

3
12
7
5
7
5
Rabbet for piece 11
4
12
4
12
17 1/2"
12
(Back View)

Top Exploded View

Material List – Top Subassembly

		T x W x L
21	Laminated Top Pieces (9)	1¼" x 3⅝" x 79½"
22	Splines (8)	½" x 1" x 79½"
23	Side Rails (2)	1¼" x 2⅞" x 79½"
24	Cross Braces (3)	1¼" x 1½" x 32⅜"
25	Long Cleats (2)	1¼" x 1½" x 79½"
26	Endcaps (2)	1¼" x 2⅞" x 34⅞"
27	Draft Vent (1)	¾" x 20" x 36"
28	Cover (1)	¾" x 20" x 36"
29	Vise Block (1)	1¼" x 5½" x 15"
30	Vise (1)	Steel-Screw-Type

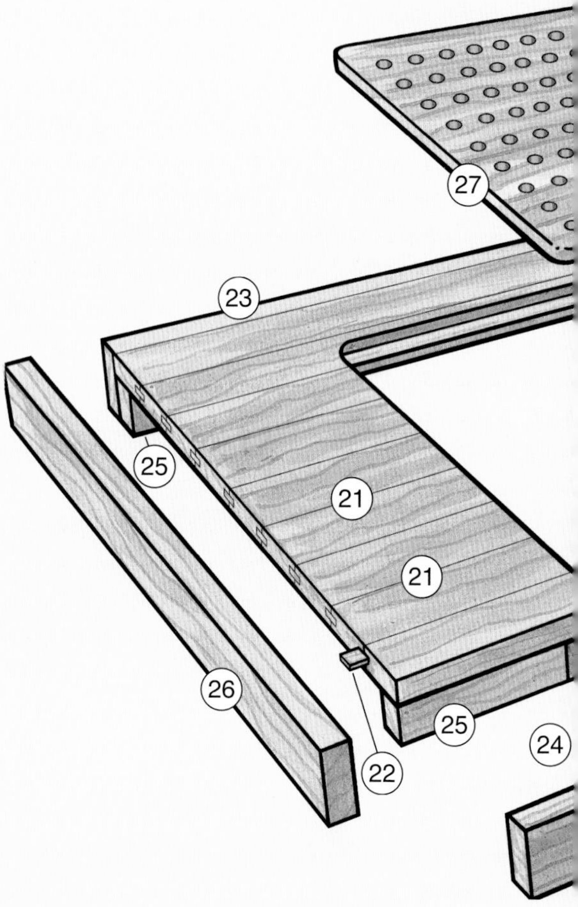

27
23
25
21
21
26
25
24
22

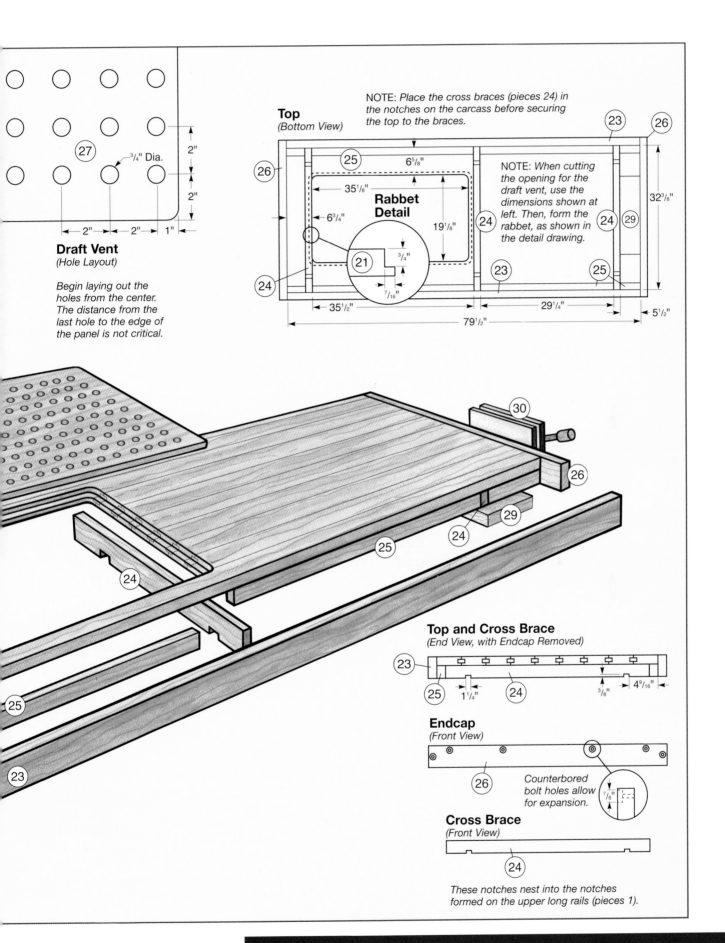

Draft Vent
(Hole Layout)

27

³/₄" Dia.

2"
2"

2" 2" 1"

Begin laying out the
holes from the center.
The distance from the
last hole to the edge of
the panel is not critical.

Top
(Bottom View)

NOTE: Place the cross braces (pieces 24) in
the notches on the carcass before securing
the top to the braces.

23 26

26

25 6⁵/₈"

35¹/₈"

**Rabbet
Detail**

6³/₄"

21

24

24

NOTE: When cutting
the opening for the
draft vent, use the
dimensions shown at
left. Then, form the
rabbet, as shown in
the detail drawing.

19¹/₈"

³/₄"

7/₁₆"

24 29

32³/₈"

23 25

35¹/₂"

29¹/₄"

5¹/₂"

79¹/₂"

30

26

29

24

25

24

25

23

Top and Cross Brace
(End View, with Endcap Removed)

23

25 24

1¹/₄" ³/₈" 4⁹/₁₆"

Endcap
(Front View)

26

Counterbored
bolt holes allow
for expansion.

7/₈"

Cross Brace
(Front View)

24

These notches nest into the notches
formed on the upper long rails (pieces 1).

Now, predrill the counterbored screw holes though the front and back stiles, and test fit the carcass together (this is another process that a helper will make much easier). Once everything fits together, assemble the carcass with glue, screws, and clamps. While the carcass is clamped up and the glue is curing, make the spacers, feet, cleats, and dust shield (pieces 12 through 15). As shown in the elevation drawings, the feet have tapers on their inside faces and a rabbet on the opposing faces. When the carcass is out of its clamps, attach the feet, cleats, and spacers with glue and screws. Plug all the exposed screw holes, and then sand them flush.

Sanding Dogs

When using the downdraft table, you'll find these sanding dogs very useful. They fit into the vent holes and keep your stock from moving during sanding.

Monster Moldings

The filters, sliding doors, and spare insert are all held in place with molding. It's not hard to make; you just need to make a bunch of it. First, rip enough stock to make the large and small molding (pieces 16 and 17), and then get your table saw set up with a dado blade and featherboard. Plow the rabbet into the large molding stock, as shown in the drawings. Readjust the saw setup to make the small molding, and create enough to make the two pieces required to hold the second sliding door.

Now is also a good time to make the door cap, door stop, and sliding doors (pieces 18 through 20). The door stop and cap are simply sticked-up hardwood, but one of the doors has a couple of rabbeted edges, and both have finger holes to be machined. Look to the elevation drawings for these details. Again, predrill counterbored screw holes, and mount the molding and assorted parts as shown in the exploded view and elevation drawings. Now, plug the screw holes, sand them flush, and get ready to do some laminating.

A Laminated Top

The glued-up maple top on this bench is a substantial bit of work. The basic top is made of nine pieces of maple (pieces 21), with splines (pieces 22) to help align the glue-up (see the Material List on page 62). Take care to surface this wood to very close tolerances—it will help you in the long run. Once you glue up the top and trim it to size, you will need to determine how you will flatten it. See Flattening a Benchtop on page 66 for techniques to help with this process.

When the top is flat, glue the side rails (piece 23) in place. Scrape the squeeze-out off, and install the cross braces (pieces 24). As mentioned earlier, the cross braces have notches cut into them that fit into the notches you formed earlier in the long rails (pieces 1). You'll need to rip the long cleats (pieces 25) from solid stock and then cut and fit them once the cross braces are in place. Gluing and clamping are sufficient to secure these cleats in place.

Next, form the endcaps (pieces 26), boring the two-step holes for the lag bolts that attach the endcaps to the top. Make the through holes for the bolts oversize to accommodate seasonal wood movement.

The Downdraft Opening

Cutting a huge hole in a perfectly good top is an admittedly disturbing task, but you can't have a downdraft table without it. Use a straight bit in your handheld router, and make a template (see the drawings on pages 62–63 for the proper opening size) to guide the router to the dimension of the inside of the opening. Use several passes to cut through the top. Then, switch to a rabbeting bit to create a rabbet around the upper edge of the opening. The rabbet will hold the draft vent.

Make the draft vent and cover (pieces 27 and 28) to fit your opening.

Figure 2: *After a little experimentation, I arrived at the perfect number of holes for the draft vent top. See the draft vent hole drawing on page 63.*

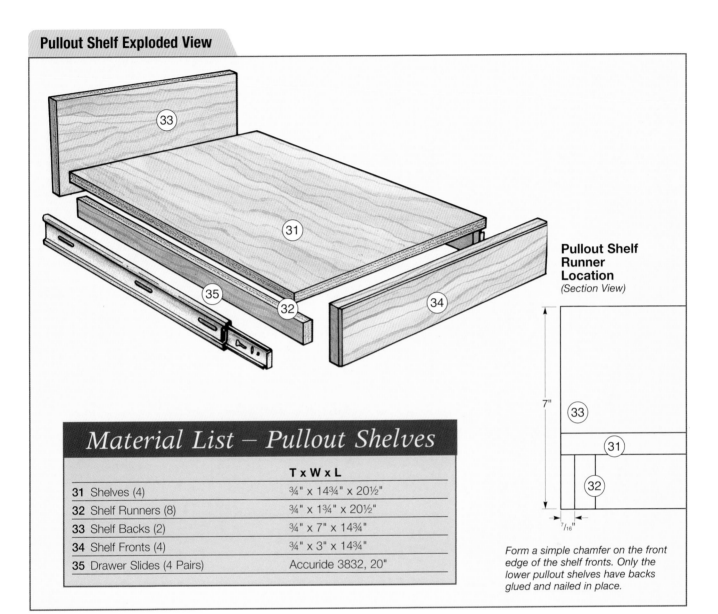

Material List – Pullout Shelves

		T x W x L
31	Shelves (4)	¾" x 14¾" x 20½"
32	Shelf Runners (8)	¾" x 1¾" x 20½"
33	Shelf Backs (2)	¾" x 7" x 14¾"
34	Shelf Fronts (4)	¾" x 3" x 14¾"
35	Drawer Slides (4 Pairs)	Accuride 3832, 20"

**Pullout Shelf
Runner
Location**
(Section View)

7"

⁷⁄₁₆"

Form a simple chamfer on the front edge of the shelf fronts. Only the lower pullout shelves have backs glued and nailed in place.

Lay out the vent holes, and use a sharp Forstner bit to bore them (see Figure 2). Follow behind with your router and a roundover bit to soften the upper edges of the vent holes. Bore a single finger hole in the cover, and round over the top and bottom edges of that hole. If you choose to put an end vise on the top, install the vise block and vise (pieces 29 and 30), as shown in the drawings on page 63.

Pullouts and Shelves

Pullout shelves make it possible to store tools in this bench without also having to climb in to get them. The top shelves serve as a little extra tabletop to place your in-use tools on, and the bottom pullouts feature a high back to keep power tools from shifting and falling off the back.

Cut the shelves, runners, fronts, and backs (pieces 31 through 34) to size (see the Material List, above), and set up a mini-assembly line to build them. Before you continue, ease the sharp edges and ends of the front pieces with a chamfer bit in the router. Use finish nails and glue to attach the runners and fronts to the shelves. Inset the runners ⁷⁄₁₆" from the edge of the shelves to

accommodate the drawer slides (pieces 35). On the two lower pullouts, glue and screw the backs in place. Mount the drawer slides in their proper places, and you are ready to move on to the final details.

Now is as good a time as any to do a once-over sanding and surface preparation. I sealed my bench with several coats of a hard-drying oil finish. I wanted something that would seal the wood but that would also be easy to retouch whenever necessary. Don't use linseed or mineral oil, because neither cures hard enough to repel dust.

Flattening a Benchtop

With a straightedge, establish and mark the low areas of the glued-up top with a pencil.

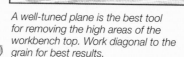

A well-tuned plane is the best tool for removing the high areas of the workbench top. Work diagonal to the grain for best results.

Another option is to use coarse-grit sandpaper and your belt sander to remove the high spots. Work in the pattern shown below.

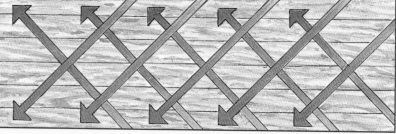

First, mark the low areas in the glued-up top. Next, with your plane or belt sander, remove the high areas as you work in an opposing diagonal pattern. Again, using your straightedge, mark the low areas once more, and repeat the pattern. Repeat this process until you flatten the top.

A dead-flat work surface is an essential element in any workbench. Flattening a glued-up top is not too hard if you take it one step at a time. You can cart your glued-up top to a cabinet shop and have it surfaced on a large stationary belt sander, but if you choose to do it yourself, simply follow the above tips.

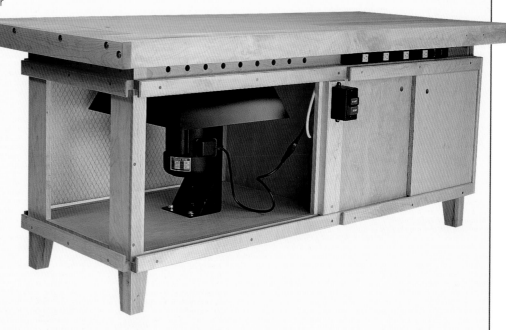

High-Tech Hardware

The downdraft hardware and power strip are final touches that make this project sing (or at least hum). You can get these items, as well as the finishing supplies and drawer slides, by contacting Rockler Woodworking and Hardware at 800-279-4441 or *www.rockler.com*.

I mounted the power strip over the pullout shelves and eventually mounted a second strip on the back side of the table, as well. There's no limit to how much access to power you can have—especially at the workbench. For more convenience, wire the power strip through the on/off switch of the downdraft unit, so there will be a single power cord exiting the bench.

Add-Ons and Personal Preferences

Workbenches should be tailor-made to suit the main user. Bench height is one area where people differ. Most woodworkers prefer the benchtop to sit at half their height. If you are 6' tall, the top should be 36".

Perhaps you would like bench dogs in your workbench. This top is designed so that bench dogs are an option. You can drill additional holes, or you can use the sanding dogs shown on page 64, along with your vise, to secure longer stock or panels while machining.

*Quick*Tip

Holder for a Drafting Lamp

Having supplemental task lighting at the workbench is essential, especially for spotting flaws during finishing and for doing other detail work. Here's a quick way to retrofit a drafting lamp onto any workbench with bench dog holes. Just take a piece of 2" x 4" and drill two holes several inches apart. One should fit the lamp base, while the other should be the same diameter as a bench dog. Glue a dowel into the second hole so you can mount your lamp into any hole on the benchtop. From there, the hinged arm allows you to focus light wherever you need it most.

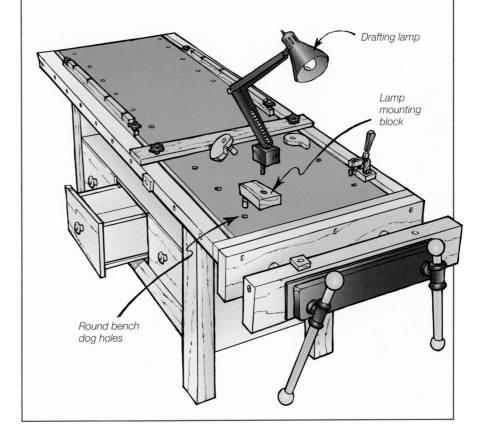

Drafting lamp

Lamp mounting block

Round bench dog holes

All-Purpose Shop Table

Just one sheet of plywood and a handful of screws build this rugged, useful worktable. It's perfect for assembly and finishing jobs, or you could even use it for broad outfeed support at the table saw.

by Keith Hettinger

You may hear a different story about the brass at the Pentagon, but our guys in uniform sure know how to squeeze a dime for all it's worth. As a GI during World War II, I helped build thousands of these all-purpose tables at bases throughout the south Pacific. The design calls for only one sheet of 4' x 8' plywood, and judging from the cutting diagram on page 69, every inch gets used, short of the sawdust left on the ground. If you need a sturdy workshop table, this one truly has been certified by the test of time.

Step 1: *After cutting the plywood into sections (see the diagram on page 69), follow the layout and the Material List to cut the individual pieces to size.*

Step 2: *Make a tapering jig from scrap wood, as shown in the taper jig layout drawing on page 69, and rip the leg panels to size and shape.*

Step 3: *Drill counterbored pilot holes in the wider leg pieces, and then glue and screw the legs into four corner brackets. Glue plugs into the counterbores.*

Step 4: *Glue and screw the aprons to the leg brackets, making sure to secure the end aprons first to get the correct overlap at the corners.*

Step 5: *Assemble the pieces for all of the support brackets, and install the middle apron. Next, mount the remaining brackets to the aprons.*

Step 6: *Band the top with hardwood strips, and lay it on your workbench. Position the base on the top, check for squareness, and screw the base to the top.*

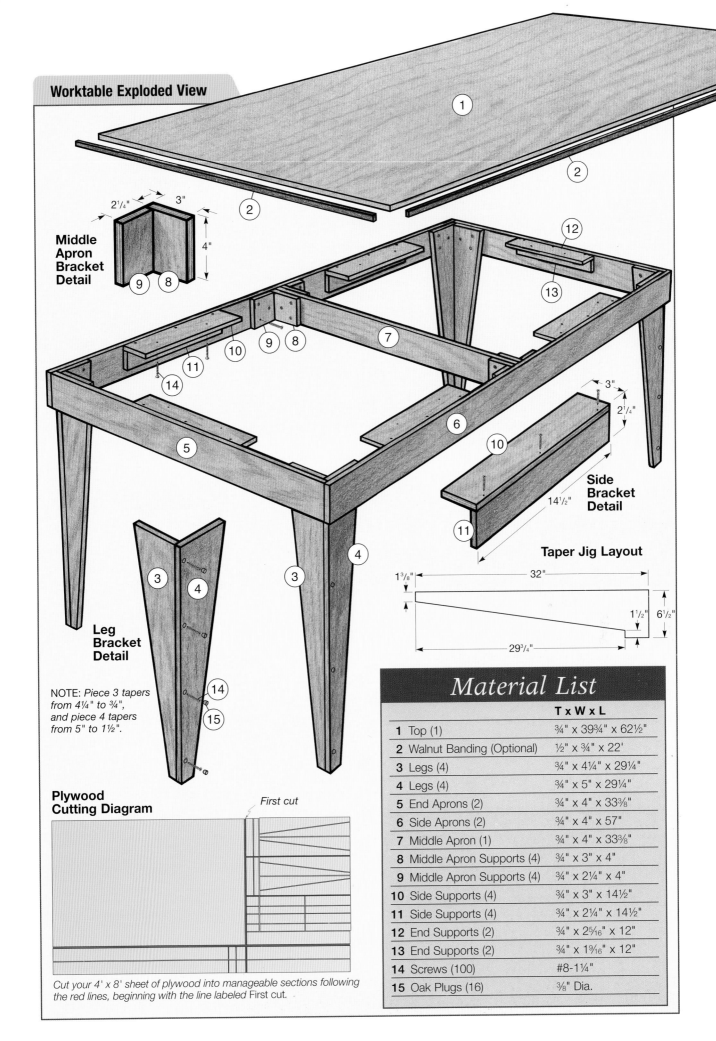

Worktable Exploded View

Middle Apron Bracket Detail
2¼"   3"
4"

Side Bracket Detail
3"
2¼"
14½"

Taper Jig Layout
1³⁄₈"
32"
1½"
6½"
29¾"

Leg Bracket Detail

NOTE: *Piece 3 tapers from 4¼" to ¾", and piece 4 tapers from 5" to 1½".*

Plywood Cutting Diagram

First cut

Cut your 4' x 8' sheet of plywood into manageable sections following the red lines, beginning with the line labeled First cut.

Material List

		T x W x L
1 Top (1)		¾" x 39¾" x 62½"
2 Walnut Banding (Optional)		½" x ¾" x 22'
3 Legs (4)		¾" x 4¼" x 29¼"
4 Legs (4)		¾" x 5" x 29¼"
5 End Aprons (2)		¾" x 4" x 33⅜"
6 Side Aprons (2)		¾" x 4" x 57"
7 Middle Apron (1)		¾" x 4" x 33⅜"
8 Middle Apron Supports (4)		¾" x 3" x 4"
9 Middle Apron Supports (4)		¾" x 2¼" x 4"
10 Side Supports (4)		¾" x 3" x 14½"
11 Side Supports (4)		¾" x 2¼" x 14½"
12 End Supports (2)		¾" x 2⁵⁄₁₆" x 12"
13 End Supports (2)		¾" x 1⁹⁄₁₆" x 12"
14 Screws (100)		#8-1¼"
15 Oak Plugs (16)		⅜" Dia.

Accessories Cart

Here's a useful shop project you can easily complete in a weekend. You'll never have to look far for your shop supplies and accessories again—just roll them right up to wherever you are working. It's like having a shop assistant at your beck and call!

by Brad Becker

Recently, during a particularly big project, I realized that we were missing an important fixture in the *Woodworker's Journal* shop. Our shop has plenty of storage space and lots of benches. But when you're working on a project, the little accessories and supplies have a tendency to spread out all over the place. Sound familiar? That's okay when it comes to major subassemblies, but if you're installing a lot of hardware or other small parts, or if you need ready access to a set of bits or chisels, you want them close at hand as you move around the shop. Otherwise, it's too easy to lose track of things.

This little accessory cart, like a kid brother, will follow you all around the shop. It has industrial-grade wheels that can be locked in place, a drawer that stays shut, and a replaceable top that's enclosed by its apron so nothing rolls off. As an afterthought, I added a tool holder and power strip to give it a little extra versatility as a small assembly table or recharging station for cordless tools.

In terms of construction, it's light, it's fast, and it fills a big need for the project builder. The design doesn't cut any corners, but it's still a project you could easily make out of the scrap wood and spare stock lying around your shop.

Figure 1: *The rabbets on the outside faces of each leg can be formed on the table saw. Here, a tenoning jig makes quick work of the task.*

Material List

		T x W x L			T x W x L
1	Legs (4)	1¾" x 1¾" x 30"	**8**	Base Cleats (4)	¾" x 7½" x 7½"
2	Front/Back Aprons (4)	¾" x 3" x 30"	**9**	Walnut Plugs (48)	⅜"
3	Side Aprons (4)	¾" x 3" x 20½"	**10**	Casters (4)	3" Locking
4	Slide Mounts (2)	½" x 4" x 19½"	**11**	Drawer Back (1)	½" x 3⅛" x 23⅜"
5	Drawer Front and Rear Cover (2)	½" x 4" x 25⅝"	**12**	Drawer Bottom (1)	¼" x 24" x 18¼"
6	Tool Hanger (1)	¾" x 2⅜" x 25⅝"	**13**	Drawer Sides/Slides (2)	Metal, Premade
7	Top and Base Shelf Inserts (2)	¾" x 19" x 28½"	**14**	Drawer Pulls (2)	Walnut

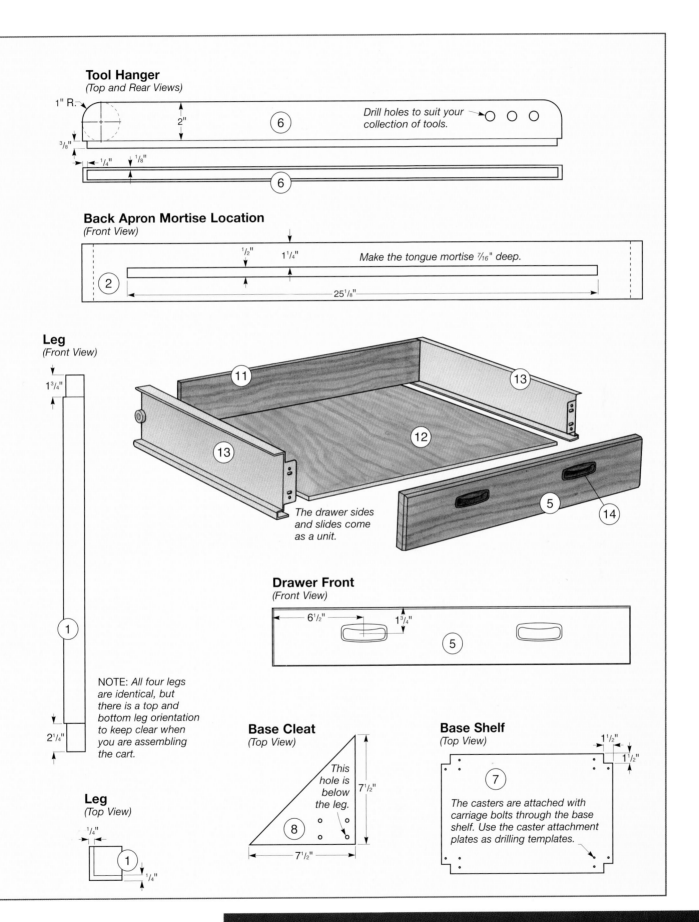

Tool Hanger
(Top and Rear Views)

1" R.

2"

⑥

Drill holes to suit your collection of tools.

³/₈"

¼"   ⅛"

⑥

Back Apron Mortise Location
(Front View)

½"   1¼"

Make the tongue mortise ⁷/₁₆" deep.

②

25⅛"

Leg
(Front View)

1³/₄"

①

2¼"

NOTE: *All four legs are identical, but there is a top and bottom leg orientation to keep clear when you are assembling the cart.*

⑪   ⑬

⑬   ⑫

The drawer sides and slides come as a unit.

⑤   ⑭

Drawer Front
(Front View)

6½"   1³/₄"

⑤

Leg
(Top View)

¼"

①

¼"

Base Cleat
(Top View)

This hole is below the leg.

7½"

⑧

7½"

Base Shelf
(Top View)

1½"

1½"

⑦

The casters are attached with carriage bolts through the base shelf. Use the caster attachment plates as drilling templates.

Figure 2: *You don't want to scrimp on the wheels when you're in a shop setting. This brute features ball bearings and easy-to-use locks. In 20 years, it'll still be on the job.*

Starting with the Legs and Aprons

The Material List on page 72 outlines all the parts for this project, and, with the exception of the tool hanger, everything is square. The first pieces to cut to size are the legs and aprons (pieces 1 through 3). The legs are rabbeted on two sides of their tops and bottoms, creating a notch for the aprons. This material can be removed on your table saw with a dado blade installed or, as shown in Figure 1 on page 71, with

a tenoning jig. (Check the elevation drawings on pages 72–73 for details.) There are two different-size aprons and a number of holes to be drilled and countersunk. The last step is to miter the ends.

Bringing the Legs and Aprons Together

With the legs and aprons cut and machined, turn to your plug cutter to create some fancy plugs for the screw holes. I used oak for my cart, so I made the plugs from walnut scrap. Use some of your clamps to bring the legs and

Figure 3: *The slides for this shop project do double-duty as sides and make drawer assembly a breeze. Magnets are used to keep the drawer shut.*

aprons together, and extend pilot holes into the legs. Now, glue and screw the legs and aprons together, checking for square as you go. Next, cut the slide mounts (pieces 4) to size, and install them inside, as shown in the exploded view on page 72. Cut the drawer front and rear drawer cover (pieces 5) to size, and then chamfer their edges—but don't install these pieces yet.

Cut the tool hanger (piece 6) to size, and clamp it in position as you drill pilot holes from the inside. There's a stopped tongue on the tool hanger and a stopped groove in the apron (see the elevation drawings). I drilled a few holes to hold screwdrivers right away, but you may want to let your tool selections dictate the number, size, and proximity of these holes.

Cut the melamine top and base shelf (pieces 7) to size, and create the notches at the corners of the base shelf, as shown in the elevation drawings. Cut the cleats (pieces 8) to size, and clamp them in position as you drill pilot holes and countersink holes for their plugs (pieces 9) through the aprons.

Install the cleats, and test fit the melamine bases. The top one sits right on top of the legs; the bottom one sits on the cleats. Chamfer the bottom edges of both pieces of melamine to ensure a smooth friction fit.

While the bottom is in place, position your wheels (pieces 10) on the bottom of the cleats, and drill all the way through for the hefty bolts. Note on the elevation drawings that one of the holes goes right into the leg bottom—use a large screw for this location. Install the wheels (see Figure 2), and turn the unit back upright.

Cut the drawer back and bottom (pieces 11 and 12) to size, and assemble the drawer, as shown in

Installing the Pulls

Creating mortises for the pulls was a simple, two-step process. First, make a hardboard template with a jigsaw and sandpaper. Then, rout the mortise with a short bearing-guided bit. The pull features a slight shoulder to cover minor slips.

I used simple fabricated walnut pulls that feature a tiny lip for this drawer. If you have pulls left over from another drawer, they'll do just fine, but I wanted the plugs and pulls to match. Follow the simple process shown above to rout mortises in the drawer front for the pulls. The key here is to get the template right. Use a jigsaw to cut the template opening. Sand exactly to the lines using sandpaper wrapped around a ¾" dowel. Then, clamp the template in place on the drawer front, and rout the openings. Fix each pull into its mortise with a little glue, and you're done.

Figure 3. I used drawer slides that come complete as metal drawer sides (piece 13). These sides simply screw to the drawer front and back, and then the drawer bottom slides into place. It's a slick and sturdy system, especially for quick shop projects like this.

Wrapping Up

Follow the instructions in Installing the Pulls, above, to create mortises for the pulls (pieces 14) and install them on the drawer front. Sand everything down through 220 grit. Fit the drawer slides on the slide mounts, and test fit your drawer. I added some magnets on the ends of the slide mounts and on the back of the drawer front to keep the drawer from opening up as the cart is wheeled around a corner. When you're happy with the fit, apply a coat of finishing oil to all the wood parts.

When the finish dries, reinstall the top—remember, it's a friction fit, so it's easy to replace when the melamine wears out. Now, find your most common tool companions, and introduce them to their hanger or new drawer—they're going for a ride!

Mobile Clamping Cart for the Small Shop

Necessity is the mother of invention. In some shops, that's not just a clever proverb—it's a design philosophy. Assembly supplies start to pile up, so you design a storage fixture for them. This one is a great solution for organizing clutter in a small shop.

from the Woodworker's Journal *Shop*

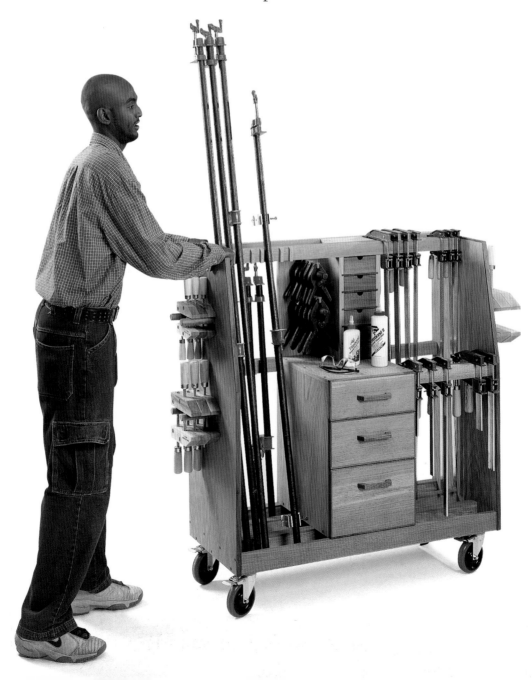

S
R
T
o

Sessions by cutting the cart's sides and bottom (pieces 1 and 2) to size on the table saw, as shown in Figure 1. Create the angle on the front corner of the sides (see the drawings on page 78) with a handheld circular saw guided by a straightedge. Rip solid stock to make pieces 3 through 6. While you're at the saw, rip the walnut banding (piece 7), too. Apply the banding to the sides, and allow the glue to cure.

Now, form the rabbet on the front rail with a dado head in your table saw, and notch one of the long rails, as shown in the drawings. Clamp and glue pairs of long and short rails together, and after the glue has cured, cut them to length. Attach the appropriate rails and cabinet support to the cart bottom with glue and screws. To assemble the sides and bottom, predrill counterbored screw holes, and, with the help of a friend,

...ces together. Secure just ...ng rail at this time (see the ... details).

Making the Center Cabinet

A clamp cart should hold more than just clamps; you also need glue, biscuits, screws, and other fasteners. The center drawers on this cart should tidy things up well. Begin making the center storage cabinet by cutting its plywood parts (pieces 8 through 11) to size and shape (form the notch to accommodate the back rail, as well). Rip some oak banding (piece 12), and use it to cover the exposed edges of the plywood pieces. Predrill counterbored screw holes, assemble the cabinet (without the back), and slide it into place on the cart subassembly. Secure it to the rails with screws. Now, go ahead and secure the back with glue and screws.

Cut the parts for the tray bank sides and top (pieces 13 and 14), and band their edges. Notch the upper corner for the rails. Put a ¼" dado head in your table saw, and plow a series of ⅜"-deep dadoes to accept the dust-proof tray bottoms, as shown in the drawings. Locate and cut the biscuit joints on the cabinet top and the tray bank sides. From ¼" hardboard, cut the tray bank divider (piece 15). Now, install the tray

bank sides and divider, with glue, screws, and biscuits securing the joints.

With that subassembly in place, you can install the remaining rails, both long and short. Next, cut all 10 clamp dowels (pieces 16) to length, and mount them to best accommodate the clamps you own. Do the same with the pipe dividers (pieces 17)—remember to check whether you have ¾"- or ½"-diameter pipe clamps before attaching the dividers. The drawer slides, casters, and hinge (pieces 18 through 20) will be mounted a bit later.

Building Drawers and Trays

The drawer faces (pieces 21 through 23) are cut from ¾" plywood and edged with the walnut banding. Drill two holes in each face for its drawer pull (see Figure 2 on page 79). The drawer sides, fronts, and backs (pieces 24 through 29) are made from ½" plywood with locking corner joints (see the detail drawing on page 79). Plow the dadoes in the sides and fronts for the drawer bottoms (pieces 30), and you're ready to assemble the drawers.

The tray sides, fronts, and backs (pieces 31 and 32) are assembled with the same corner joints as the drawers. Their bottoms (pieces 33) are glued and pin-nailed in place. Note that the overhanging edges of the bottoms fit into the dadoes you cut in the tray bank sides.

The walnut tray faces (pieces 34) are made in pairs. First, drill the finger hole, and then slice the blank down the center (see the drawing of the tray face blank layout on page 79). Attach the tray faces with screws.

Figure 1: *Rip the large plywood pieces first. The sides and bottom form the shell of this rolling cart.*

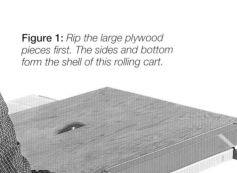

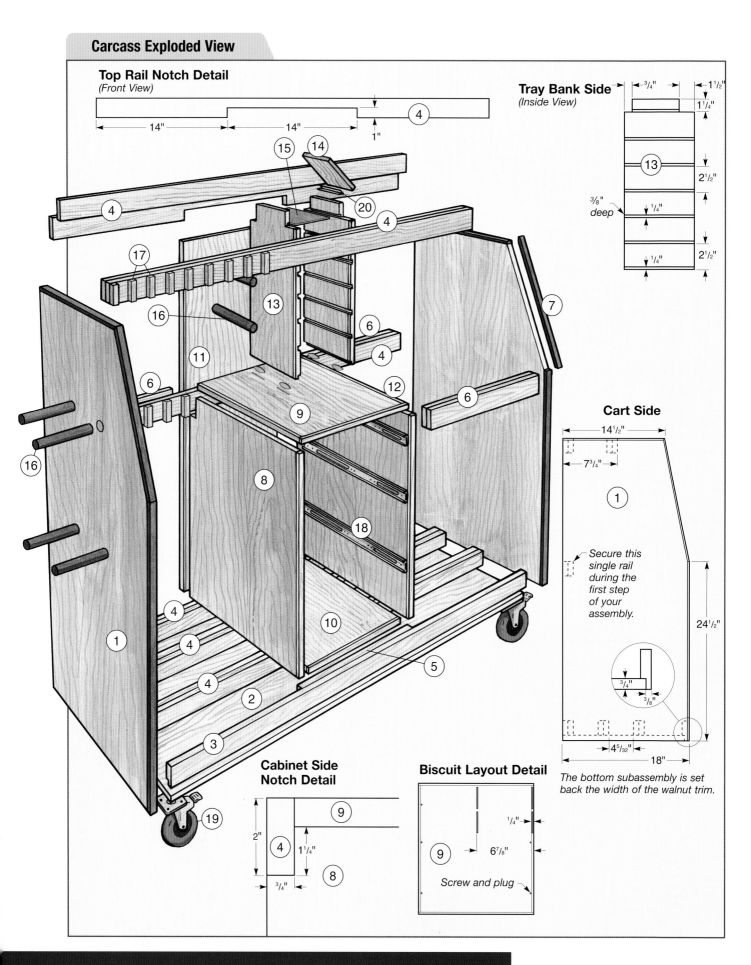

Top Rail Notch Detail
(Front View)

14"

14"

1"

4

Tray Bank Side
(Inside View)

3/4"   1 1/2"

1 1/4"

13

2 1/2"

3/8"
deep

1/4"

1/4"   2 1/2"

15

14

20

17

4

4

7

16

13

6

4

11

6

12

Cart Side

9

14 1/2"

7 3/4"

1

16

8

18

6

Secure this
single rail
during the
first step
of your
assembly.

24 1/2"

4

10

3/4"

3/8"

4

5

2

3

19

4 5/32"

18"

*The bottom subassembly is set
back the width of the walnut trim.*

**Cabinet Side
Notch Detail**

9

2"

4

1 1/4"

8

3/4"

Biscuit Layout Detail

9

1/4"

6 7/8"

Screw and plug

Material List – Carcass

	T x W x L
1 Sides (2)	¾" x 17¾" x 41½"
2 Bottom (1)	¾" x 17⅜" x 42"
3 Front Bottom Rail (1)	¾" x 2¾" x 42"
4 Long Rails (11)	¾" x 2" x 42"
5 Cabinet Support (1)	¾" x 2" x 14"
6 Short Rails (4)	¾" x 2" x 14"
7 Walnut Banding (1)	¼" x ¾" x 260"
8 Cabinet Sides (2)	¾" x 16" x 21"
9 Cabinet Top (1)	¾" x 13½" x 15¼"
10 Cabinet Bottom (1)	¾" x 12½" x 16"
11 Cabinet Back (1)	¾" x 13½" x 38"
12 Oak Banding (1)	¼" x ¾" x 115"
13 Tray Bank Sides (2)	¾" x 7" x 16½"
14 Tray Bank Top (1)	¾" x 4¾" x 7"
15 Tray Bank Divider (1)	¼" x 6¼" x 4¾"
16 Clamp Dowels (8)	1" Dia. x 8"
17 Pipe Dividers (30)	½" x ½" x 2"
18 Drawer Slides (3 Sets)	16" Full Extension
19 Casters (4)	Locking
20 Piano Hinge (1)	Brass

Now, mount the drawer pulls (pieces 35), casters, and hinge on the tray bank top, and you are nearly done. Cover all exposed screw holes with walnut plugs, and topcoat with a penetrating finish.

You will likely want to modify the cart to suit your specific clamp collection. Keep in mind that you can fit a lot in those drawers—that's where all my C-clamps and band clamps go.

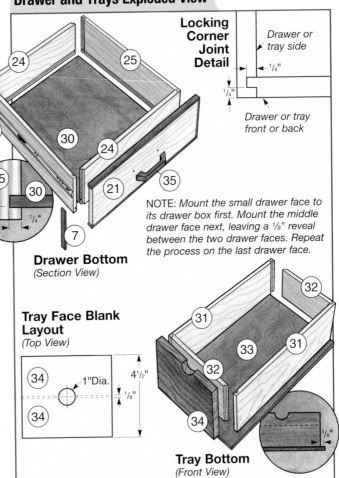

Drawer and Trays Exploded View

Locking Corner Joint Detail

Drawer or tray side

Drawer or tray front or back

NOTE: *Mount the small drawer face to its drawer box first. Mount the middle drawer face next, leaving a ⅛" reveal between the two drawer faces. Repeat the process on the last drawer face.*

Drawer Bottom (Section View)

Tray Face Blank Layout (Top View)

1"Dia.

4½"
⅛"

Tray Bottom (Front View)

3/8"

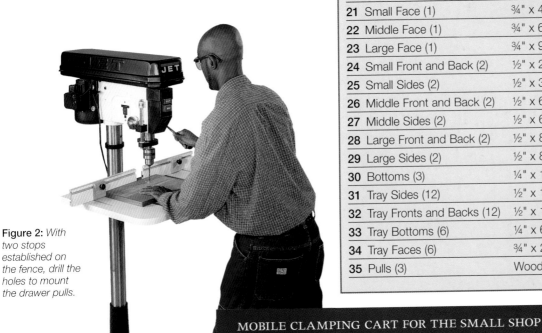

Figure 2: *With two stops established on the fence, drill the holes to mount the drawer pulls.*

Material List – Drawers and Trays

	T x W x L
21 Small Face (1)	¾" x 4¼" x 13½"
22 Middle Face (1)	¾" x 6¼" x 13½"
23 Large Face (1)	¾" x 9¼" x 13½"
24 Small Front and Back (2)	½" x 2½" x 11"
25 Small Sides (2)	½" x 3¾" x 15½"
26 Middle Front and Back (2)	½" x 6" x 11"
27 Middle Sides (2)	½" x 6" x 15½"
28 Large Front and Back (2)	½" x 8" x 11"
29 Large Sides (2)	½" x 8" x 15½"
30 Bottoms (3)	¼" x 11" x 15"
31 Tray Sides (12)	½" x 1¾" x 6¼"
32 Tray Fronts and Backs (12)	½" x 1½" x 4⅞"
33 Tray Bottoms (6)	¼" x 6¼" x 7"
34 Tray Faces (6)	¾" x 2³⁄₁₆" x 5½"
35 Pulls (3)	Wood

Ultimate Clamping Station

Organize all your clamps and glue-up supplies within arm's reach, and enjoy the advantages of the space-saving fold-down clamping table—you'll never have to scrape glue off your workbench again.

by Rick White

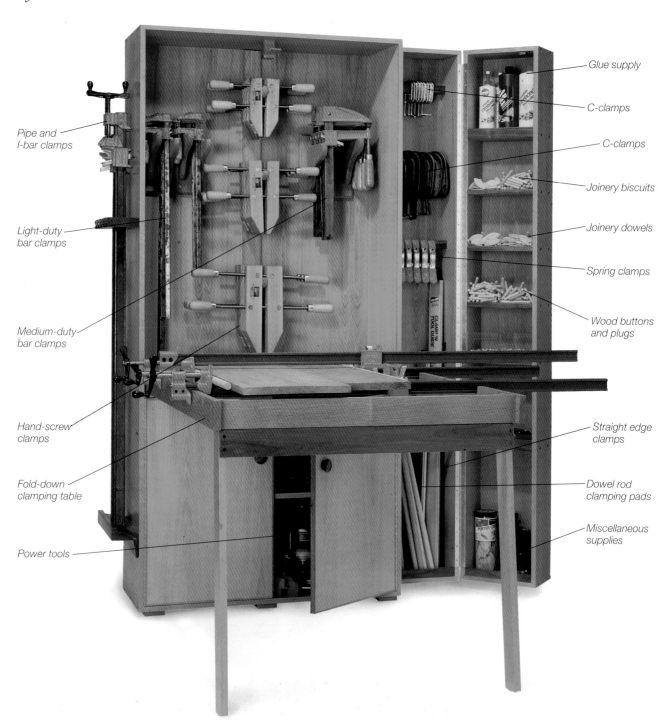

Pipe and I-bar clamps

Light-duty bar clamps

Medium-duty bar clamps

Hand-screw clamps

Fold-down clamping table

Power tools

Glue supply

C-clamps

C-clamps

Joinery biscuits

Joinery dowels

Spring clamps

Wood buttons and plugs

Straight edge clamps

Dowel rod clamping pads

Miscellaneous supplies

If you have a typical home shop, you probably store clamps wherever you can find a little spare space. Glue bottles are on a far-off shelf, dowels and biscuits are in a cupboard, and your clamping pads are stored in a box. Sound familiar?

Maybe a deluxe clamping station isn't the top project on your to-do list, but it could centralize your clamping supplies and put an end to the mad scrambles you might go through just before a glue-up. Better yet, the days of giving up your workbench for use as a clamping table are over.

Figure 1: *After you're finished with a glue-up, the clamping station closes flat and takes on a clean, modular appearance that blends in nicely with other shop cabinetry. You'll appreciate this if floor space is in short supply in your shop.*

Cutting Your Plywood to Size

The bulk of the clamping station is made of white-oak plywood. Lay out your panels, as shown on the plywood cutting layouts on page 89. Cut the pieces slightly oversize with a circular saw and straightedge, and then recut the pieces to final size on a table saw (see the Material List on page 82). This makes the sheets more manageable to break down and also bumps up cutting accuracy a nudge.

Now, rip banding (pieces 1), and glue it to the front edges of the left side panel, divider, right side panel, top, bottom, and fixed shelf (pieces 2 through 7). In addition, band both edges of the panels for the side door (pieces 8 and 9), with one exception: On the right side panel, band the front edge completely, but only glue banding to the 2" at each end of the back edge, as shown in the exploded view on page 84. The unbanded edge will provide the mortise for the piano hinges.

Continue working with the panels by plowing the rabbets and dadoes for the joints with your table saw and a ¾" dado blade, as shown in the carcass and side door elevation drawings on pages 87–88. Next, slip each joint together, and drill counterbored pilot holes for #8-1½" screws (pieces 10), temporarily driving the screws as you go. After drilling all the holes, take the assemblies apart, spread glue in the joints, and permanently screw the pieces together again. Glue walnut plugs (pieces 11) into the counterbores, and sand them flush.

Slip the back panel (piece 12) into the carcass assembly, and drill pilot holes through the walls, top, and bottom for the screws. Glue and screw the back into place, and cover the screw heads with walnut plugs. Trim the door front (piece 13), and glue it into the side door assembly. You may want to use a hand plane to shave the door front's edges to get a perfect slip-fit.

Completing the Carcass

Cut plywood for the cupboard doors (pieces 14), and glue oak banding to three edges of each panel (see the exploded view on page 82). Cover the fourth edge with walnut banding (pieces 15).

Cut two piano hinges (pieces 16) to length for the cupboard doors, and install the doors and hinges in the cabinet. Make sure the doors swing shut without banging into each other—plane the walnut edges if necessary. Next, mount the magnetic door catches (pieces 17), and drill pilot holes for the door knobs (pieces 19), as shown in the carcass elevation.

Inside the the cupboard, drill rows of ¼" holes (see the carcass elevation) for the shelf supports (pieces 20), using a strip of pegboard as a template. After drilling the holes, cut plywood for the adjustable shelf (piece 21), and glue oak banding to its front edge. Wrap up the carcass by cutting the feet (pieces 22) to size and screwing them to the underside of the bottom panel.

Making the Clamping Table

The clamping table is a great space saver. When it's not in use, it swings out of the way (see Figure 1); yet, when you need to clamp a panel together, it's right at your fingertips, with all your clamps still within reach. You'll also appreciate the fact that the table supports a panel at a comfortable working height—much better than clamping at the bench or down on the floor.

To build the clamping table, cut oak for the sides, front, and legs, and cut walnut for the stop (pieces 23 through 26; see the Material List on page 83). Shape the ends of the legs with a jigsaw, as shown in the elevation drawings on page 83. Cut the bottom

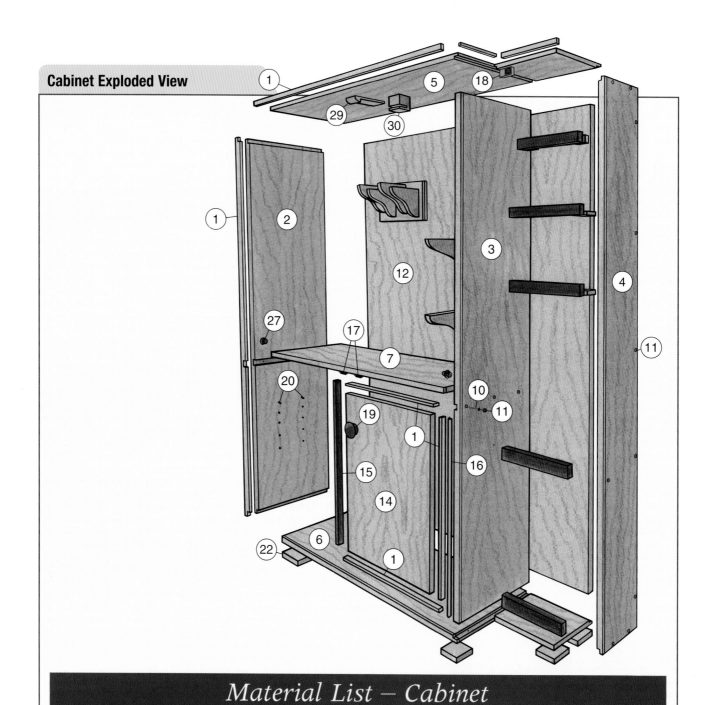

Material List – Cabinet

	T x W x L		T x W x L
1 Oak Banding (10)	¼" x ¾" x 96"	**12** Back (1)	¾" x 48" x 75¼"
2 Left Side (1)	¾" x 13¾" x 76"	**13** Box Door Front (1)	¾" x 10¾" x 75¼"
3 Divider (1)	¾" x 13" x 75¼"	**14** Cupboard Doors (2)	¾" x 17¼" x 26½"
4 Right Side (1)	¾" x 7" x 76"	**15** Walnut Banding (1)	¼" x ¾" x 60"
5 Top (1)	¾" x 13¾" x 48¼"	**16** Piano Hinges (4)	1½" x 36" (Brass Finish)
6 Bottom (1)	¾" x 13¾" x 48¼"	**17** Door Catches (3)	Magnetic
7 Fixed Shelf (1)	¾" x 13" x 36½"	**18** Block (1)	¾" x 1¼" x 2"
8 Box Door Sides (2)	¾" x 6¾" x 76"	**19** Door Knobs (3)	1¾" Dia. (Beech)
9 Box Door Top/Bottom (2)	¾" x 6¾" x 10¾"	**20** Shelf Supports (4)	¼" Dia. Posts
10 Screws (100)	#8-1½"	**21** Adjustable Shelf (1)	¾" x 12½" x 35¾"
11 Walnut Plugs (100)	⅜" Dia.	**22** Feet (6)	¾" x 2¾" x 2¾"

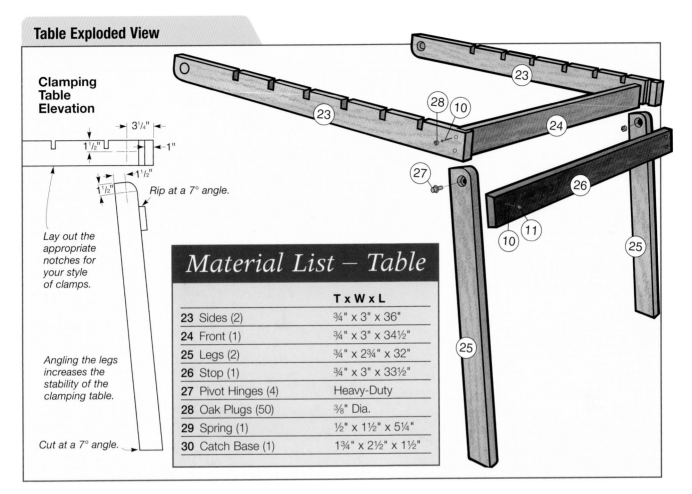

**Clamping
Table
Elevation**

3¼"

1½"

1"

1½"

1½"

Rip at a 7° angle.

*Lay out the
appropriate
notches for
your style
of clamps.*

*Angling the legs
increases the
stability of the
clamping table.*

Cut at a 7° angle.

Material List – Table

		T x W x L
23	Sides (2)	¾" x 3" x 36"
24	Front (1)	¾" x 3" x 34½"
25	Legs (2)	¾" x 2¾" x 32"
26	Stop (1)	¾" x 3" x 33½"
27	Pivot Hinges (4)	Heavy-Duty
28	Oak Plugs (50)	⅜" Dia.
29	Spring (1)	½" x 1½" x 5¼"
30	Catch Base (1)	1¾" x 2½" x 1½"

end of each leg at a 7° angle so
that it's more difficult to accidently
kick the legs out from under the
table. Use the jigsaw to notch the
frame sides to form holders for
your bar or pipe clamps (see the
drawings and Figure 2), and then
cut the dado near the end of each
piece with your table saw and a ¾"
dado blade.

Now, drill holes for the pivot
hinges (pieces 27) in the frame sides,
legs, and carcass, as shown in the
clamping table elevation drawing,
above, and in the other carcass
elevation drawings. Install the frame
sides in the carcass with the hinges,
and then glue the front rail into the
side rail dadoes. Drill counterbored
pilot holes into these joints, drive the
screws, and then cover the screws
with oak plugs (pieces 28). Next, join
the legs to the frame sides with the

pivot hinges, and mount the walnut
stop to the front legs with screws
and plugs.

The catch (pieces 29 and
30) for holding the clamping table
closed is shown on page 85. Lay
out the spring shape on the edge
of some oak stock, and band
saw it to shape. Sand the piece
smooth, and cut the base to size.
Kerf the base with a table saw
blade to fit the spring, and glue the
pieces together. Glue and screw
the catch to the roof of the main
cabinet compartment.

Adding Clamp Supports
and Storage Bins

All the fixtures you can
make for the side door and side
compartment are versatile enough
to hold a variety of clamps and
shop supplies. You may need

Figure 2: *With notches holding the bar clamps or pipe
clamps steady, the fold-down clamping table is ideal
for gluing up panels. You'll get even better results using
dowel pads that direct the clamping pressure exactly at
the center of the panel's edge.*

Storage Strategy

In addition to storing glue, dowels, biscuits, and light-duty clamps, keep some ¾" dowels on hand for use as clamping pads. When gluing up a panel, the dowels direct the clamping pressure right where it's needed.

Storage bins
with acrylic fronts and dividers keep small joinery supplies organized and in full view.

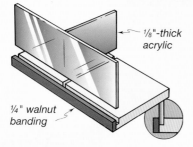

⅛"-thick acrylic

¼" walnut banding

Storage shelves
with a tall front lip are ideal for holding extra glue bottles, solvents, and band clamps.

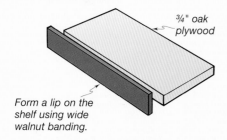

¾" oak plywood

Form a lip on the shelf using wide walnut banding.

Right Door Exploded View

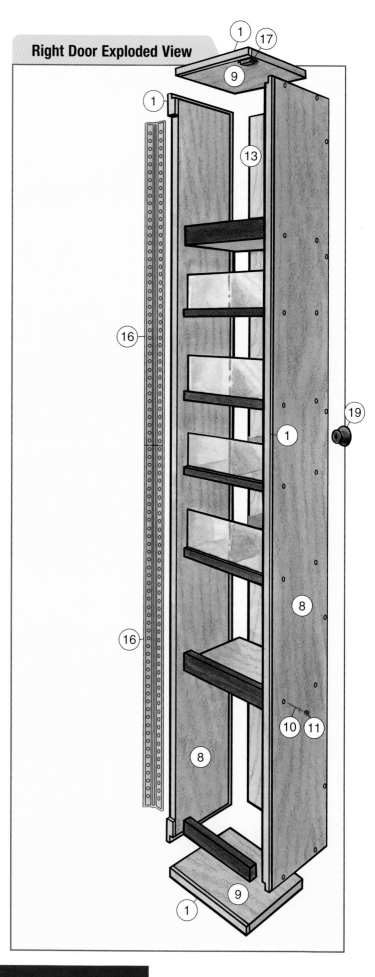

to redesign some of them or come up with designs of your own to suit your tools. In addition, I recommend that you use these fixture sizes and layouts as a guide (they're not in the Material List) and spend time figuring out the best position for each bracket according to your needs.

Begin by making the fixtures for the side door. Install shelves and bins in the door for holding all sorts of glue-up odds and ends, including glue bottles, a scraper, fluted and spiral dowels, biscuits, band clamps, cleanup rags, and a can or two of solvent. Build the shelves and bins to span the width of your door, as shown on page 84. The walnut strip on the front of each shelf rises 1" above the plywood to prevent your supplies from falling off. The see-through acrylic bin fronts and dividers (acrylic sheets are available at most building supply centers) slip nicely into ⅛" grooves cut with a standard table saw blade. Be sure to cut the grooves in the plywood before adding the walnut strip to the front edge (otherwise, you'll cut through the walnut).

Mount the shelves and bins by driving screws through the door sides into the plywood base of each fixture. Remember to counterbore all the pilot holes and fill them with walnut plugs.

My piano hinge lengths were 36", so I butted two hinges end-to-end in order to mount the side door to the cabinet. Once the door is in place, screw the magnetic catch to the top panel, and cut a block (piece 18) for holding the strike plate in the side compartment. Screw the strike plate to the block, and then glue this assembly into the compartment so the strike plate is just a hair past the front edge of the cabinet. This will allow the catch to fully contact the strike plate. Finally, drill a pilot hole for the door knob (piece 19).

Outfitting Your Clamping Station

Table Catch
The wood spring lock allows quick release of the fold-down clamping table.

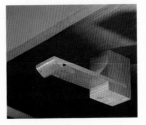

Glue into the base, and then screw the catch to the cabinet.

Simplicity is the key to designing clamp supports and other clamping station fixtures. If they work in different situations and are easy to make and install, you'll get the most mileage out of the design. Once you've made the fixtures, move them around to find the best arrangement in your cabinet. Keep your heavy-duty clamps close to the clamping table, where they're used most often, and put the light-duty clamps and other supplies in the side compartment and door.

Spring Clamps and C-Clamps
Simple wood bars are sufficient for hanging these light-duty clamps. Be sure to size the backup blocks to accommodate the clamp sizes in your shop.

Drive screws through the block into the back of the cabinet.

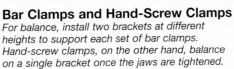

Bar Clamps and Hand-Screw Clamps
For balance, install two brackets at different heights to support each set of bar clamps. Hand-screw clamps, on the other hand, balance on a single bracket once the jaws are tightened.

Offset brackets keep the clamps level.

Pipe and I-Bar Clamps
Because they're heavy and unsteady, these clamps should be stored in individual slots. The lower bracket carries the weight while the upper bracket assembly pins the clamps in for safekeeping.

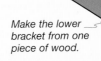

Screws hinge the retainers to the upper bracket.

Make the lower bracket from one piece of wood.

Now, make the fixtures for the side compartment, as shown on page 85. Cut walnut bars and blocks for the C-clamp and spring clamp hangers, and glue them together. Drill counterbored pilot holes, and screw the hangers to the back of the compartment.

Cut two more walnut bars for the dowel bin, and install them by driving screws through the divider and right side wall into the ends of the bars. (In case you're wondering, I use dowels as clamping pads on panel glue-ups because they direct the pressure right at the middle of the boards' edges.)

To make the fixtures for the main compartment, lay out and cut the clamp brackets to shape (see the elevation drawings on page 89), band sawing as many as you think you'll need. Screw the brackets to base plates, as shown on page 85 and on the bracket elevation drawings, and then screw the base plates to the back panel. Fill the counterbores with oak plugs.

The best place for storing pipe and I-bar clamps is on the outside of the cabinet. For the upper clamp bracket, glue two pieces of walnut face-to-face,

and then lay out notches, as shown in the pipe clamp fixture elevation drawing on page 89. Use a Forstner or spade bit to drill the ends of each notch, and then remove the rest of the waste with your table saw. Next, rip a ½" x ½" strip of walnut for the retainers, and cut them to length for spanning each notch. Screw the retainers into place. Cut the lower bracket out of one thick piece of walnut (see the pipe clamp fixture elevation drawing). Screw the brackets to the side of the cabinet, and plug the holes.

Finishing Up

Stain the door knobs dark brown to match the walnut parts of the project, and give the clamping station two coats of varnish or lacquer to protect it from glue drips. Slide the cabinet into position, and screw it to the wall to prevent any chance of it tipping forward once the clamps are loaded up.

After you get all your clamps and supplies organized, you'll probably notice that your shop feels a little roomier. Mostly, though, you'll appreciate how this station lowers your stress levels at glue-up time.

QuickTip

Storing Plywood and Other Sheet Goods

When working with manufactured panels such as plywood and particleboard, store them flat or vertically—never at an angle, or they'll warp. Vertical storage economizes space. Sheet materials can also de-laminate in severely damp or moist locations, so run a dehumidifier in your basement if you store sheet goods there. Better yet, buy only what you need for a particular project, use it up, and then buy fresh sheet goods for the next project.

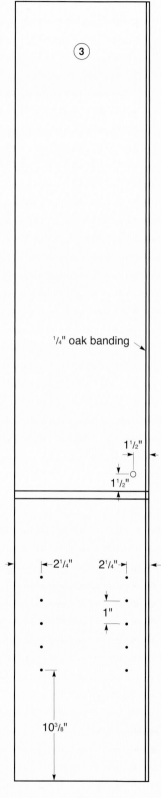

¼" oak banding

1½"

1½"

2¼"   2¼"

1"

10³⁄₈"

Divider Elevation

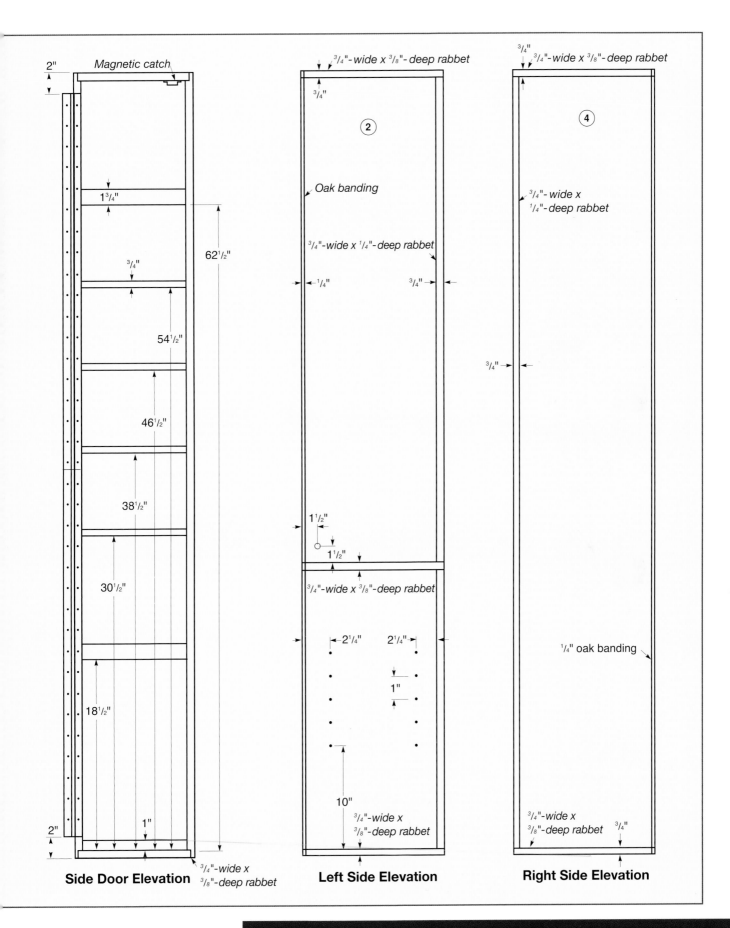

Side Door Elevation

2"

Magnetic catch

1³/₄"

³/₄"

62¹/₂"

54¹/₂"

46¹/₂"

38¹/₂"

30¹/₂"

18¹/₂"

1"

2"

³/₄"-wide x ³/₈"-deep rabbet

Left Side Elevation

³/₄"-wide x ³/₈"-deep rabbet

³/₄"

②

Oak banding

³/₄"-wide x ¹/₄"-deep rabbet

¹/₄"

³/₄"

1¹/₂"

1¹/₂"

³/₄"-wide x ³/₈"-deep rabbet

2¹/₄"   2¹/₄"

1"

10"

³/₄"-wide x ³/₈"-deep rabbet

Right Side Elevation

³/₄"

³/₄"-wide x ³/₈"-deep rabbet

④

³/₄"- wide x ¹/₄"-deep rabbet

³/₄"

¹/₄" oak banding

³/₄"-wide x ³/₈"-deep rabbet

³/₄"

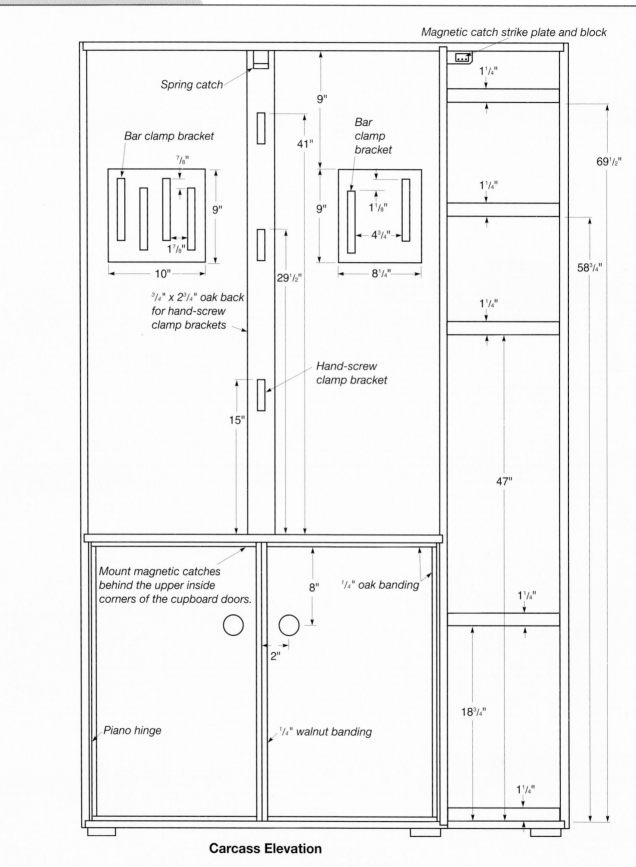

Carcass Elevation

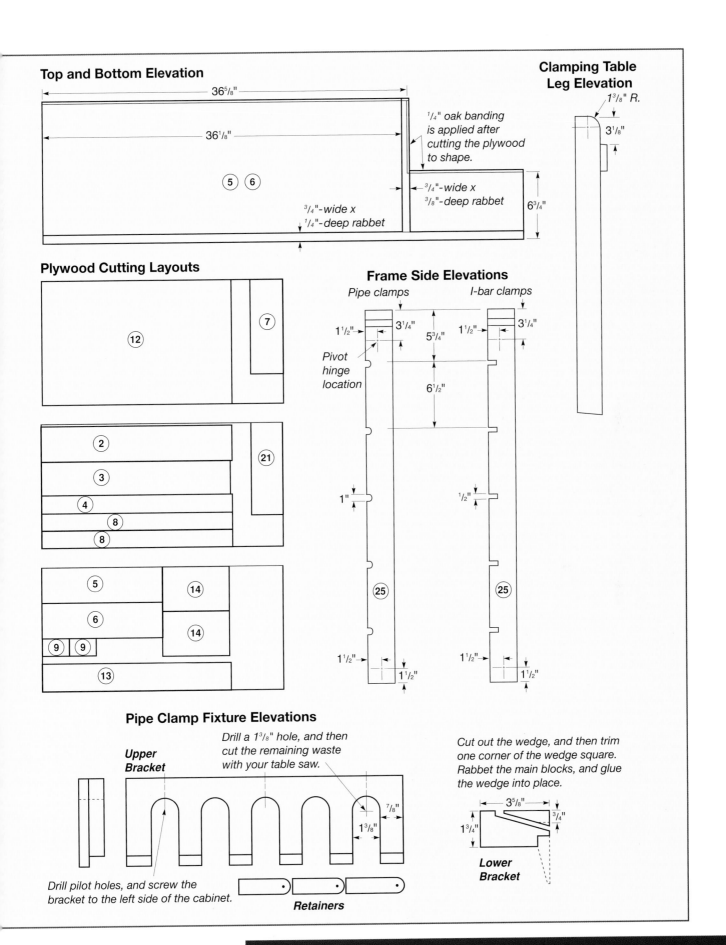

Top and Bottom Elevation

36⁵/₈"

36¹/₈"

⑤ ⑥

¹/₄" oak banding
is applied after
cutting the plywood
to shape.

³/₄"-wide x
³/₈"-deep rabbet

6³/₄"

³/₄"-wide x
¹/₄"-deep rabbet

Clamping Table
Leg Elevation

1³/₈" R.

3¹/₈"

Plywood Cutting Layouts

⑫ ⑦

② ②①
③
④
⑧
⑧

⑤ ⑭
⑥
⑨ ⑨ ⑭
⑬

Frame Side Elevations

Pipe clamps   I-bar clamps

1¹/₂" 3¹/₄"   1¹/₂" 3¹/₄"

5³/₄"

Pivot
hinge
location

6¹/₂"

1"   ¹/₂"

②⑤   ②⑤

1¹/₂"   1¹/₂"

1¹/₂"   1¹/₂"

Pipe Clamp Fixture Elevations

**Upper
Bracket**

Drill a 1³/₈" hole, and then
cut the remaining waste
with your table saw.

⁷/₈"

1³/₈"

Drill pilot holes, and screw the
bracket to the left side of the cabinet.

Retainers

Cut out the wedge, and then trim
one corner of the wedge square.
Rabbet the main blocks, and glue
the wedge into place.

3⁵/₈"

1³/₄"   ³/₄"

**Lower
Bracket**

Ultimate Sharpening Station

There seems to be a strong correlation between the amount of time woodworkers spend in the shop and the shape of their tools. Novices rarely sharpen, while the pros are almost fanatical about slurries, grits, and bevel angles. Trouble is, the tools and supplies are likely to be so widely scattered around the shop that an otherwise calming activity—sharpening—becomes more and more of a headache. It's time to stop searching for your stuff and start building it a proper home.

by Rick White

Starting with the Carcass

Melamine-coated particleboard is a great choice for the carcass of this station because it's durable, inexpensive, and resistant to the fluids involved in sharpening. It's heavy, too, and this extra weight doesn't hurt—the station needs to be solid to absorb the vibrations of machines and the elbow grease of a determined woodworker.

Begin construction by cutting the parts to the dimensions given in the Material List on page 92. After counterboring and predrilling for the screws (see the technical drawings on pages 94–95 for locations), glue and screw the bottom trim (pieces 1) to the bottom edge of two of the sides (pieces 2). Use three 2" screws (pieces 3) to secure each piece of trim.

The remaining side serves as a center divider and is attached to the bottom (piece 4) with screws. Lay out and predrill the countersunk holes in the bottom, as shown in the technical drawings. Before attaching it, bore countersunk holes through two faces of the divider cleat (piece 5), and mount it to the back end of the divider, as shown in

the carcass exploded view on page 93. Attach the center divider to the bottom, using care to keep the pieces square.

Next, glue and clamp trim (pieces 6 and 7) to the side and bottom edges of the back (piece 8). Now, with the T-shaped subassembly on a large flat surface, glue and clamp both sides to the bottom.

After the glue cures, glue and clamp the back to the sides and bottom. Next, make sure the center divider is perfectly square within the cabinet cavity, and then drive screws into the back through the remaining holes in the divider cleat. To keep the assembly from moving, tack a temporary cleat across the top of the three sides with short brads. You can remove it once the face frame is in place.

The left-hand bay of your new carcass receives a shelf (piece 9), supported by four cleats (pieces 10 and 11). Predrill three of the cleats for 1¼" screws (pieces 12) at the locations shown in the technical drawings, and then fasten the cleats in place. Drive screws up through the cleats to secure the shelf. The last cleat will be attached to the face frame later.

Making the Face Frame

With the rough treatment this sharpening station will receive over the years, it makes sense to construct the face frame (pieces 13 through 17) out of a tough hardwood. I chose white oak because of its durability and good looks. All the joints are simple butts, each kept in line with a pair of ⅜" fluted dowels (pieces 18). Dry fit all the parts according to the face frame layout in the technical drawings, test their fit on your assembled carcass, and when everything looks right, glue and clamp your frame together. Note that the right edge of the center stile lines up flush with the right face of the center divider. Make sure the frame remains flat and square during clamping.

Let the glue dry overnight. Then, remove the clamps, and sand the frame smooth. Chisel out any excess glue in the inside corners. Make sure the lower edge of the face frame is flush with the bottom of the carcass. Then, predrill for countersunk screws (pieces 3), and join the subassemblies. Glue ⅜" oak plugs (pieces 19) in all the counterbored screw holes in the carcass, and sand them flush.

Melamine

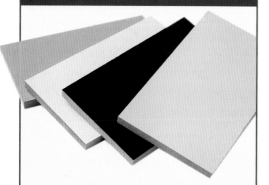

If you happen to have a chemistry lab attached to your shop, heat up a bucket of dicyandiamide, and you'll have the chief component for making melamine resin. Add formaldehyde, and you're on your way to a nice laminated plastic. Now all you have to do is impregnate some kraft paper with phenolic resin and bond it to your melamine layer.

Too much? The alternative is to walk into a building supply center and ask for melamine board. They'll show you a stack of particleboard with a plastic covering that works great for projects like this sharpening center. Melamine comes in several colors and is sold oversize at 49" x 97" to allow for trimming.

Four Steps to Chip-Free Cutting

1. Use a zero-clearance insert.
2. Cut pieces slightly oversize.
3. Use a straightedge and a sharp knife to score the material at the exact size you need.
4. Put a carbide plywood-cutting blade (very slight set on the teeth) in your table saw, and cut to exact size.

A zero-clearance insert is the real key to creating clean, chip-free edges when cutting melamine-coated materials on a table saw.

Material List – Carcass and Drawers

		T x W x L
1	Bottom Trim, Sides (2)	¾" x 1½" x 24"
2	Sides (3)	¾" x 24" x 28½"
3	Large Screws (50)	#8 x 2"
4	Bottom (1)	¾" x 24" x 35½"
5	Divider Cleat (1)	¾" x ¾" x 28½"
6	Back Trim, Sides (2)	¾" x ¾" x 29¼"
7	Back Trim, Bottom (1)	¾" x ¾" x 37"
8	Back (1)	¾" x 28½" x 37"
9	Shelf (1)	¾" x 14½" x 24"
10	Shelf Cleats, Sides (2)	¾" x ¾" x 22½"
11	Shelf Cleats, Front and Back (2)	¾" x ¾" x 14½"
12	Small Screws (50)	#6 x 1¼"
13	Frame Top and Bottom Rails (2)	¾" x 1½" x 35½"
14	Frame Side Stiles (2)	¾" x 1½" x 29¼"
15	Frame Middle Stile (1)	¾" x 1½" x 26¼"
16	Frame Left Rail (1)	¾" x 1½" x 13"
17	Frame Right Rails (3)	¾" x 1½" x 21"
18	Frame Dowels (26)	⅜" Dia. Fluted
19	Trim Plugs (26)	⅜" Oak Face Grain
20	Drawer Spacers (7)	¾" x 2½" x 20⅝"
21	Drawer Slides (6 Pairs)	22" Blum ¾ Extension
22	Tray (1)	¾" x 20" x 23¼"
23	Tray Liner (1)	¼" x 20" x 23¼"
24	Tray Front (1)	¾" x 1½" x 20⅞"
25	Left Drawer Front and Back (2)	¾" x 14" x 10½"
26	Left Drawer Sides (2)	¾" x 14" x 22"
27	Left Drawer Bottom (1)	¼" x 12" x 22"
28	Left Drawer Face (1)	¾" x 12½" x 14½"
29	Upper Drawer Front and Back (2)	¾" x 4½" x 18½"
30	Upper Drawer Sides (2)	¾" x 4½" x 22"
31	Upper Drawer Bottom (1)	¼" x 20" x 22"
32	Upper Drawer Face (1)	¾" x 5¾" x 20½"
33	Large Drawer Front and Back (2)	¾" x 6¼" x 18½"
34	Large Drawer Sides (2)	¾" x 6¼" x 22"
35	Large Drawer Bottom (1)	¼" x 20" x 22"
36	Large Drawer Face (1)	¾" x 7½" x 20½"
37	Small Drawer Fronts and Backs (4)	¾" x 1¾" x 18½"
38	Small Drawer Sides (4)	¾" x 1¾" x 22"
39	Small Drawer Bottoms (2)	¼" x 20" x 22"
40	Small Drawer Faces (2)	¾" x 2½" x 20½"
41	Drawer Face Trim (1)	¼" x ¾" x 264"
42	Drawer Edge Tape (1)	¹⁄₃₂" x ¾" x 384"
43	Drawer Pulls (5)	Wood
44	Drawer Knob (1)	Wood

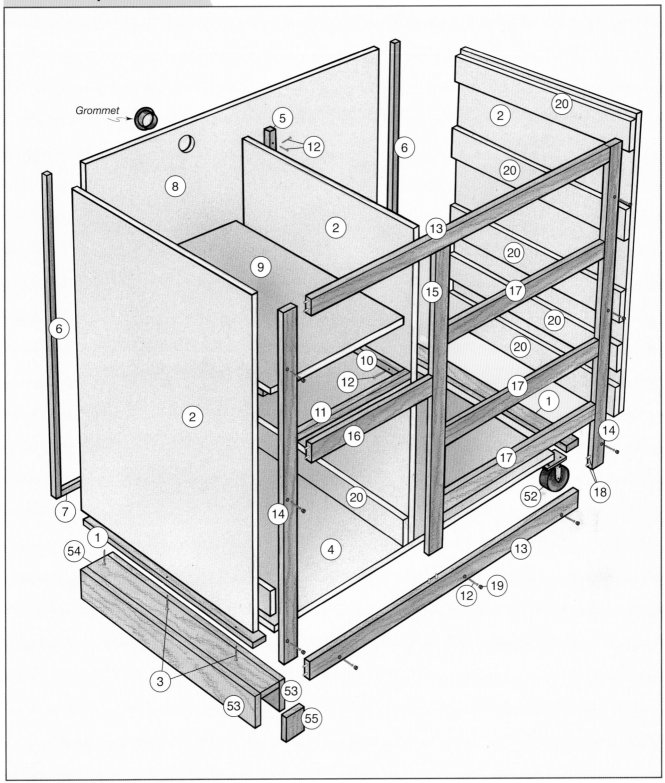

Grommet

Carcass Joinery: Cleat and Spacer Locations
(Front View)

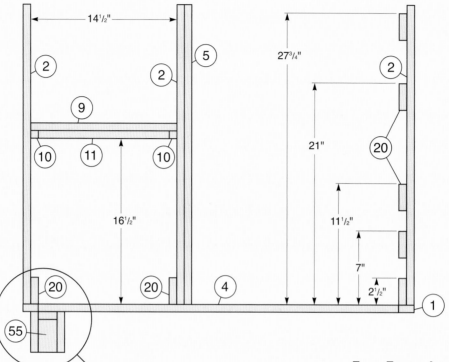

Foot Detail
(Section View)

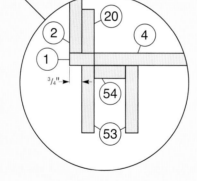

Chamfer the front edges of the tray front.

Tray Assembly
(Side View)

Face Frame Layout
(Front View)

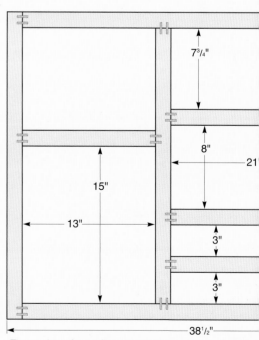

The worktop frame fits outside the carcass and rests on the work frame supports.

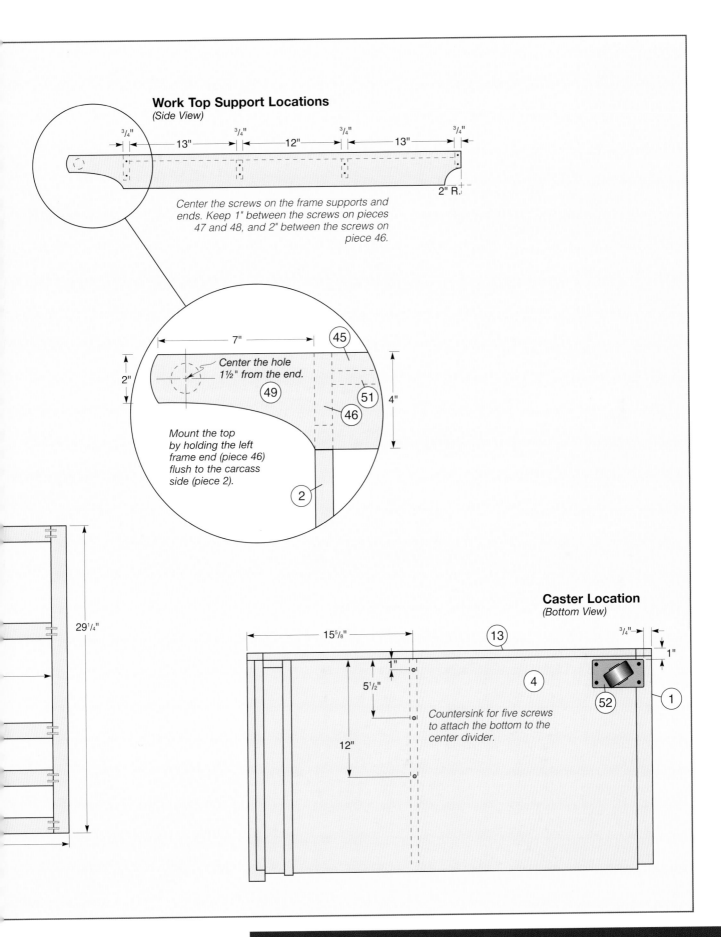

Work Top Support Locations
(Side View)

$^3/_4$" 13" $^3/_4$" 12" $^3/_4$" 13" $^3/_4$"

2" R.

Center the screws on the frame supports and ends. Keep 1" between the screws on pieces 47 and 48, and 2" between the screws on piece 46.

7"

(45)

Center the hole 1½" from the end.

2"

(49)

(51)

4"

(46)

Mount the top by holding the left frame end (piece 46) flush to the carcass side (piece 2).

(2)

29¼"

Caster Location
(Bottom View)

15⅝"

(13)

$^3/_4$"

1"

(4)

1"

5½"

(52)

(1)

12"

Countersink for five screws to attach the bottom to the center divider.

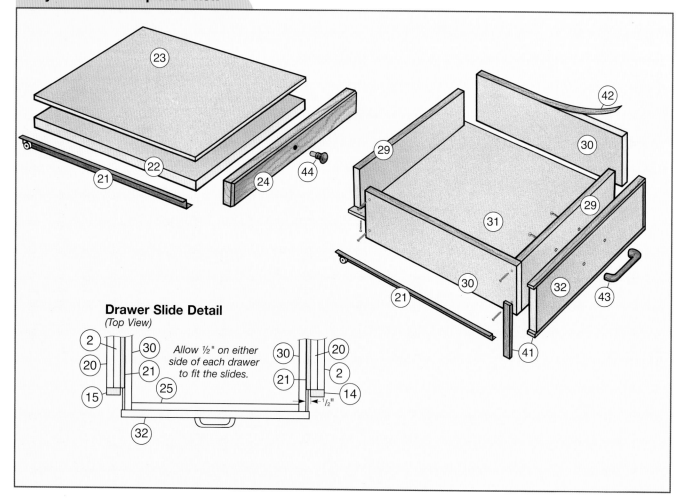

Drawer Slide Detail
(Top View)

Allow ½" on either side of each drawer to fit the slides.

Adding Some Inside Details

The face frame is flush with the left side of the large carcass opening, but you'll need to build out the right side before installing the drawer slides. Glue and screw these spacers (pieces 20) in place now, following the locations on the technical drawings. Attach the remaining shelf cleat to the face frame at this time.

Building the Drawers

Storage is a primary concern with sharpening supplies, so this station features five drawers and a slide-out tray. All six units are mounted on 22" drawer slides (pieces 21). The tray (piece 22) is ¾"-thick melamine with a ¼" melamine liner (piece 23) glued to its top face. Place a heavy weight on it while the glue dries. Chamfer the front edges of the tray front (piece 24) with a chamfering bit

chucked in your router, as shown in the technical drawings. Attach the front to the tray with glue and finish nails, predrilling pilot holes for the nails and then setting and filling the heads.

All five drawers (pieces 25 through 40) are built alike, and all are flush mounted. This is a workshop project, so I kept the construction process simple. Butt the fronts and backs to the sides, securing them with glue and screws. Attach the bottoms with glue and screws, and then trim all four edges of each face with ¼" hardwood stock (piece 41). Attach this trim with glue and 3d finish nails driven through predrilled pilot holes, setting and filling the heads as you go.

Center the drawer faces on the drawers (see the drawings on page 96 and How to Install Drawer Slides on page 97), and then attach the faces from the

inside, after predrilling the screw holes. Next, seal the exposed top edges of the drawer sides, fronts, and backs with iron-on hardwood tape (piece 42), and drill holes in each drawer face for the pulls (pieces 43). Install the pulls and tray knob (piece 44), slide the drawers in place, and you're all set to start on the worktop.

Constructing the Worktop

Review the Material List on page 98. The worktop (piece 45) is a slab of ¾"-thick melamine-coated particleboard surrounded by a hardwood frame. The frame is composed of two ends (pieces 46 and 47), a pair of supports (pieces 48), two shaped sides (pieces 49), and a towel bar/handle (piece 50).

Transfer the profile of the sides from the elevation drawings on page 95 to your stock, and then band saw them to shape. Clean up the saw cuts with a drum sander, and drill the stopped holes on their insides for the handle. The worktop is surrounded by the hardwood frame and held securely by glue blocks (pieces 51) and screws, as shown in the exploded view on page 98.

Building the Frame Assembly

The white-oak frame is held together with screwed butt joints. Temporarily clamp the frame elements together, and then counterbore and predrill for the large screws (see the technical drawings for locations). While you have the frame clamped, dry fit it to the carcass. A half inch of the face frame's top rail should be peeking out below the bottom of the shaped sides. When everything fits, glue and screw the top frame together, trapping the handle as you do. Plug the screw holes as you did earlier, and make sure the handle remains free to turn.

Place the frame on top of the carcass, locating it as shown on the drawings. Then, glue and screw it in place, driving the screws from the inside of the cabinet into the frame.

Wrapping Up the Details

While you won't be moving this station around too much, it's always nice to be able to rearrange the workshop to accommodate new tools or big projects. Have a friend help you lift the project onto a couple of sawhorses, and then bolt a pair of swivel casters (pieces 52) to one end of the bottom, at the locations shown in the technical drawings.

Bolt a matching foot on the other end: This is a simple hollow box made up of two sides, a top, and two ends (pieces

How to Install Drawer Slides

This sharpening station uses Blum's low-profile, ¾-extension slides. This all-purpose, bottom-mounted steel slide features an epoxy coating and is self-closing, a nice feature on a project like this. Rated at up to 100 pounds per drawer, this is one of the easiest slides on the market to mount—just follow the four steps below. Remember, you'll need ½" on each side of the drawer to accommodate your slides.

Step 1. *With this sharpening center (and many other cabinet projects), spacer blocks are installed to provide a mounting surface flush with the face frame.*

Step 2. *Once the spacers are installed, use a drill to mount the inside slide component to the bottom edge of the drawer bottoms. Be sure to drill pilot holes first.*

Step 3. *With the drawer components in place, move on to the casework components, and mount them to the spacer blocks or cabinet sides, predrilling your pilot holes.*

Step 4. *Locate the drawer fronts on the drawers. An old trick is to use double-sided tape to tack the drawer face in place before you secure it with screws.*

53 through 55). Butt joint, glue, and clamp the foot together; then, glue and screw it in place to complete the footings.

There isn't a lot of finishing to this project. Start by filling any nail holes you missed, and then glue hardwood plugs over the tops of all the counterbored screws. Mask the melamine along all the hardwood edges, and clamp a square or a metal ruler along these same edges while you lightly sand the wood. Apply three coats of clear satin varnish to the hardwood, and then install the drawers, adding the pulls and knob. If you have a power sharpening system and plan to use

a magnifying lamp for better viewing (a good idea, by the way), bore an access hole through the worktop for running the power cords neatly behind the station. Protect the cords from abrasion with a grommet inserted in the access hole (see the exploded view on page 98).

Now, the fun begins. Search through your shop for all your containers of oil and mineral spirits, emery paper, stones, and files. You'll probably be amazed at how much you've accumulated over the years. While you're at it, pick a couple of plane irons and chisels to give your new sharpening station a christening.

Material List – Top Subassembly

		T x W x L
45	Worktop (1)	¾" x 25⅝" x 40½"
46	Worktop Frame Left End (1)	¾" x 3" x 25⅝"
47	Worktop Frame Right End (1)	¾" x 2" x 25⅝"
48	Worktop Frame Supports (2)	¾" x 1⅞" x 25⅝"
49	Worktop Frame Sides (2)	¾" x 4" x 48"
50	Towel Bar/Handle (1)	1¼" Dia. x 26⅜"
51	Glue Blocks (8)	¾" x 2" x 2"
52	Casters (2)	3⅞" Swivel
53	Foot Sides (2)	¾" x 3⅞" x 24"
54	Foot Top (1)	¾" x 1⅞" x 24"
55	Foot Ends (2)	¾" x 1⅞" x 3⅛"

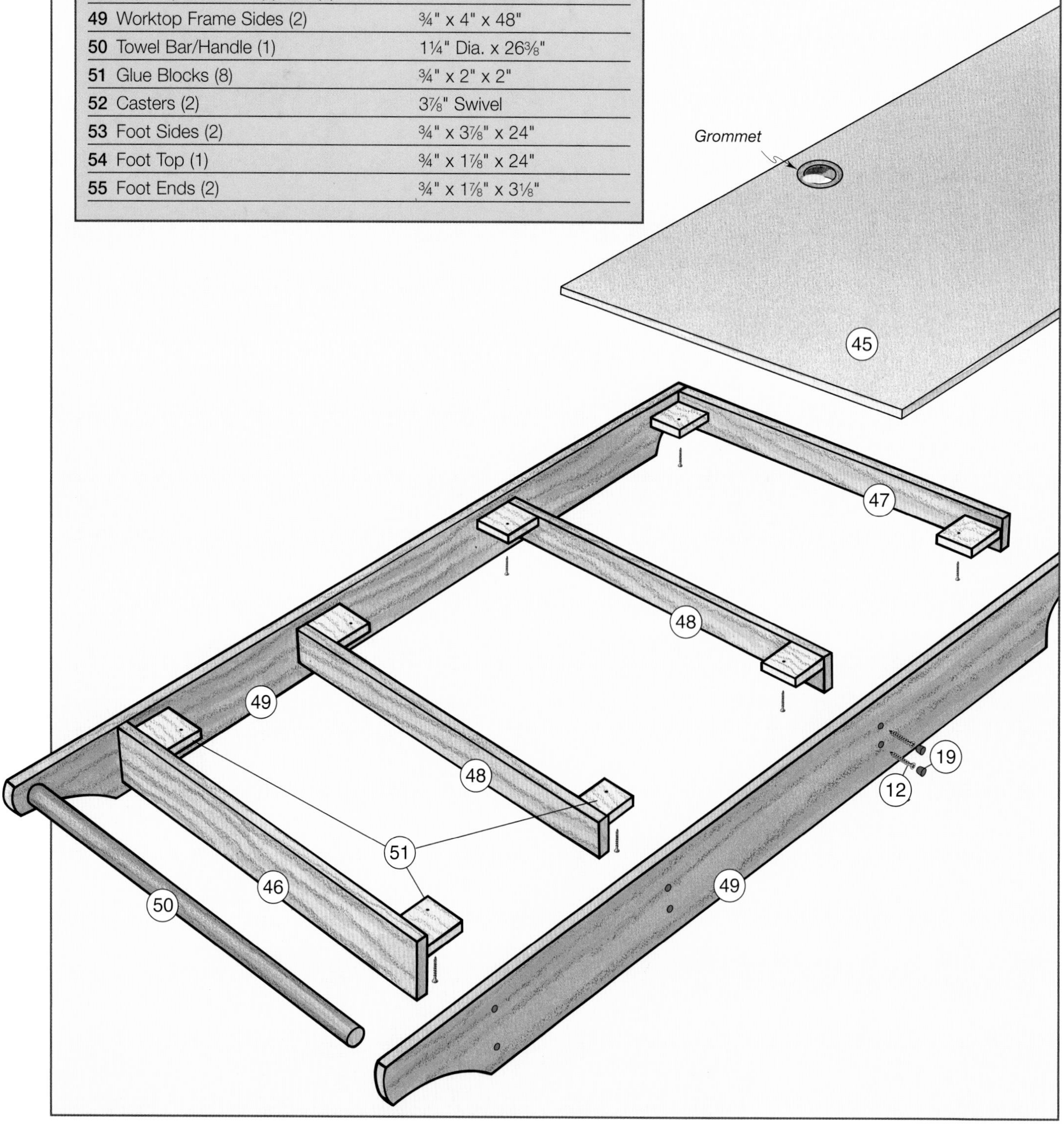

Grommet

Use a Doweling Jig

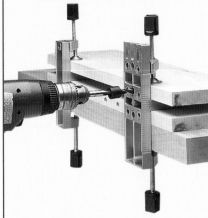

Dowels are easier to install accurately for face frame and other joinery if you can drill their holes squarely. Fixtures such as the Dowel Pro Jig shown here are a slick and easy way to use dowels like a pro. They provide drilling guides, and most also center the holes automatically on the thickness of your material.

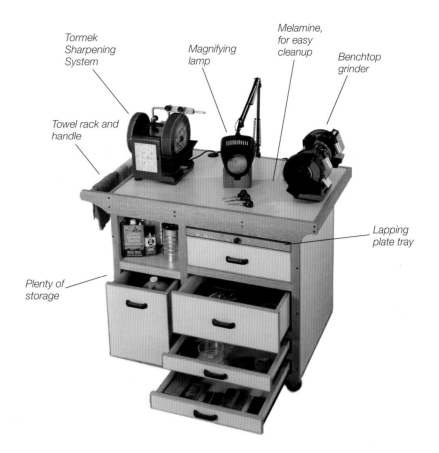

Tormek Sharpening System

Magnifying lamp

Melamine, for easy cleanup

Benchtop grinder

Towel rack and handle

Lapping plate tray

Plenty of storage

The Tormek Sharpening System

One of the premier sharpening machines on the market, the Tormek sells for about $400. At that price, it may not be for everyone, but its versatility demands a look. Replete with gizmos to put an edge on everything from a curved gouge to a long planer knife, this British import is the real deal. Pair it with a traditional grinder, and the only thing you won't be able to sharpen is your wits.

Two auxiliary sharpening aids team up to hone curved gouges, making a difficult task much easier.

Keep the knives of your benchtop planer or jointer razor-sharp on the water-bathed honing wheel.

Key Features

- Two dust collection ports
- Adjustable fence with T-slot bolts and easy-grip locking knobs
- Movable lower fence faces that sllide to accommodate various diameter bits
- Accessory tall fence for added support while vertical routing
- Reversible fence to support larger workpieces
- Aluminum T-tracks in fence for stops, hold-downs, featherboards, and guards
- Aluminum table track for miter gauge, tenoning sleds, and to hold featherboards
- Thick, laminated, always-flat table
- Cabinet storage compartments
- Doors that open to 120°
- Doors that close with pneumatic cushions
- Six drawers to hold tools and bits
- Full-extension drawer slides
- Infeed-side on/off switch
- Built-in shop-made mobile base
- Machine that rolls easily on dual low-profile casters
- Rubber-bottomed levelers
- Heavy, solid platform for routing
- Table overhang for easy clamping

Adjustable Fence

Super-Accurate Lift

...ter Table

In this router table, two lifts are much better than one. One raises and lowers the router, while the other makes the cabinet mobile.

by Bruce Kieffer

You may find this hard to believe, but my old router table was merely a router hung from a discarded countertop sink cutout, with a board clamped on as a fence. This is quite a change!

Actually, I shunned router tables for many years, but with the advent of finely machined router lifts, powerful variable-speed routers, and many new "router table only" router bits, I began rethinking the usefulness of this tool. So, a year ago, I broke down and bought a router lift, a monster variable-speed router, and a premade router table and fence. I was quickly converted. I loved the speed and precision of the lift, the ease of changing bits, and the quality of the routed work the system produced.

Still, I wanted more. The router table and fence I bought were not up to my standards, and I found myself using the system more than I figured I would, so I yearned for a better, more "dedicated" system. So, off to the drawing board I went. I defined three goals: a rock-solid and versatile table and fence, storage for related tools and bits, and a mobile base so I could move the machine off to the side when it was not in use. After many days of designing and refining, I came up with the table you see here. And the more I use it, the more I like it.

The Components

The machine consists of four major components: the base, the cabinet, the table, and the fence. The materials used to build the machine are a combination of solid maple, maple-veneered MDF (medium-density fiberboard), blank MDF, Baltic birch plywood, and white plastic laminate. The unique hardware and router lift are available by mail order (see the supply lists on pages 103 and 106).

The base houses the lift that raises the machine up by pushing the dolly down. The cabinet is screwed to the base. All of the spare space inside the cabinet is used for storage. The table holds the lift and router, and it's centered over the cabinet and screwed in place. The fence is mounted to the table with T-slot bolts secured in T-tracks.

I used a JessEm Mast-R-Lift for the router lift and a Porter Cable 3¼ hp variable-speed router. The Mast-R-Lift is fit for that router, but there are adapter sleeves made for other routers. I chose to buy my router with a handheld base, in case I ever needed to use it that way. The cost difference was minimal, but if you want, you can buy the motor only.

The dust collection ports are set for 2½" hose on the fence and 4" hose on the cabinet. The hose on the cabinet serves two purposes, the obvious being dust collection, and the other being ventilation. Big routers like the one used in this machine generate a lot of heat, and the space where the router goes is very tight. Keeping the router cool by ventilating it with an airflow will greatly increase its life.

Figure 1: *Effortless cranking raises this heavy machine onto its casters so it can be rolled around the shop.*

Base Lift Mechanics

The idea of shop-made mobile bases has been rumbling around in my head for what seems like a hundred years. I messed around making some lever-operated ones, but the levers needed to move great distances to lift heavy loads, and that consumed a lot of space. All in all, I was never really happy with that system. So, I set out to develop a crank-operated mobile base. I remembered reading about the virtues of Acme threads. They have flat tops and bottoms and slightly angled sides, and they work great for moving heavy loads. So, an Acme threaded rod became a part of my design. The lift you see here is my second generation.

Here's how the system works: Look at the exploded view on page 103. The lift is captured so it can only move horizontally, and the dolly is captured so it can only move vertically. Turning the crank moves the lift 3" from start to finish. Since the ramps have a 3-to-1 incline, that makes the dolly move down 1" and puts the base up on the casters (see Figure 1 on page 101).

Building the Base

Making the base requires precise alignment of the parts so those that move can do so without binding. Be careful to make everything square and sized correctly. Labeling parts will help you keep track of things.

Build the housing (pieces 1 and 2; see the Material List at right). Cut the cover rabbets in the four pieces, and drill the hole for the flange bushings (pieces 21) in the housing right side. Glue one corner at a time, and dry fit the rest. Use band clamps to clamp the assembly together. Round over the edges. Drill the holes for the screw-on T-nuts and levelers. If your saw is not up to the task of mitering the ends of the dense maple, then adjust the

Figure 2: *One of the keys to success with the bottom crank is chopping hexagon-shaped holes in the ramp supports for the Acme nuts. These holes tightly capture the nuts so the lift moves as the crank is turned.*

Figure 3: *Glue and screw the ramp supports to the lift ramps. Then, glue and clamp the ramp guides to the sides of the lift ramps. The guides keep the dolly ramps tracking in line with the lift ramps. Note the track guides attached to the underside of the base housing cover in the background.*

Material List – Base, Lift, and Dolly

	T x W x L
Base	
1 Front and Back (2)	1½" x 8" x 30½"
2 Sides (2)	1½" x 8" x 22¼"
3 Cover (1)	¾" x 20¼" x 28½"
4 Track Guides (4)	³⁄₁₆" x ¾" x 27½"
5 Dolly Cleats (2)	¾" x 1¼" x 16"
6 Lift Cleats (2)	¾" x ¾" x 27½"
7 Levelers (4)	⅜"-16 tpi x 1¾"
8 Screw-On T-Nuts (4)	⅜"-16 tpi
9 Flathead Screws (24)	#8 x 1½"
Lift	
10 Platform (1)	¾" x 19⅛" x 24½"
11 Tracks (2)	¼" x 1½" x 24½"
12 Ramps (4)	1½" x 3" x 9"
13 Ramp Supports (2)	1½" x 3" x 15⅝"
14 Ramp Guides (8)	½" x ¾" x 9½"
15 Cover Plates (2)	½" x 2" x 4"
16 Flathead Screws (4)	#8 x 1¼"
17 Crank Handle (1)	¾" x 1¾" x 5"
18 Crank Knob (1)	1⅝" Dia. x ⅜"-16 tpi
19 Acme Threaded Rod (1)	½"-10 x 30⅞"
20 Acme Nuts (6)	½"-10 x 30¾"
21 Bronze Flange Bushings (2)	½" x ⅝" x ⅝"
22 Star Lock Washers (3)	½"
23 Hexhead Bolt (1)	⅜"-16 tpi x 1½"
24 Washers (2)	⅜" Dia.
25 Flathead Screws (8)	#8 x 1½"
26 Flathead Screws (4)	#8 x 1¾"
27 Flathead Screws (8)	#8 x 2½"
Dolly	
28 Platform (2)	½" x 19⅛" x 27⅜"
29 Ramps (4)	1½" x 3" x 9"
30 Casters (4)	Dual 2" Dia., Low Profile
31 Lag Bolts and Washers (16)	⁵⁄₁₆" Dia. x 1"
32 Flathead Screws (8)	#8 x 1½"

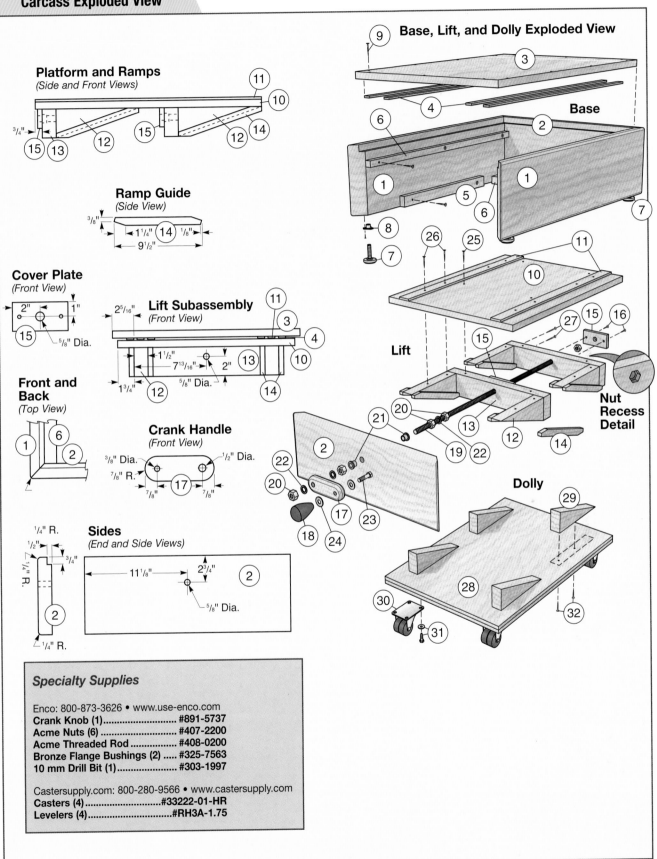

Platform and Ramps
(Side and Front Views)

Ramp Guide
(Side View)

Cover Plate
(Front View)

Front and Back
(Top View)

Sides
(End and Side Views)

Crank Handle
(Front View)

Lift Subassembly
(Front View)

Base, Lift, and Dolly Exploded View

Base

Lift

Nut Recess Detail

Dolly

Specialty Supplies

Enco: 800-873-3626 • www.use-enco.com
Crank Knob (1) .... #891-5737
Acme Nuts (6) .... #407-2200
Acme Threaded Rod .... #408-0200
Bronze Flange Bushings (2) ..... #325-7563
10 mm Drill Bit (1) .... #303-1997

Castersupply.com: 800-280-9566 • www.castersupply.com
Casters (4) ....#33222-01-HR
Levelers (4) ....#RH3A-1.75

Figure 4: *Screw the lift cleats to the base housing. Place temporary cardboard shims between the cleats and lift platform to create a bit of clearance. A right-angle drill attachment is helpful here.*

Figure 5: *Screw the dolly cleats flush with the bottom edges of the base housing. These cleats keep the dolly from dropping out of the housing when you flip it over.*

lengths of the pieces, overlap the front and back pieces over the sides, and join the corners with biscuits.

Attach the track guides (pieces 4) to the cover (piece 3). I used scrap MDF to make spacers to position the parts. I cut one 11⅛"-wide center spacer and two 1⁹⁄₁₆" outside spacers (see the drawings on page 103). Then, I laid the spacers, track guides, and tracks (pieces 11) across the width of the underside of the cover. I trimmed the width of the outside spacers equally, until the total width of everything was equal to the cover's width. I clamped the spacers down, and glued and tacked the track guides in place.

Screw the cover to the base housing. Temporarily screw the tracks to the lift platform (piece 10), using more MDF spacers as guides. Remove the tracks, trim a bit off each side of each track, and then reattach them. This will give them a little clearance so they won't bind inside the track guides. Make the rest of the lift and dolly parts (pieces 12 through 15, plus pieces 17, 28, and 29). Drill ⅞"-diameter x ½"-deep holes in the ramp supports (pieces 13) for the Acme threaded nuts. Chop open the

⅞"-diameter holes so the nuts fit in snugly (see Figure 2 on page 102). Drill the remaining rod, bolt, and screw holes in the lift and dolly parts, and round over the edges of the crank handle (piece 17).

Glue and screw the ramp supports to the lift ramps (see Figure 3 on page 102). Place a 12⅝"-wide spacer between the ramps to align them when you insert the screws. Insert the Acme nuts, and attach the cover plates (pieces 15). Screw the forward ramp assembly to the underside of the lift platform. Align the bottom pointed ends of the ramps with the leading edge of the lift platform, and use spacers to align the width. Position, but don't screw, the rear ramp assembly to the lift platform. Thread the Acme rod through both ramp support nuts. This is done to align the threads of both nuts with those of the rod. Now, screw the rear ramp assembly in place. Turn the Acme rod to make sure it rotates freely, and then remove the rod and set it aside.

Set the lift into the base housing, and position it tight to the housing left side (no rod hole). Temporarily align and adhere the dolly ramps to the lift ramps with double-sided tape. Set the

dolly platform into the base housing, align it so there's a ¹⁄₁₆" gap all around, and screw it to the dolly ramps. Then, unscrew it and remove it. Now, remove the dolly ramps. Sand a bit off each side, check that they slide freely through the lift ramp guides, and then rescrew them to the dolly platform. Attach the casters to the dolly platform so they are tight in the corners but can turn 360° without hitting the base housing.

Set the flange bushings in the base housing rod hole, and insert the threaded rod. I had to open the hole on my base housing a bit to get the rod to align with the nuts in the lift. Put the inside Acme nuts and star lock washer on the rod as you thread it in place. With the lift still tight to the housing left side, thread the rod in until it just peeks out of the rear cover plate hole. Run the front nut up against the inside thrust bushing, back it off ever so slightly, and then jam the rear nut against the front nut. Assemble and attach the crank, attach the lift cleats (see Figure 4), insert the dolly, attach dolly cleats (see Figure 5), and test the lift. Make any necessary adjustments, and set the base aside.

Building the Cabinet

Making the cabinet is fairly straightforward. Referring to the Material List on page 107, cut the sheet stock parts to size (pieces 33 through 39). Note that you will need to adjust for the nominal thickness of your sheet stock; it will not be exactly ¾".

Now, cut the square hole in the top, and drill the holes in the back for the dust port and power cord. Glue ⅛"-thick edging (pieces 41) to the front edges of all the cabinet parts, and biscuit and glue the rear corner edging (pieces 40) to the

Figure 6: *A shop-made guide can help when drilling the centered 10 mm Blumotion door cushion holes on the front edge of the cabinet top.*

sides of the back. Cut the biscuit grooves in all of the cabinet parts except the back. Drill the Blumotion door cushion holes in the top front edge (see Figure 6), the screw holes in the top and bottom, and the shelf pin holes in the sides and upper vertical dividers. Finish sand the insides of the cabinet parts. I drilled screw holes through all the horizontal parts in line with the biscuit grooves so I could screw those joints together rather than clamp them. After all that drilling, I'm not sure I actually saved any time!

Figure 7: *Fit, biscuit, glue, and clamp the cabinet back to the cabinet. Biscuits are placed around the outside of the back only.*

Assemble the cabinet in this order: Attach the upper vertical dividers to the fixed shelf, and then attach the lower vertical divider to the fixed shelf. Attach the top and bottom to the vertical dividers, with one side dry fit in place to make sure the parts align. Attach the sides, fit and attach the back (see Figure 7), and then round over the rear corners.

Doors and Drawers

Fitting the doors and drawer faces is time-consuming and finicky work, but getting the fit to look good is worth the effort. The gaps are all ¹⁄₁₆" wide. Here's the way I do it: Cut the drawer faces slightly oversize (pieces 55, 59, and 63).

Make the doors (pieces 68 through 71). Lay the cabinet on its back, and set the doors and drawer faces in place. Cut some long, ¹⁄₁₆"-thick strips of wood (it's best to cut these off the edges of wide boards so the skinny piece drops away from the table saw blade). Use the strips as spacers, and trim the door and drawer faces' edges slowly until everything fits.

Drill the holes for the pull mounting screws (pieces 52 and 67), and round over the outside edges of the drawer faces and outer doors. You'll need to drill recess holes in the backs of the drawer faces for the heads of the pull screws, and you will need to shorten the screws a bit or buy shorter ones.

Next, mount the doors. I used a Jig It guide for drilling the hinge mounting plates (see Figure 8). It was fast and easy. Drill the hinge cup holes on the backs of the doors. Test your drilling setups on scrap wood.

Assemble the drawers (pieces 51, 56 through 58, 60 through 62, and 64 through 66). Mount the drawer slide drawer members to the drawers,

Figure 8: *Use a Jig It drilling guide to position the holes for the hinge mounting plates inside the cabinet. A right-angle drill attachment is required here.*

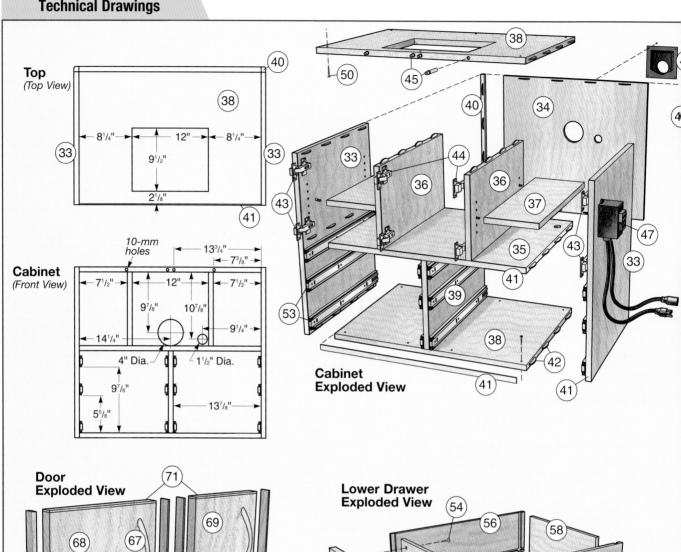

Top
(Top View)

8¹/₄" 12" 8¹/₄"
9¹/₂"
2¹/₈"

Cabinet
(Front View)

10-mm holes
13³/₄"
7³/₈"
7¹/₂" 12" 7¹/₂"
9⁷/₈" 10⁷/₈"
14¹/₄" 9¹/₄"
4" Dia. 1¹/₂" Dia.
9⁷/₈"
5⁵/₈" 13⁷/₈"

**Cabinet
Exploded View**

**Door
Exploded View**

**Lower Drawer
Exploded View**

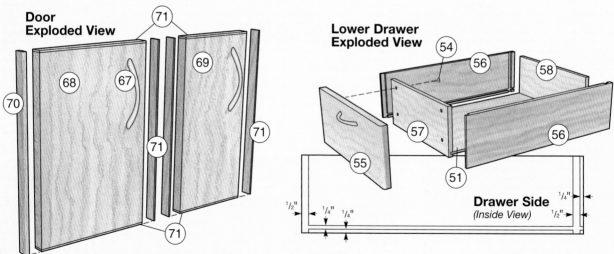

Drawer Side
(Inside View)
¹/₄"
¹/₂" ¹/₄" ¹/₄" ¹/₂"

Hard-to-Find Hardware and Supplies

The following supplies for completing the router table are available from *Woodworker's Journal*:

Screw-On T-Nuts (1 pack)........................#68387	T-Slot Bolts and Washers (10)........................#83311
Full Overlay Hinges (2 pairs)........................#55793	Ergo-Style Wing Nuts (6)........................#26748
Half Overlay Hinges (2 pairs)........................#55801	Round Knobs (2)........................#34134
Blumotion Cushions (2 packs)........................#31680	Tapered Knobs (2)........................#81505
Dust Hood........................#21025	4-Piece Router Accessory Kit........................#53756
Router Table Switch........................#63026	Jig It Mounting Plate Template-A........................#31350
Shelf Pins (1 pack)........................#30437	Bit Safety Guard........................#67157
20" Slides (6 pairs)........................#37406	Stop Block Kit........................#83337
Drawer/Door Pulls (10)........................#36399	Mast-R-Lift Template........................#60804
24" T-Track (2 lengths)........................#21739	¹/₂" Pattern Bit........................#33536
36" T-Track (3 length)........................#21746	T-Slot Bit........................#26099
36" Miter Gauge Track........................#63018	Mast-R-Lift Mechanism w/ Attached Plate........................#22788

To check on availability and to order supplies, call 800-610-0883 and mention code W5123.

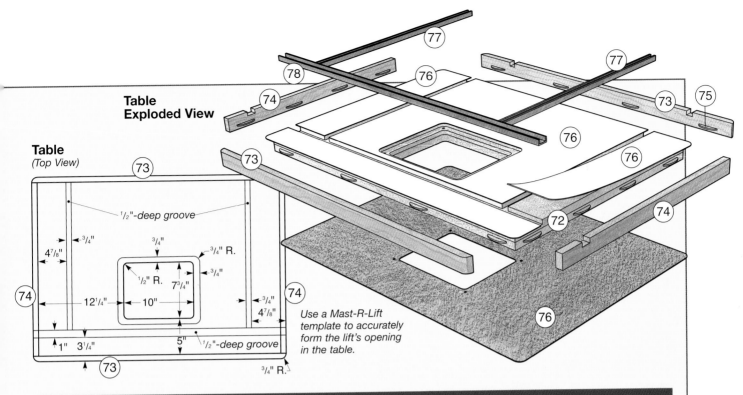

Table Exploded View

Table *(Top View)*

½"-deep groove

4⅞" ¾" ¾" ¾" R.

½" R. 7¾" ¾"

½" R. ¾"

12¼" 10" ¾"

4⅞"

1" 3¼" 5" ½"-deep groove

¾" R.

Use a Mast-R-Lift template to accurately form the lift's opening in the table.

Material List – Cabinet, Drawers, Doors, and Table

	T x W x L			T x W x L
Cabinet			**Middle Drawers**	
33 Sides (2)	¾" x 20⅟₁₆" x 25¾"		59 Faces (2)	¾" x 4¼" x 14³¹⁄₃₂"
34 Back (1)	¾" x 28½" x 25¾"		60 Sides (4)	½" x 4" x 20"
35 Fixed Shelf (1)	¾" x 20⅟₁₆" x 28½"		61 Fronts (2)	½" x 4" x 12⅜"
36 Vertical Divider (2)	¾" x 20⅟₁₆" x 11⅛"		62 Backs (2)	½" x 3½" x 12⅜"
37 Shelves (2)	¾" x 20" x 7⅜"			
38 Top and Bottom (2)	¾" x 20⅟₁₆" x 28½"		**Upper Drawers**	
39 Vertical Divider (1)	¾" x 12⅜" x 20⅟₁₆"		63 Faces (2)	¾" x 2¾" x 14³¹⁄₃₂"
40 Rear Corner Edging (2)	¾" x ¾" x 25¾"		64 Sides (4)	½" x 2¼" x 20"
41 Edging (20 Lineal Feet)	⅛" x ¾"		65 Fronts (2)	½" x 2¼" x 12⅜"
42 Biscuits (60)	#20		66 Backs (2)	½" x 1¾" x 12⅜"
43 Hinges (2 Pairs)	120° Full Overlay			
44 Hinges (2 Pairs)	120° Half Overlay		**Doors**	
45 Blumotion Cushions (2 Pairs)	10 mm x 50 mm		67 Door Pulls (4)	4½" x 1"
46 Dust Fitting (1)	8" x 8" with 4"-Dia. Hole		68 Outer Door Panels (2)	¾" x 8⁷⁄₃₂" x 11¹⁵⁄₁₆"
47 Router Table Switch (1)	18 amp		69 Inner Door Panels (2)	¾" x 6⅟₁₆" x 11¹⁵⁄₁₆"
48 Shelf Pins (8)	¼" Dia.		70 Edging (2)	¼" x ¾" x 12³⁄₁₆"
49 Flathead Screws (8)	#8 x 1¼"		71 Edging (10 Lineal Feet)	⅛" x ¾"
50 Flathead Screws (6)	#8 x 1½"			
			Router Table	
Drawers and Doors			72 Substrates (2)	¾" x 24" x 34½"
51 Bottoms (6)	¼" x 12⅜" x 19¼"		73 Front and Back Edging (2)	¾" x 1½" x 36"
52 Drawer Pulls (6)	4½" x 1"		74 Side Edging (2)	¾" x 1½" x 24"
53 Slides (6 Pairs)	20" Self-Closing		75 Biscuits (18)	#20
54 Washerhead Screws (20)	#6 x 1"		76 Plastic Laminate (2)	25" x 37"
			77 T-Track (2)	½" x ¾" x 21¼"
Lower Drawers			78 Miter Gauge Track (1)	½" x 1" x 36"
55 Faces (2)	¾" x 6¼" x 14³¹⁄₃₂"		79 Mast-R-Lift Mechanism (1)	For P-C 7518 Router
56 Sides (4)	½" x 5⅜" x 20"			
57 Fronts (2)	½" x 5⅜" x 12⅜"			
58 Backs (2)	½" x 4⅞" x 12⅜"			

Figure 9: *Fit the hole in one of the table substrates to the router lift. That fit hole will be used as a template to rout the other substrate hole after the two substrates are glued together.*

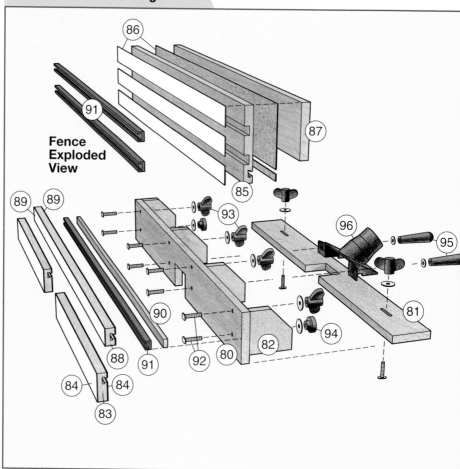

Fence Exploded View

Figure 10: *Plastic laminate is adhered with contact cement to both sides of the table. Use ½"-diameter dowels to hold the laminate away from the substrate. Align the pieces, remove the dowels, and press the laminate down.*

centered ¾" up from the bottom edges. Mount the drawer slide cabinet members. I used MDF spacers to align the heights of the upper slides and then the middle slides (see the drawings on page 106).

Building the Table and Fence

Cut one table substrate to size and the other ½" oversize in both length and width (pieces 72). On the sized piece, cut the opening for the router lift (see the drawings on page 107). Trim the opening until the lift fits (see Figure 9). Don't worry if the lift is a little loose—there are "snugger bars" underneath the lift to snug it in the opening.

Rough cut the opening in the oversize substrate, and then glue and clamp the substrates together. Use a flush-trimming router bit to trim the oversize substrate to match the sized one. Machine

the table edgings (pieces 73 and 74) so their widths match the thickness of the substrate. Cut the biscuit grooves, and attach the edgings. Shape the ¾"-radius corners of the table. I trimmed away most of the waste with a handsaw, and then I used the ¾"-radius outside corners of the Mast-R-Lift template (used later for routing the lift ledge) and a flush-trimming bit to finish the shaping.

Figure 11: *A store-bought template and top-bearing pattern bit are used to rout the ledge in the table for the router lift. Double-sided tape holds the template in place.*

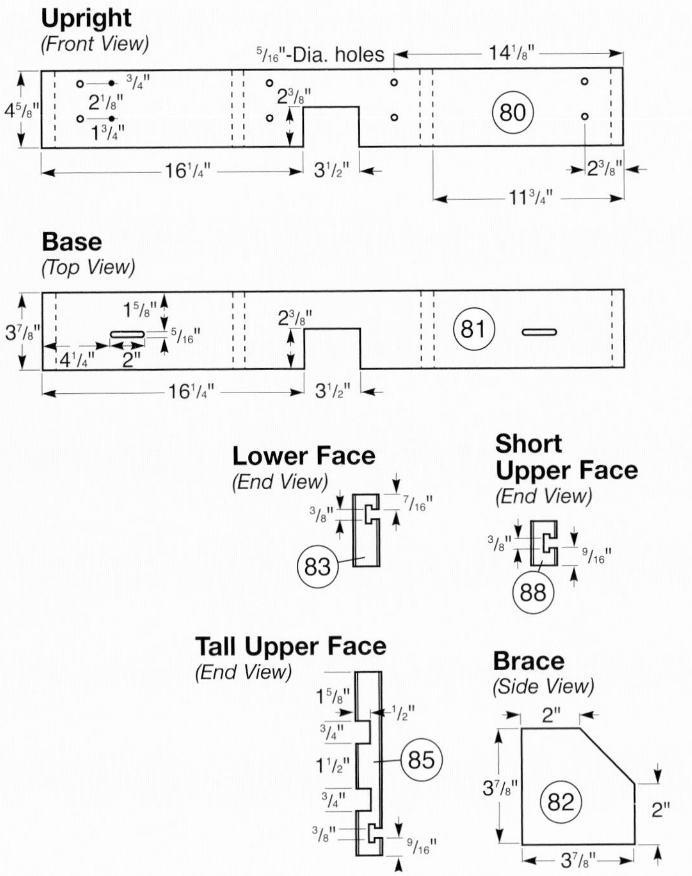
Upright
(Front View)
5/16"-Dia. holes
14 1/8"
4 5/8"
3/4"
2 1/8"
1 3/4"
2 3/8"
80
16 1/4"
3 1/2"
2 3/8"
11 3/4"
Base
(Top View)
3 7/8"
1 5/8"
5/16"
4 1/4"
2"
2 3/8"
81
16 1/4"
3 1/2"
Lower Face
(End View)
3/8"
7/16"
83
Short
Upper Face
(End View)
3/8"
9/16"
88
Tall Upper Face
(End View)
1 5/8"
1/2"
3/4"
1 1/2"
85
3/4"
3/8"
9/16"
Brace
(Side View)
2"
3 7/8"
82
2"
3 7/8"

Material List – Fence

		T x W x L
80	Upright (1)	¾" x 4⅝" x 36"
81	Base (1)	¾" x 3⅞" x 36"
82	Braces (4)	¾" x 3⅞" x 3⅞"
83	Lower Faces (2)	¾" x 2⅜" x 18"
84	Plastic Laminate (4)	3⅜" x 19"
85	Tall Upper Face (1)	¾" x 6⅛" x 36"
86	Plastic Laminate (2)	7⅛" x 37"
87	Stiffener (1)	¾" x 4⅝" x 36"
88	Short Upper Face (1)	¾" x 1½" x 36"
89	Plastic Laminate (2)	2½" x 37"
90	Fill Strip (1)	⅜" x ¾" x 36"
91	T-Track (3)	½" x ¾" x 36"
92	T-Slot Bolts/Washers (10)	5/16"-18 tpi x 1½"
93	Ergo-Style Wing Nuts (6)	5/16"-18 tpi
94	Round Knobs (2)	1⅜" Dia. x 5/16"-18 tpi
95	Tapered Knobs (2)	4½" x 5/16"-18 tpi
96	Router Accessories (1 Kit)	Dust Port/Featherboards

Apply the plastic laminate to the substrate on both sides (see Figure 10), and trim away the waste. Set the lift in its opening, and adjust the snugger bars if necessary. Place double-sided tape on the underside of the Mast-R-Lift template, set it over the lift, and press it down to the table. Remove the lift, and rout the ledge using a short, ½"-diameter pattern bit (see Figure 11). Rout the ledge slightly deep. The lift has built-in plate levelers to adjust it flush with the table. Drill holes in the corners of the ledge and through the table so you can insert an Allen wrench and adjust the level of the lift while it's in the table.

Rout the miter track and T-track dadoes. I used a plunge router with an edge guide and a ½" straight bit. I clamped scrap wood to the edges of the table to stop blowout, aligning those scrap pieces to add some bearing surface for the edge guide at the beginning and end of my cuts. First, I cut the outsides of the dadoes, and then I moved the edge guide farther from the bit and cut the insides of the dadoes. Now, attach the miter and T-tracks.

Referring to the Material List above, make the fence (pieces 80 through 96).

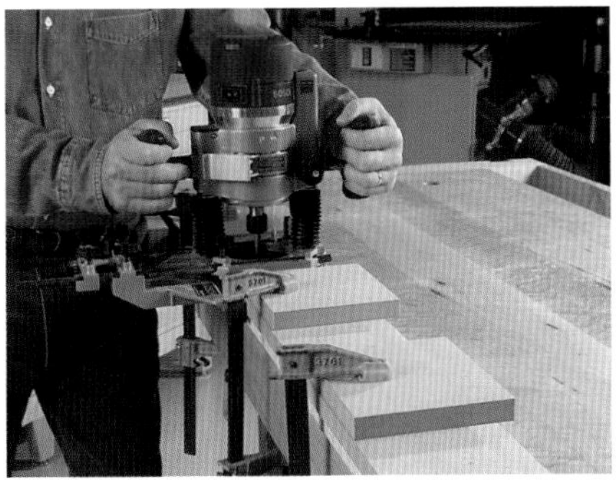

Figure 12: *The elongated T-bolt slots in the fence base are cut using a plunge router, a 5/16"- diameter straight bit, and a mess of clamped-on stops. Set the whole thing up on top of a sacrificial board.*

Be precise when drilling the holes for the T-bolts (see Figure 12), and make sure the fence is assembled dead-on at 90°.

Finishing and Final Assembly

Apply whatever finish you choose to the exposed wood. Do the drawers, too, if you want. I used finish wax on mine. Apply paraffin wax to the bearing surfaces of the lift, and reassemble the base. Trim the length of the Acme rod if necessary, apply Loctite thread-locking solution on the crank handle nuts, and attach the crank. Screw the cabinet to the base, and the table to the cabinet. Push the Blumotion cushions in place. Attach the big dust port and the switch—and that's it.

Now, I just need to find the right place in my shop for my table. It sure beats a discarded countertop sink cutout!

Deluxe Drum Sander

If you want to build a better mousetrap, the best starting point is a list of the limitations of your old one. As far as drum sanding on a drill press goes, most sanding jigs lack dust control, and the drums tend to clog too soon. This jig addresses both problems: It has a built-in dust collection port, and the drum can be raised or lowered through the tabletop, so you can work with a new, unclogged part of the sleeve as often as needed.

by Dick Dorn

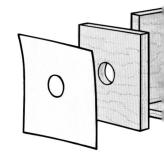

There's another advantage to this jig: The cube in the center can be revolved to present different-size holes for various drum diameters, so it supports the workpiece right up to the drum. That makes it easier to sand thin or delicate stock that might otherwise break off or get trapped.

The inner cube measures 4" on all sides, and I built it from ½" Finnish birch plywood. Measure your six most frequently used drums, and drill appropriately sized holes in the cube. Then, construct the main box (also ½" stock) so that the 4" cube is absolutely flush with its top.

The vacuum port in the jig is standard 1¼" I.D. plastic plumbing pipe, but you'll have to adjust that to fit your own shop's dust collector hose.

Two dozen ¾"-diameter rare-earth magnets hold the jig to the drill press table, eliminating the need for clamps. Drill ⅜"-deep holes in the bottom for these magnets, and secure them with silicone adhesive. Finally, cover the bottom with nonslip rubber (the type used on steps or ramps), and you're ready to start sanding.

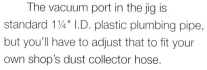
½" plywood

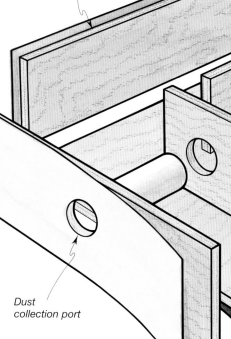
Dust collection port

Nonslip rubber

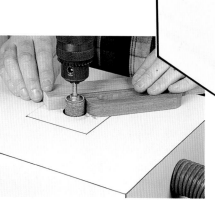

Overall dimensions

12¹⁄₂"

5"

5"

4"

12¹⁄₂"

Plastic laminate

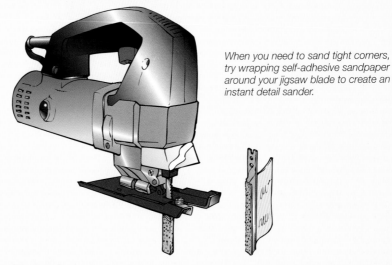

When you need to sand tight corners, try wrapping self-adhesive sandpaper around your jigsaw blade to create an instant detail sander.

Jig Sander

One way to power sand those intricate cuts that no sander can reach is to wrap a piece of self-adhesive sandpaper around your jigsaw blade. You'll have to open the cooling blocks on the jigsaw for this trick to work, and you'll need to use a stiff blade. There's no need to wrap the blade with excess paper—just two wraps should do it.

Budget Bushings

When a number of perpendicular holes have to be drilled, drill bit guide bushings sure come in very handy. If you're ever caught without one, try grabbing an appropriate-size T-nut instead. Install one in a piece of scrap, and drill it out for the correct-size drill bit. This trick won't hold up in daily use, but it sure works well for 10 to 20 holes.

Pizza Pedestals

Save the plastic spacers that come with your home-delivered pizza. After you collect a few, use them as handy supports for elevating small projects when spraying or brushing on a finish. This sure beats excess finish sticking a project to the newspaper that it's sitting on.

Options for Drawing a Smooth Curve

An old band saw blade works wonderfully for drawing smooth curves. Drive nails at key spots along the waste side of the curve, and bend the blade against the nails to draw the final curve. Another option for scribing smooth curves is to use a piece of stiff electrical wire. Ten- to six-gauge wire will provide enough stiffness for the wire to hold its shape but still be flexible enough to bend easily to shape.

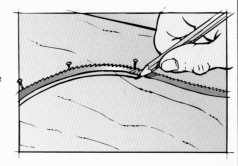

Drum Sanding Station

Take the chore out of sanding curves—and give your drill press a facelift—with this versatile sanding station.

by Chris Marshall

Woodworking doesn't involve much drudgery, but I can think of three tedious chores: Scraping dried glue, cleaning pitch off saw blades, and, of course, sanding. Concerning that last one, sanding curves is the worst type—especially when you have to do it by hand. If you're still wrapping sandpaper around dowels and sanding till your arm goes numb, it's time to convert your drill press into a drum sander.

There's a low-tech approach to drum sanding that I didn't adopt here. You could just chuck the sanding drum and lower it partially into a hole in a board clamped to your drill press table. That option didn't work for me. I needed a place to store all the different drum sizes and sanding sleeves that come with a drum sanding kit. I also needed to stash my Forstner bits, hole cutters, and other drilling doodads, so a drawer seemed in order. Equally important, the sanding-drum-and-board approach doesn't keep dust at bay—and that's a real issue if you have lots of curves to clean up.

My sanding station satisfies all these needs. Essentially, it's a two-compartment cabinet with an oversize top and a base that clamps to your drill press. The top compartment serves as a dust extraction chamber with an adapter port that attaches to a 2½" shop vacuum hose. The lower compartment houses a storage drawer just big enough to hold a healthy collection of sanding

Figure 1: *Slip a pair of 4¹⁄₁₆"-wide spacers inside the cabinet to position the divider while installing it. The spacers ensure that the 4" drawer sides will slide smoothly.*

sundries. Although I could have cut an oversize hole in the worktop to make room for the sanding drum, I installed a router table plate instead. Because it lifts off, it gives you plenty of access to the dust collection chamber whenever a sanding drum or drill bit accidentally slips down inside. Plus, most plates, including the Rockler aluminum router plate I use for my setup, come with interchangeable inserts. Just bore one out to fit around each size of sanding drum you own.

One other benefit to this project is that you can use it for either sanding or routine drilling. I never take mine off the drill press. The worktop overhangs provide plenty of room for clamping a fence or drilling jig in place. You should know that I've sized this project to suit my drill press's large table. If it's too big as is for your drill press table, just bolt a piece of plywood to your machine's table, and clamp the station to that. Or adjust the dimensions in the Material List on page 115 to make a smaller station.

Cabinet Assembly
(Side View)

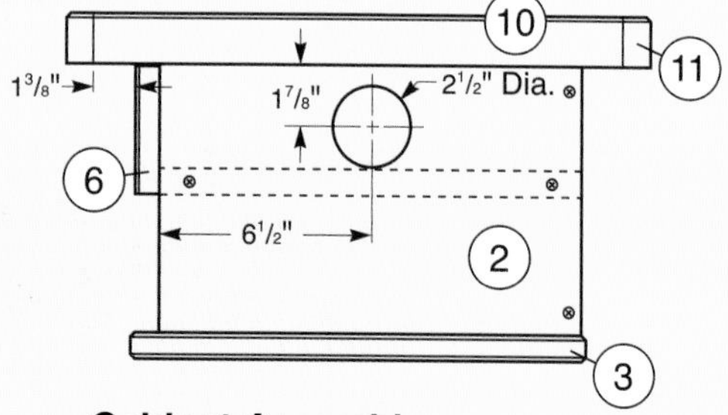

$1^{3}/_{8}$"

$1^{7}/_{8}$" $2^{1}/_{2}$" Dia.

$6^{1}/_{2}$"

(10)
(11)
(6)
(2)
(3)

Cabinet Assembly
(Front View)

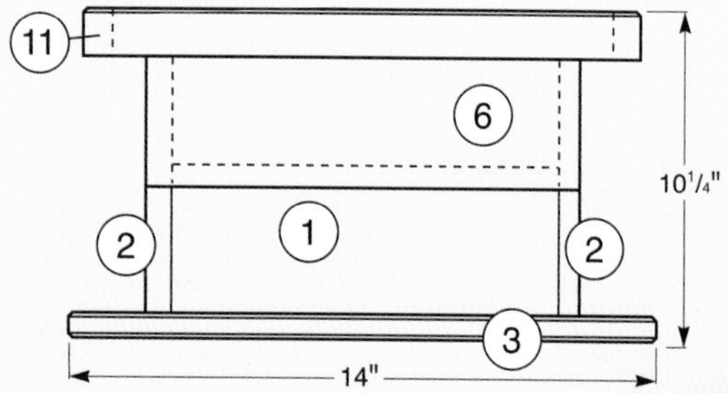

(11)
(6)
(2)   (1)   (2)
(3)

$10^{1}/_{4}$"

14"

Cabinet Assembly
(Section View)

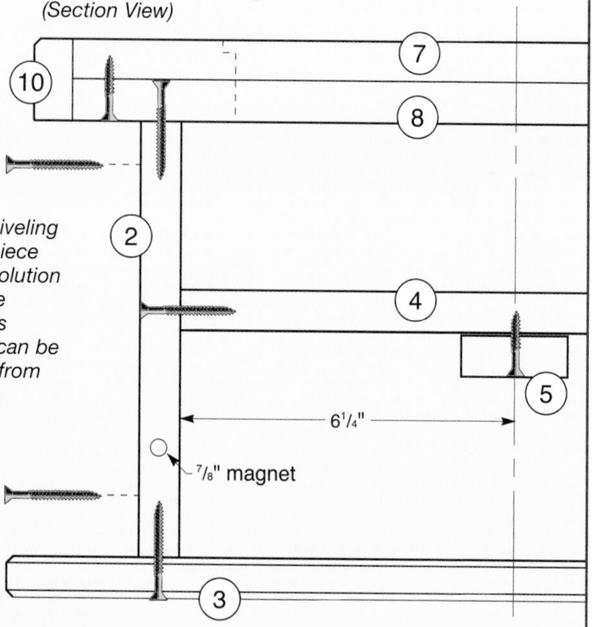

(10)
(7)
(8)
(2)
(4)
(5)
(3)

$6^{1}/_{4}$"

$^{7}/_{8}$" magnet

NOTE: *The swiveling drawer stop (piece 5) is a clever solution for shop fixture drawers. In this application, it can be mounted 3½" from the front edge.*

(9)
(7)
(13)
(8)
(11)
(10)

Cabinet Exploded View

(2)
(1)
(4)
(2)
(6)
(12)
(5)
(3)

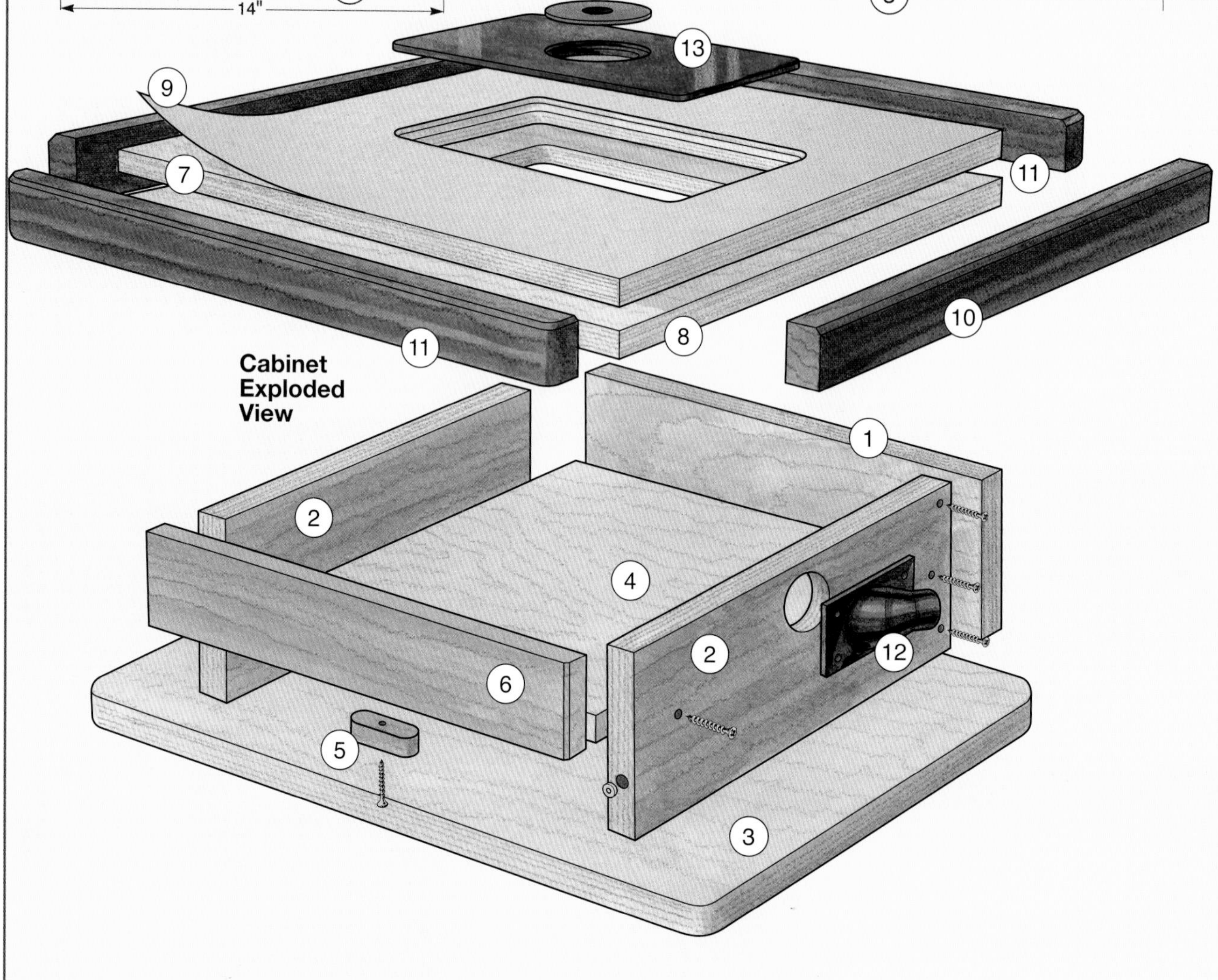

Material List – Cabinet

		T x W x L
1	Back (1)	¾" x 8" x 12½"
2	Sides (2)	¾" x 8" x 13"
3	Base (1)	¾" x 14" x 19"
4	Divider (1)	¾" x 12¼" x 12½"
5	Drawer Stop (1)	¾" x 1" x 2"
6	Front Panel (1)	¾" x 3⅞" x 14"
7	Work Surface (1)	¾" x 16½" x 16½"
8	Subtop (1)	¾" x 16½" x 16½"
9	Plastic Laminate (1)	Larger than work surface
10	Side Edging (2)	¾" x 1½" x 16½"
11	Front/Back Edging (2)	¾" x 1½" x 18"
12	Vacuum Port (1)	2½"-Dia. Opening
13	Router Table Insert Plate	¼" x 8" x 11"

Basic Building with Baltic Birch

Get construction underway by cutting the back, sides, base, and divider (pieces 1 through 4) to size. I used Baltic birch plywood for these and most of the cabinet parts (the drawer front and front panel are solid birch). Round the corners of the base to keep it from scraping your thighs, and chamfer the back outside edges of the sides and the sharp edges of the base to minimize splintering. Bore a 2½"-diameter hole in one side piece to serve as the dust port access (see the drawings on page 114 to locate this hole position). Fasten the sides to the back with screws and glue, and tack the base to the carcass with a couple of screws. You'll remove it later on, so no glue here.

To limit the travel of the drawer, I fashioned a swiveling stop (piece 5) that functions like a turnbuckle. As you can see in the drawings on page 117, a notch in the drawer back allows the drawer to slide past the stop for removal when the stop faces front to back. Turning the stop sideways locks the drawer in the cabinet. Make the stop, and install it on the divider with a single flathead wood screw. Drill the countersunk screw hole in the stop slightly oversize so the stop swivels easily on the screw. With the stop in place, fasten the divider to the carcass assembly. I used 4¹⁄₁₆"-wide spacers to hold the divider in place during installation (see Figure 1 on page 113). It needs to be positioned carefully so it will clear the top edges of the drawer. Wrap up the carcass assembly by cutting and nailing the front panel (piece 6) to the carcass.

Preparing the Worktop

The worktop consists of a buildup of plastic laminate and two layers of plywood. Cut the work surface and subtop to size (pieces 7 and 8), making sure the proportions match. Apply a few dabs of hot-melt glue or ordinary wood glue to the center of these panels, confining the glue to about a 4" area. Sandwich the panels, and fasten them together with four screws, one at each corner. Apply an oversize piece of plastic laminate (piece 9) to the worktop with contact cement (see Figure 2), and trim it to size with a router (see Figure 3). Once that's done, wrap up by marking the worktop to locate the router insert plate.

Figure 3: *Trim the laminate flush with a piloted flush-trim bit, holding the workpiece in place on an antislip mat.*

Routing the Insert Plate Recess

I recommend using an MDF (medium-density fiberboard) template to rout a perfectly sized recess for the router plate. You'll find the template, plate, and other items you'll need in the supply list on page 116. It's worth the extra investment, especially if you also plan to build a new router table someday and reuse the template. For this project, I used the template and a piloted pattern bit to rout the router plate lip that holds it flush to the worktop (see Figure 4 on page 116).

Figure 2: *Apply plastic laminate to the worktop with contact adhesive, and press it flat. I opted for a board wrapped in a towel, instead of a J-roller, for this job.*

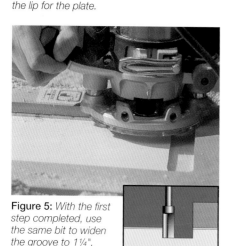

Figure 4: *Using a template and a bearing-guided pattern bit (bearing on top), cut a ¼"-deep groove to form the lip for the plate.*

Figure 5: *With the first step completed, use the same bit to widen the groove to 1¼", taking multiple passes.*

Figure 6: *Remove the template, switch to a rub collar and a ½" straight bit, and remove the waste in the middle, forming a lip for the plate.*

Step-by-Step Routing

Hold the template in place for routing with double-sided tape. Once this cut is complete, use the same bit to widen the cut to about 1¼" (see Figure 5). To remove the inner waste area, remove the template, install a 1" O.D. rub collar on your router, and switch to a long, ½"-diameter straight or spiral upcut bit. The offset between the rub collar and bit establishes the ¼" width of the router plate lip. Make a series of progressively deeper passes to rout all the way down through the worktop and subtop and remove the waste (see Figure 6).

Installing the Worktop

Once you've cut the router plate recess into the work surface and subtop, remove the screws that hold these parts together, and attach the subtop to the cabinet with screws. Unscrew and remove the base. Then, line up the work surface and subtop, and reattach these parts with glue and screws. Install the base permanently with more screws and glue. Position the worktop in place, wrapping it with hardwood edging (pieces 10 and 11), and then glue and nail it in place. Round the outer corners of the edging, and chamfer the top edges.

Making the Drawer

There are no surprises in the drawer construction. The front joints are sliding dovetails, and the rear joints are rabbet-and-dado joints. The biggest challenge is sizing the drawer width to leave just enough slip space so it slides in the cabinet without binding but doesn't feel sloppy. Start by cutting the drawer front and sides (pieces 14 and 15) to shape. Before you make the front joints, determine the precise drawer width by clamping a drawer side to each inside wall of the cabinet. Slip a scrap of plastic laminate in between the cabinet sides and drawer sides to serve as a spacer. With

everything clamped, set the drawer front in position, and mark the locations of the drawer sides on it. Lay out and cut these sliding dovetail joints with a ⅜" dovetail bit on the router table.

Once the front drawer joints are cut, confirm the length of the drawer back (piece 16), and then cut it to size. Make the notch in the drawer back for clearing the drawer stop. Cut the rabbet-and-dado joints to join the drawer back and sides, and then dry assemble the drawer box and check its fit in the cabinet. Once it slides in and out satisfactorily, disassemble the parts, and rout slots for the drawer bottom (piece 17). Chamfer the front outer ends of the drawer front. I used four ⅜"-diameter rare-earth magnets (pieces 18) to hold the drawer closed. Install one pair in the back face of the drawer front at the overlaps, and a second pair in the cabinet sides where they meet the drawer. Drill shallow holes with a Forstner bit, add a drop of epoxy in each, and press the magnets into place (make sure to check for correct polarity between each pair first). Now, glue up and clamp the drawer box joints, and check the drawer for square by measuring the diagonals. When the glue cures, slide the drawer bottom in dry, and tack it to the drawer back. Complete the drawer by installing the pull (piece 19).

Finishing Up

All that stands between you and a proper drum roll is to apply a coat of finish and add the vacuum port and insert plate (pieces 12 and 13) to the cabinet.

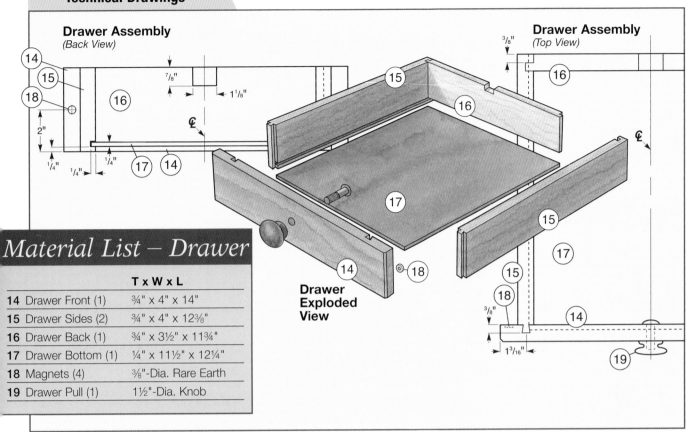

Drawer Assembly
(Back View)

Drawer Assembly
(Top View)

Drawer Exploded View

Material List – Drawer

	T x W x L
14 Drawer Front (1)	¾" x 4" x 14"
15 Drawer Sides (2)	¾" x 4" x 12⅜"
16 Drawer Back (1)	¾" x 3½" x 11¾"
17 Drawer Bottom (1)	¼" x 11½" x 12¼"
18 Magnets (4)	⅜"-Dia. Rare Earth
19 Drawer Pull (1)	1½"-Dia. Knob

Mechanical Joints for Added Strength

Step 1: *Rout ⅜" dovetail slots in the back of the drawer front on the router table. I used a backup board instead of a miter gauge to steady the workpiece for these two cuts.*

Step 2: *Complete the sliding dovetail joints for the drawer by forming pins on the sides. Again, I used a backup board here to prevent rocking.*

Step 3: *Once the drawer joints are assembled, slip the bottom panel into its slots (no glue), and then nail it to the drawer back.*

Shop-Built Disc Sander

A dedicated disc sander is a useful addition to any shop, but it's another tool expense that often falls down the list of must-haves until it never gets purchased. What you may not know is that an ordinary bench grinder is easy to convert into a disc sander by simply replacing a grinding wheel with a plywood disc and a spacer. Once you've made that switch, your new "sander" will need a sturdy platform and sanding table—the genesis for this project. If you're the resourceful sort or if you feed your woodworking hobby from a lean budget, this shop-built disc sander should have instant appeal!

by Jeff Jacobson

If you decide to build this project, use a grinder that revolves at 1,725 rpm to avoid burning your wood. The slow-speed variety used for sharpening turning tools is ideal.

Making the Base Cabinet

Get started on the cabinet by cutting the bottom, shelf, top, sides, front, and back (pieces 1 through 7) from a sheet of oak-veneered plywood (see the Material List on page 120 for dimensions). And while you're at the table saw, make the storage bin shelves (pieces 8) from ¼" plywood.

While most of the milling on this project takes place on the edges of the stock, there is a little routing required. Chuck a ¾" straight bit in your router and clamp a straightedge in place to plow the dado in the cabinet back for the cabinet shelf (see the drawing on page 121 for its location). Switch to a ¼" bit, and mill the dadoes for the storage bin shelves on the inside faces of the upper sides.

All the panels are trimmed to some degree with ¼"-thick solid walnut (piece 9), and some of this trim must be attached before you start milling grooves. See Figures 1 through 3 on page 120 for

the technique for attaching trim to the back edge of the cabinet top, the front edge of the shelf, and both the front and back edges of the cabinet bottom.

When the glue is dry, mount a ⅜" dado head in your table saw, and mill the appropriate dadoes, grooves, and rabbets (see the drawings). The grooves will be captured by the hardwood edging. As you assemble the cabinet, the method behind this construction technique will become clear.

Assembling the Base

Glue and clamp walnut trim (ripped to ¼" thickness) along the remaining plywood edges of the cabinet pieces, as shown in the exploded view on page 121. Note that the trim stops short of the rabbets on the front, back, and shelf. Dry fit and temporarily clamp the front, back, bottom, and shelf together. Double-check the size and fit of the lower side and upper sides. The sides are installed with biscuits, so you can mark their locations and cut their slots now. Glue up and clamp the cabinet, dropping the lower side (and its biscuits) in place as you do.

Next, install the upper sides and the top with glue, clamps, and biscuits, capturing the storage bin shelves. Check for squareness as you tighten the clamps.

Converting the Grinder

Here's how to convert your grinder to a sander: I decided to retrofit mine with a 12" disc to match the standard-size stick-on discs available through catalogs and home improvement centers. Use plywood for making the disc (piece 10); MDF (medium-density fiberboard) and particleboard are not structurally stable enough for this application. Start with a plywood blank, and drill a step-down center hole to match the diameter of your grinder's arbor, as well as the nut and washer. Then, cut the disc to size on the band saw. Stay just outside your layout lines, and finish to the center of the pencil line with a belt sander.

Apply plastic laminate (piece 11) to the sandpaper side of the disc, using a good-quality contact adhesive, and trim it to size with a bearing-guided flush-trim bit in a router. Break the sharp edges of the disc with sandpaper, and don't forget to remove the laminate over the center hole.

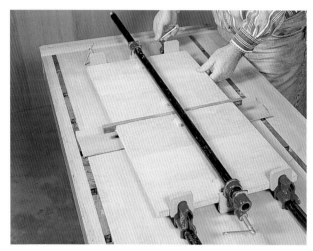

Figure 1: *Start by gluing and clamping a strip of solid hardwood between two pieces of plywood. With this approach, the clamping pressure is even and strong across the entire joint.*

Figure 2: *Rip the assembled pieces down the middle, leaving two securely attached strips of hardwood in place. The strip is machined to be a bit thicker than the plywood.*

Figure 3: *Now, simply spin the plywood panels around, and repeat the process. Whenever your trim is likely to get abuse, this method of glue-up provides a stronger bond.*

Material List – Carcass

		T x W x L
1	Cabinet Bottom (1)	¾" x 16" x 15½"
2	Cabinet Front (1)	¾" x 16" x 16½"
3	Cabinet Shelf (1)	¾" x 16" x 15⅜"
4	Cabinet Lower Side (1)	¾" x 16⅛" x 14½"
5	Cabinet Upper Sides (2)	¾" x 12¼" x 12½"
6	Cabinet Top (1)	¾" x 16" x 12¾"
7	Cabinet Back (1)	¾" x 16" x 29¾"
8	Storage Bin Shelves (2)	¼" x 15¾" x 11⅞"
9	Walnut Trim (1)	¼" x ¾" x 400"
10	Disc (1)	¾" x 12"
11	Disc Laminate (1)	1/32" x 13" x 13"
12	Disc Spacer (1)	Cut to fit
13	Grinder Sub-Base (1)	Cut to fit
14	Table (1)	1½" x 12" x 18"
15	Walnut Table Edging (1)	½" x 1½" x 43"
16	Table Laminate (1)	1/32" x 13" x 19"
17	Miter Gauge Channel (1)	Aluminum; Trim to length
18	Table Mounting Blocks (2)	1½" x 5" x 12"
19	Block Bolts and Nuts (4 Sets)	5/16" x 4"
20	Table Hinges (1 Pair)	1½" Brass
21	Table Support (1)	Brass Lid Support
22	Cabinet Casters (2)	3" Dia.
23	Cabinet Feet (2)	1½" x 3" x 3½"
24	Cabinet Handle (1)	1¼" Dia. x 14½"
25	Cabinet Handle Brackets (2)	1½" x 3" x 3½"

The handle brackets and cabinet feet are shaped exactly the same. The brackets for the feet have no borings for a handle.

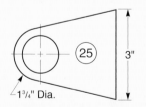
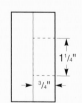

Handle Brackets
(Inside and End Views)

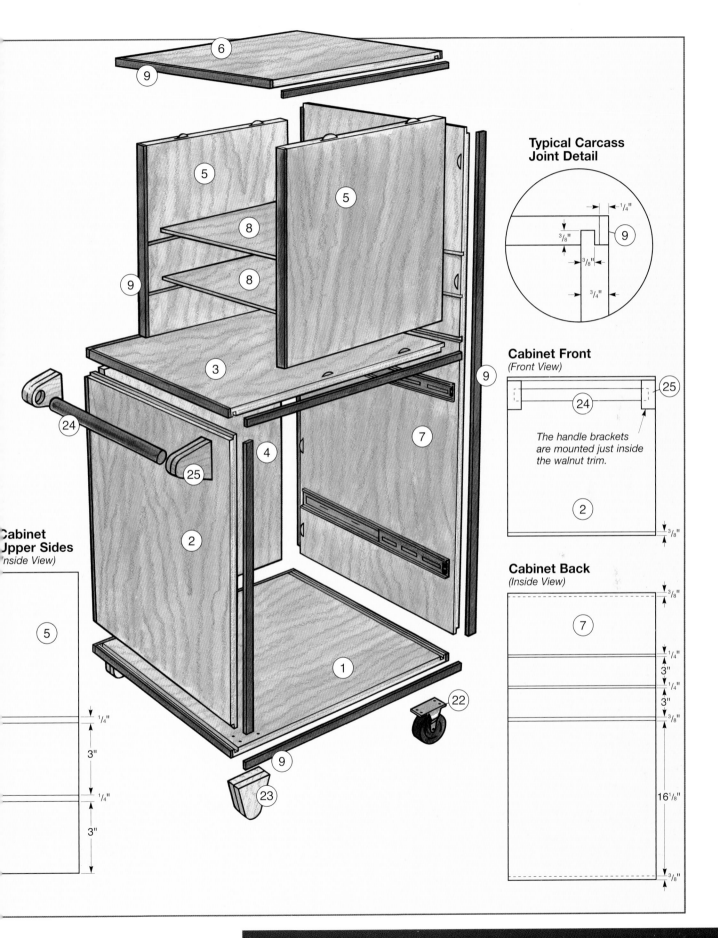

Typical Carcass Joint Detail

$1/4"$
$3/8"$
$3/8"$
$3/4"$

9

Cabinet Front
(Front View)

25
24

The handle brackets are mounted just inside the walnut trim.

2

$3/8"$

Cabinet Back
(Inside View)

$3/8"$
7
$1/4"$
3"
$1/4"$
3"
$3/8"$
$16^1/8"$
$3/8"$

Cabinet
Upper Sides
(Inside View)

5

$1/4"$
3"
$1/4"$
3"

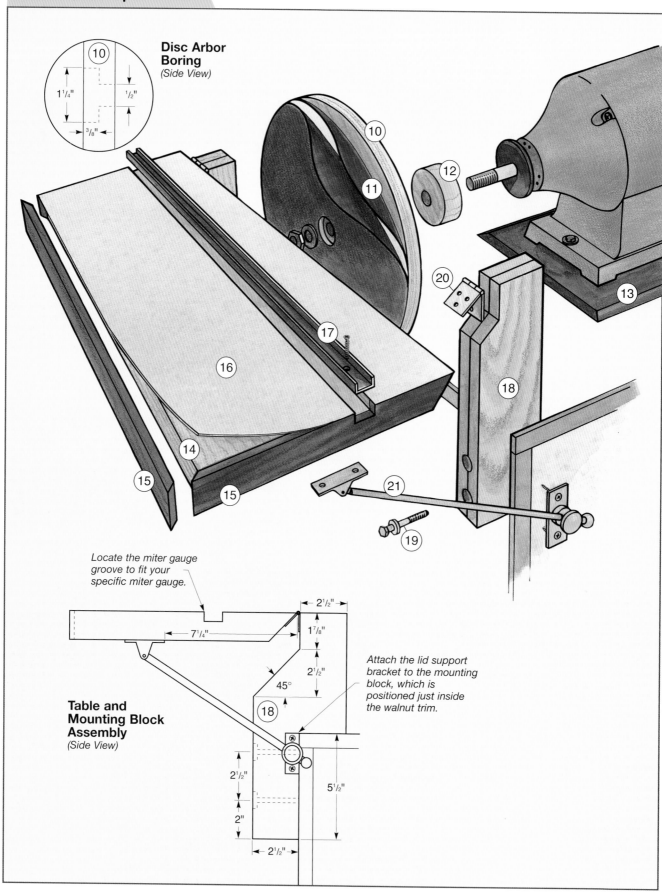

Disc Arbor Boring
(Side View)

$1^1/_4$" $^1/_2$"

$^3/_8$"

Locate the miter gauge groove to fit your specific miter gauge.

$2^1/_2$"

$7^1/_4$"

$1^7/_8$"

$2^1/_2$"

45°

Table and Mounting Block Assembly
(Side View)

Attach the lid support bracket to the mounting block, which is positioned just inside the walnut trim.

$2^1/_2$"

2"

$5^1/_2$"

$2^1/_2$"

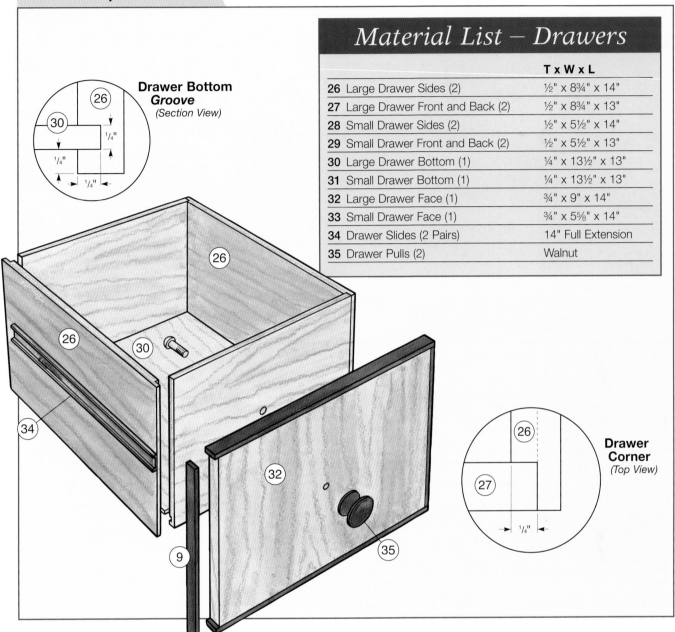

Drawer Bottom
Groove
(Section View)

Material List – Drawers

		T x W x L
26	Large Drawer Sides (2)	½" x 8¾" x 14"
27	Large Drawer Front and Back (2)	½" x 8¾" x 13"
28	Small Drawer Sides (2)	½" x 5½" x 14"
29	Small Drawer Front and Back (2)	½" x 5½" x 13"
30	Large Drawer Bottom (1)	¼" x 13½" x 13"
31	Small Drawer Bottom (1)	¼" x 13½" x 13"
32	Large Drawer Face (1)	¾" x 9" x 14"
33	Small Drawer Face (1)	¾" x 5⅝" x 14"
34	Drawer Slides (2 Pairs)	14" Full Extension
35	Drawer Pulls (2)	Walnut

Drawer Corner
(Top View)

The cylindrical hardwood spacer (piece 12) provides support for the disc, but it also takes up space on the arbor so the threads are set in from the sanding disc face. Band saw the spacer after boring the arbor hole on the drill press (to ensure that it is exactly 90° to the disc face). Slide the spacer and disc onto the arbor, and lock them in place with the nut and washer. Then, stick on an 80-grit disc, and mount the grinder on the cabinet. Depending on the model, you may have to install a sub-base (piece 13) under your grinder to achieve ¼" of

clearance between the bottom of the disc and the top of the cabinet. Alter the thickness of this piece as required by your machine.

Building an Adjustable Table
The tabletop (piece 14) is comprised of three thicknesses of ½" plywood, face glued together. The hinged edge is chamfered on the table saw at 45°, and the other three edges are laminated with ½"-thick walnut table edging (piece 15), mitered at the corners. After sanding, apply plastic laminate (piece 16) to the

top. Then, use a straight bit in your router table to plow the groove for the aluminum miter gauge channel (piece 17). Locate this groove so the edge of your miter gauge (use the one from your table saw) is about ¼" away from the disc when it's set at 60°, and then screw the channel in place (see Figure 4 on page 124).

Glue up two thicknesses of 1x stock to form blanks for the two mounting blocks (pieces 18), and band saw them to the shape shown in the drawings. Sand the blocks smooth, and then secure each to the cabinet with a pair of predrilled,

Figure 4: *By adding a miter gauge slot, this shop-built disc sander can help create compound angles.*

Figure 5: *This heavy-duty lid support allows for accurate and infinite angle adjustments. Drop the table down for storage.*

Figure 6: *Storage is always useful in the shop, and the two drawers in this cabinet will hold plenty of supplies.*

counterbored bolts (pieces 19), washers, and nuts. Attach the table to the mounts with a pair of brass hinges (pieces 20), making sure the screws are not so long that they penetrate the tabletop.

You can adjust and set the angle of the table with a heavy-duty brass lid support (piece 21). This is surface mounted by means of predrilled screws at the locations shown on the drawings (see Figure 5).

Mobilizing the Cabinet

To make your sanding center mobile, add two locking casters (pieces 22), a pair of feet (pieces 23), and a handle (piece 24). The feet and the handle brackets (pieces 25) are identical, except that the brackets feature a shallow bore to accommodate the walnut handle (see the drawings). All four parts are secured with predrilled screws driven home from inside the drawer cavity. The casters are simply screwed to the bottom of the cabinet.

Building the Drawers

The drawers in the cabinet provide handy storage space for your sanding supplies (see Figure 6). Choose high-quality, ½" plywood for the drawer sides, fronts, and backs (pieces 26 through 29). Baltic birch is an excellent choice. Cut these parts to size (see the Material List on page 123). Then, install a ½" dado head in the table saw, and plow two rabbets on the inside face of each drawer side (see the drawings). Switch to a ¼" dado head to mill a groove in each drawer side, front, and back for the drawer bottoms (pieces 30 and 31). Assemble the drawers with glue and clamps.

Both drawers fit in the same opening, so it's a good idea to install them before sizing the drawer faces (pieces 32 and 33). Use full-extension slides (pieces 34), following the manufacturer's instructions. Mount the slides after placing the drawers in the opening.

Cut the drawer faces from ¾" plywood, with the grain running vertically. Wrap the edges with walnut trim. Test fit the drawer faces using double-sided tape (allow ⅛" between the two drawers). Permanently mount the drawer faces with glue and screws. Then, drill a hole dead-center in each, and install the hardwood pulls (pieces 35).

After sanding the entire project down to 180 grit, spray or brush on three coats of satin finish. Now, you have an extremely useful addition to your woodworking tool arsenal. Better yet, half the grinder still remains for touching up those chisels or the mower blade!

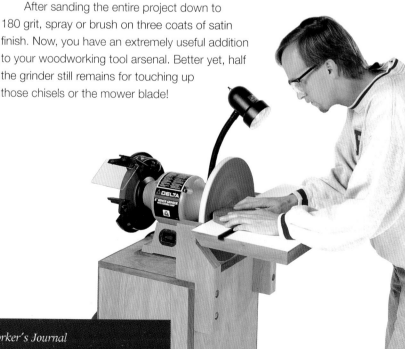

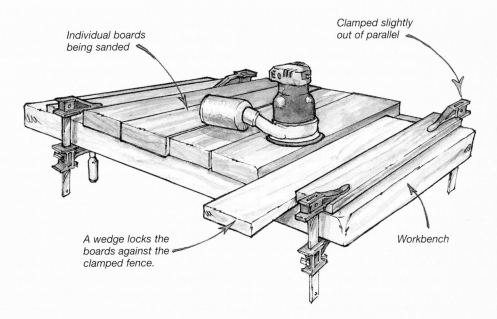

Individual boards being sanded

Clamped slightly out of parallel

A wedge locks the boards against the clamped fence.

Workbench

Sanding Jig for Multiple Boards

When you need to sand several boards of the same size, clamp two fences to your bench, leaving one at a very slight angle to the other. Then, load up the boards you need to sand, and wedge them in place between the fences with a piece of scrap. It makes for quick and easy board changes, which is great on big jobs. Just make sure the fences and wedge are thinner than the boards being sanded, so they don't get in the way along the edges of the outermost boards you're sanding.

Keep It Grounded

As dust flies through your collector hoses, it builds up static electricity on the walls of the hose. This can also occur if you use rigid plastic pipe for dust collection ductwork. To prevent sparks (and even explosions), ground metal hoses by attaching a piece of plastic-covered copper wire to the hose and to a cold-water pipe (or similar ground). Run bare wire through plastic hoses, and ground one end of this in the same fashion.

One Person's Trash. . .

Anyone who owns farm animals or small pets such as gerbils and hamsters would be delighted to get your sawdust for bedding. Just be sure you let them know what species you've been milling, and have them call their vet to make sure the

particular wood type won't harm the animals. For example, horses have been known to get colic when exposed to species such as walnut.

Making Perfectly Round Wheels

If you need a pair of wheels (or maybe even four), scribe circles on your stock and cut the wheels out on the band saw, staying just outside the lines. Drill a ¼" hole at the center of each wheel, slide the wheels onto a ¼" threaded rod, and tighten with nuts. Chuck the rod into your portable drill, clamp a wooden guide block onto the table of your disc sander, and, with the drill in reverse, sand the wheels to their final size.

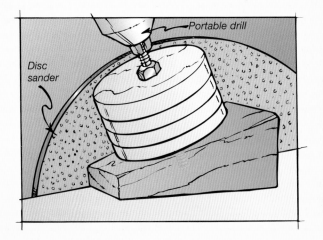

Portable drill

Disc sander

Sanding Disc Caddy

If finding a specific grit of sandpaper in your sandpaper drawer is a frustrating chore, here's an easy way to bring some order to the chaos. This handy caddy design is basically an embellishment of a simple alignment block for installing orbital sanding discs on a sander. Make several of these alignment blocks for the various grits you use and this case to store them in.

by Len Urban

The concept here is simplicity itself: Dowels on a board line up the holes on a sanding disc with your sander's pad. To install a disc, slip the orbital sander over the guide pins of the appropriate block, and press down (see Figure 1). Lift off the sander, and you're ready to sand.

The critical dimension on these blocks (pieces 1) is the location of the guide pins (pieces 2). Follow the elevation drawing on page 127, and use one of your sanding discs to verify the layout marks. Make a cardboard template, and use it as a guide for locating the pins.

The holes in the faceplate of the sander and the sanding discs are ⅜". Using ⁵⁄₁₆" dowels for the pins allows for some slight misalignment but still provides a good match between the holes in the paper and the dust extraction openings in the pad. Make enough storage blocks for the various grits you use. Five should cover it—60, 80, 100, 150, and 220 grits.

Once you've made the alignment blocks, build the storage cabinet shown in Figure 2 and in the exploded view on page 127. It simply consists of an open-faced rectangular box with a series of runners that hold the different alignment blocks.

Rather than fabricating the sides (pieces 3) individually, cut a board 13" wide x 10⅞" high. Use ¼" hardboard for the sides. Glue the five runners (pieces 4 and 5) in place at their proper locations (see the drawings). After the glue dries, cut the assembly in half vertically, and trim each half to width to make two identical case sides.

Cut the top, bottom, and back of the cabinet (pieces 6 and 7) to size. Make the back from hardboard. Glue these parts to the cabinet sides, starting with the top and bottom. You can pin the joints with brads or finish nails if you wish to hold them in place while the glue dries.

To identify the grit of the paper stored on each block, attach a label to each. The labels can be quickly made on a computer.

Figure 1: *The alignment blocks don't just store the discs, but they also make it easy to center them on your orbital sander: Just press down. The dust extraction holes line up every time.*

Figure 2: *This handy sanding caddy holds five grits' worth of sanding discs. Use the blocks to mount discs on your sander and to make each grit easy to find.*

Alignment Block
(Top View)

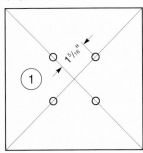

1

NOTE: *The easiest way to locate the pin holes is to draw the layout lines shown at left, lay a disk in place, and then rotate it until four of the holes intersect the lines. Or measure out from the center, as shown.*

Material List

		T x W x L
1	Alignment Blocks (5)	$^3/_4$" x $5^7/_8$" x $5^7/_8$"
2	Guide Pins (20)	$^5/_{16}$" Dia. x $1^1/_4$"
3	Sides (2)	$^1/_4$" x $5^7/_8$" x $10^7/_8$"
4	Middle Runners (8)	$^3/_8$" x $^3/_8$" x $5^7/_8$"
5	Bottom Runners (2)	$^3/_8$" x $^5/_8$" x $5^7/_8$"
6	Top/Bottom (2)	$^3/_4$" x $5^7/_8$" x $5^7/_8$"
7	Back (1)	$^1/_4$" x $6^3/_8$" x $10^7/_8$"

Storage Cabinet Side
(Section View)

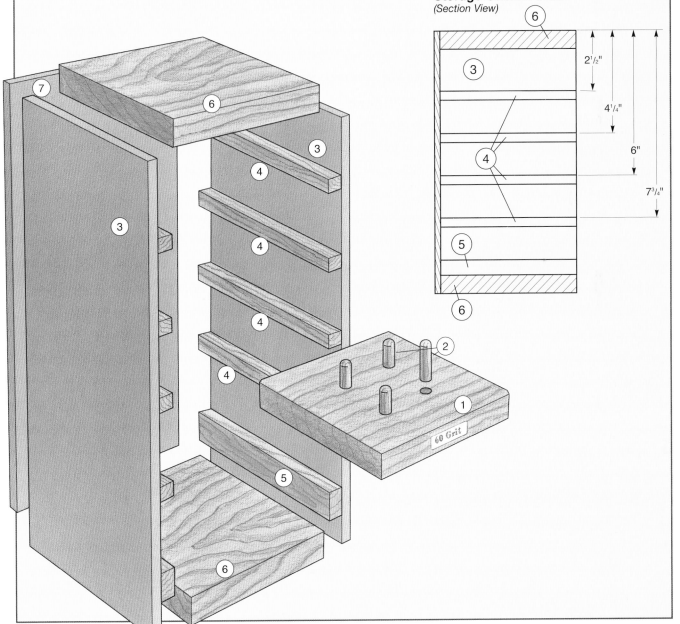

Quick and Easy Band Saw Fence

Your band sawing results will always be on the straight and narrow when you use this helpful accessory. It fits in your saw table's miter slot and clamps in place. A single-point attachment makes it perfect for resawing or for compensating for blade drift during rip cuts. Plastic laminate makes the fence face durable and slippery smooth.

by Dave Olson

For either resawing or ripping, your band saw successes will only improve with a good rip fence. This design takes just a few hours to build and can be custom-fit to any saw. This one is sized for a 14" band saw, but you can change the Material List dimensions as needed to modify the fence for your machine.

Figure 1: *For ripping operations or resawing stock that's been milled four-square, the fence alone may be all the guidance you need.*

Most band saws are equipped with decent standard features, but one of the typical weak links is the fence. Some stock fences don't adjust easily for blade drift, and most lack a point attachment for resawing. This design addresses both issues. The jig has two parts: a base and the fence. Installing the base in the saw table's miter slot automatically squares the jig to the blade. The fence fits over a pair of guides on the base so it can slide back and forth to set the width of the cut. At 5" tall, you should have ample height for typical resawing tasks on a 14" saw, and the single-point attachment makes it easy to follow a line while making adjustments for blade drift. A couple of clamps hold the assembly in place.

Baltic birch plywood is an ideal choice for this jig, since it is dimensionally stable, flat, and strong. I used hard maple for the guides and glued plastic laminate to the fence to reduce friction and improve wear resistance.

Getting Started

Begin by cutting an extralong piece of plywood 12" wide for the base and fence plate (pieces 1 and 2; see the Material List on page 130). By machining these two plates as one piece, you'll guarantee that they match perfectly. In addition, cut plywood to size for the fence and braces (pieces 3 and 4).

Now, install a ¾" dado blade in your table saw, raise it ¼", and plow the guide grooves in the plywood for the base and fence plate, as shown in the base and fence plate groove elevation on page 130. Cut this plywood into the two pieces for the jig, and plow a ⅛"-deep rabbet in the base for the band saw slot guide.

To cut a perfect groove in the back of the fence for the fence plate, match your dado blade width exactly to the thickness of your plywood (make two passes with a narrower blade if necessary), and be sure the distance from the groove to the bottom edge of the fence also equals the plywood's thickness (see the fence joint detail on page 130). Getting these measurements dead-on is the key to keeping your completed fence plumb at any position on the band saw table.

After cutting the fence groove, trace the brace pattern on page 131 onto your stock, band saw the pieces to shape, and round the top corners of the fence. Next, drill all the countersunk pilot holes for screwing the pieces of the jig together. Then, join the fence, fence plate, and braces with glue and screws (pieces 5).

Joint the edges of some ½"-thick maple, and rip these edges off the boards a hair oversize for the guides (pieces 6 and 7). Next, plane the guides to fit the grooves in the base and the saw table. I recommend experimenting with this step, using your planer and your hand plane to find a method that works best for you.

Cover the front of the fence with white plastic laminate (piece 8); it's a good preventive measure against wear and tear, as well as a nice way to brighten up the cutting area when sawing. Cut your laminate a little larger than the fence,

Figure 2: *When working with a dull blade that tends to drift or when cutting along a scribed line, add the single-point attachment so you can pivot your stock slightly for easier tracking.*

Fence Exploded View

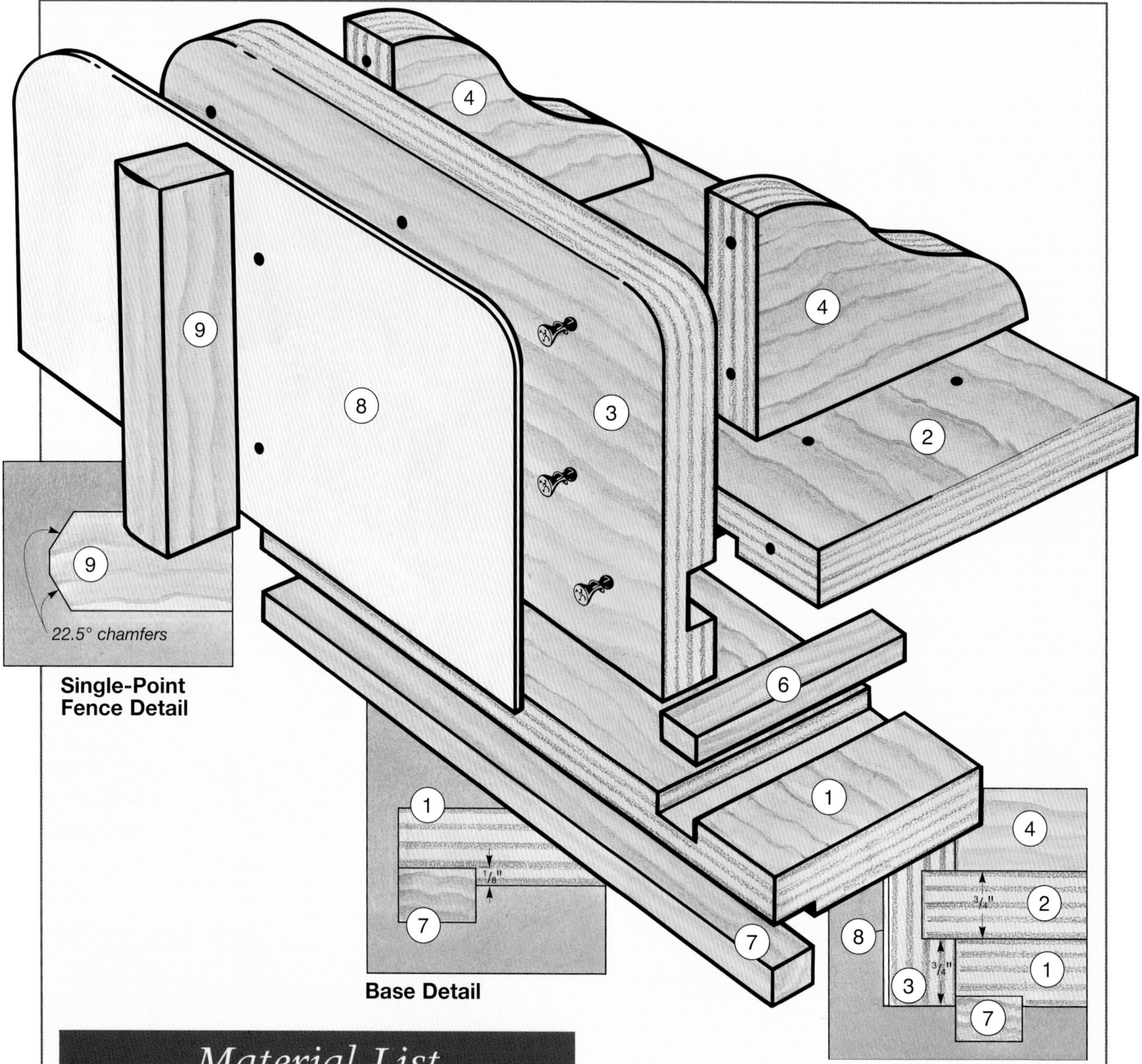

22.5° chamfers
1/8"
3/4"
3/4"

Single-Point Fence Detail

Base Detail

Fence Joint Detail

Material List

	T x W x L
1 Base (1)	¾" x 12" x 3½"
2 Fence Plate (1)	¾" x 12" x 6¼"
3 Fence (1)	¾" x 12" x 5"
4 Braces (2)	¾" x 3¼" x 5"
5 Screws (13)	#8-1½"
6 Jig Guides (2)	½" x ¾" x 3½"
7 Saw Slot Guide (1)	½" x ¾" x 12"
8 Laminate (1)	1⁄16" x 5" x 12"
9 Single-Point Fence (1)	¾" x 1½" x 5½"

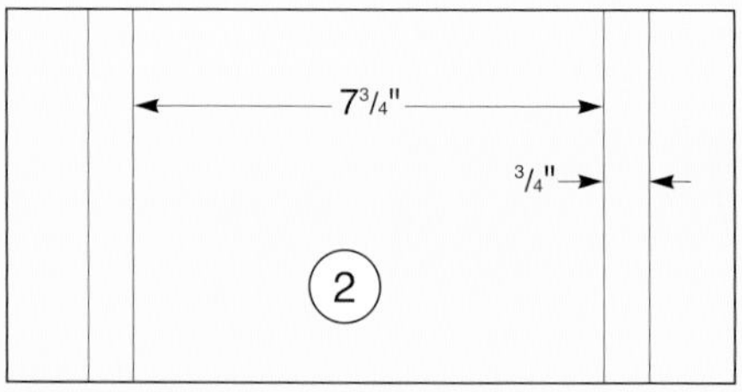

7 3/4"
3/4"
2

Base and Fence Plate Groove Elevation

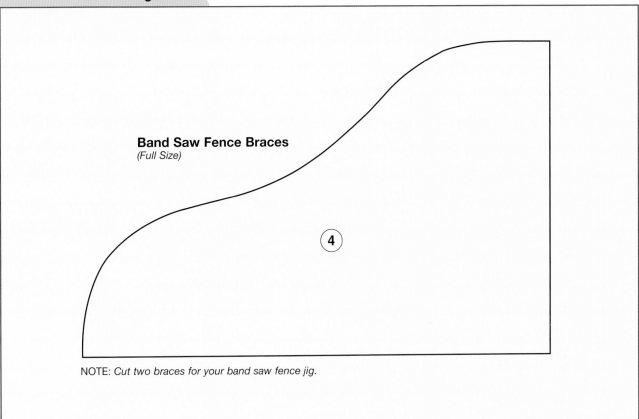

Band Saw Fence Braces
(Full Size)

④

NOTE: *Cut two braces for your band saw fence jig.*

and bond it to the plywood with yellow glue. Spread the glue evenly, and back up the laminate with a piece of scrap plywood while clamping the assembly tight. Trim the laminate with a flush-cutting router bit after giving the glue a few hours to dry.

For the single-point fence attachment (piece 9), cut a piece of maple to size, and chamfer one edge, as shown in the single-point fence detail on page 130. Sand the chamfers to improve the tracking of your stock, clamp the attachment to the fence, and fasten the parts together with screws.

Give the jig a quick sanding, and apply a protective topcoat. Avoid finishing the guides, as this may make sliding the fence more difficult. Instead, apply wax to the guides on a regular basis.

The fence works best when your saw blade is sharp and your stock is flat and square (see Figure 1 on page 129). When the blade is worn and no longer tracks accurately, or when you need to follow a line, the single-point attachment comes in handy (see Figure 2 on page 129)—as long as its crown is ⅛" ahead of the blade. Either way, this jig is bound to improve your band saw's performance.

*Quick*Tip

Sawing Straight—Consider All the Variables

It may seem counterintuitive, but if your band saw doesn't follow a straight cutting line, tightening the blade isn't necessarily the solution. Experiment with different blade tensions on scrap stock to see how performance varies. The keys to good tracking are proper blade tension, correct blade guide adjustment, and uniform blade position on the saw's flywheels. Of course, a fresh saw blade never hurts! When all of these factors harmonize, your saw should cut wood like butter.

Scroll Saw Blade Caddy

Put an end to bent or disorganized scroll saw blades when you build this simple storage caddy. Nine storage fingers tip out to hold various blade types, and interlocking cleats make the caddy easy to mount to a wall or cabinet near your saw.

by John English

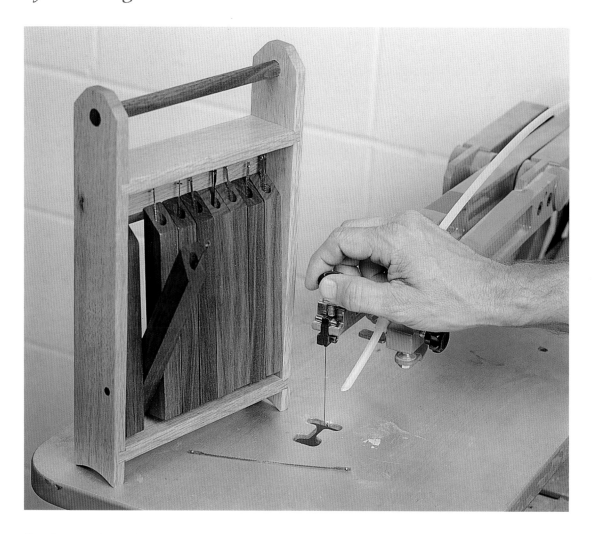

If you're a regular scroll saw user, you know that it takes more than one blade tooth configuration to cut the variety of woods, plastics, and even soft metals that you encounter in your shop projects. Trouble is, blade manufacturers don't tend to package blades in containers that hold up over the long haul. And scroll saw blades are easily bent and damaged if they're stored in a drawer with other odds and ends. My blade caddy has nine tip-out storage fingers that will keep your spare blades organized and safely stored. A hanging system consisting of a pair of interlocking French cleats makes it easy to hang it near the saw. One of these (piece 8) is attached to the wall, while the other (piece 6) is part of the caddy. Now, a fresh blade is always easy to find and just an arm's reach away.

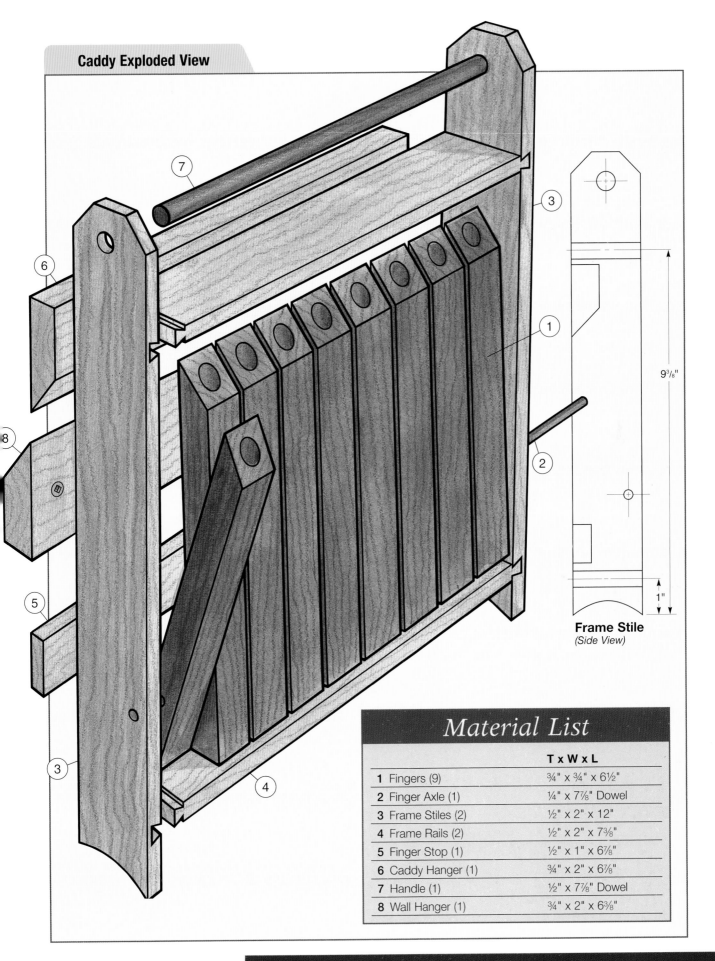

Frame Stile
(Side View)

$9^{3}/_{8}$"

1"

Material List

	T x W x L
1 Fingers (9)	$^{3}/_{4}$" x $^{3}/_{4}$" x $6^{1}/_{2}$"
2 Finger Axle (1)	$^{1}/_{4}$" x $7^{7}/_{8}$" Dowel
3 Frame Stiles (2)	$^{1}/_{2}$" x 2" x 12"
4 Frame Rails (2)	$^{1}/_{2}$" x 2" x $7^{3}/_{8}$"
5 Finger Stop (1)	$^{1}/_{2}$" x 1" x $6^{7}/_{8}$"
6 Caddy Hanger (1)	$^{3}/_{4}$" x 2" x $6^{7}/_{8}$"
7 Handle (1)	$^{1}/_{2}$" x $7^{7}/_{8}$" Dowel
8 Wall Hanger (1)	$^{3}/_{4}$" x 2" x $6^{3}/_{8}$"

Step 1: *Cut the nine ¾" square fingers (pieces 1) to size (see the Material List on page 133). Use a centering jig to drill a ⅜" hole in one end of each. Made from shop scraps, this jig is nothing more than a vertical stand that locks the workpiece into a pair of matched dadoes (see the drawings at right).*

Step 2: *On your table saw, miter the top of each finger at 45°. A long auxiliary fence equipped with a stop will ensure that all pieces are cut to the same length. Make sure you use clamps to keep your fingers away from the saw blade when working with such small parts.*

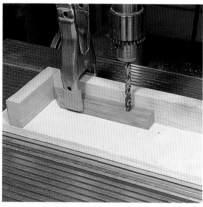

Step 3: *A simple indexing jig holds the workpiece as you drill the ⁵⁄₁₆" holes that will house the ¼" hardwood dowel axle (piece 2). Using this jig will ensure that all nine holes line up properly. Blow sawdust out of the jig between each drilling to avoid buildup.*

Step 4: *Remove most of the waste for the dovetail dadoes in the stiles (pieces 3) with a straight router bit, and then finish with a 9° x ¼" dovetail bit. To make the matching tails on the rails (pieces 4), move the fence to cover a portion of the dovetail bit (see the drawings at right).*

Step 5: *Use the drawings at right to drill ½" and ¼" dowel holes in the stiles. Then, glue and clamp the frame, including the finger stop (piece 5), caddy hanger (piece 6), and handle (piece 7). Now, dry fit the fingers and axle, and with a brace clamped behind them, sand the tops flush.*

Step 6: *Finish the fingers and all of the frame except the outsides of the stiles before final assembly. After the finish is dry, permanently install the fingers and axle. Then, sand the axle ends flush, and finish the outside faces of the caddy stiles and the wall hanger (piece 8).*

Technical Drawings

Frame Stile
(Front View)   *(Side View)*

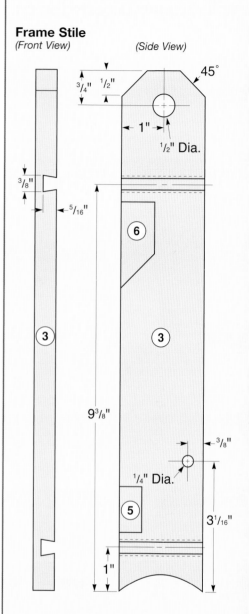

45°

¾" ½"

1"

½" Dia.

⅜"

⁵⁄₁₆"

6

3   3

9³⁄₈"

⅜"

¼" Dia.

5

3¹⁄₁₆"

1"

Frame Rail
(Front View)

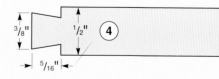

⅜"   ½"   4

⁵⁄₁₆"

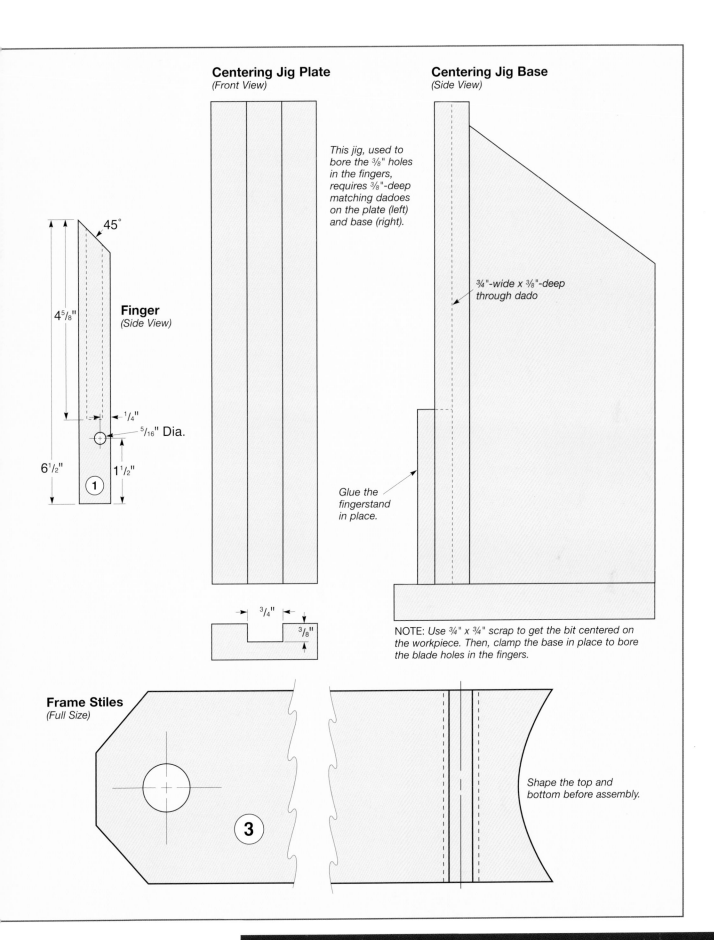

Centering Jig Plate
(Front View)

Centering Jig Base
(Side View)

This jig, used to bore the ⅜" holes in the fingers, requires ⅜"-deep matching dadoes on the plate (left) and base (right).

¾"-wide x ⅜"-deep through dado

Glue the fingerstand in place.

Finger
(Side View)

45°

4⅝"

¼"

⁵⁄₁₆" Dia.

6½"

1½"

①

¾"

⅜"

NOTE: Use ¾" x ¾" scrap to get the bit centered on the workpiece. Then, clamp the base in place to bore the blade holes in the fingers.

Frame Stiles
(Full Size)

③

Shape the top and bottom before assembly.

Sliding, Circle-Cutting Band Saw Jig

The clever use of drawer slides soups up the classic circle-cutting jig. Form circles up to 30" and larger in diameter or down to the minimum your blade will allow. Within those parameters, the jig is infinitely adjustable by using the star-knob friction locks.

by John G. Premo

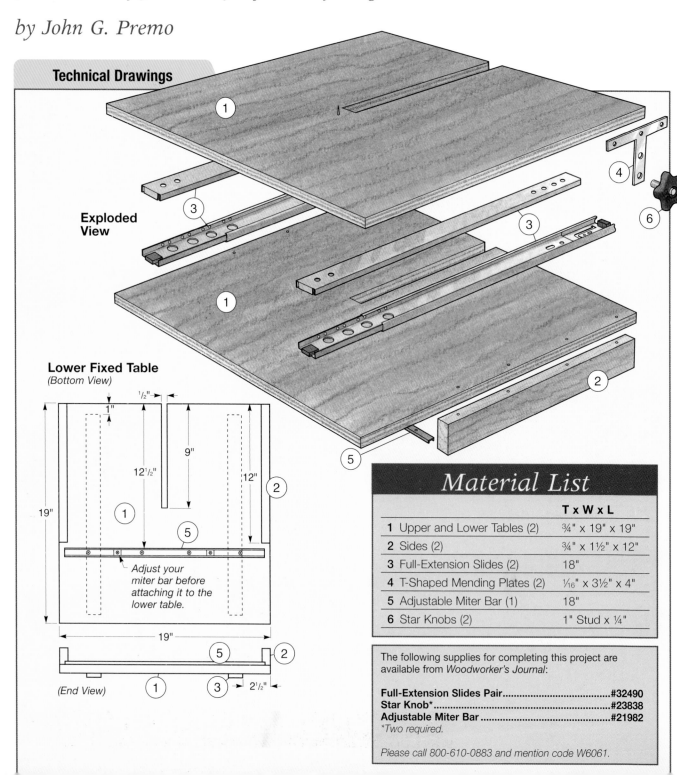

Technical Drawings

Exploded View

Lower Fixed Table
(Bottom View)

Adjust your miter bar before attaching it to the lower table.

(End View)

Material List

		T x W x L
1	Upper and Lower Tables (2)	¾" x 19" x 19"
2	Sides (2)	¾" x 1½" x 12"
3	Full-Extension Slides (2)	18"
4	T-Shaped Mending Plates (2)	1/16" x 3½" x 4"
5	Adjustable Miter Bar (1)	18"
6	Star Knobs (2)	1" Stud x ¼"

The following supplies for completing this project are available from *Woodworker's Journal*:

Full-Extension Slides Pair.........................#32490
Star Knob*..#23838
Adjustable Miter Bar ....#21982
*Two required.

Please call 800-610-0883 and mention code W6061.

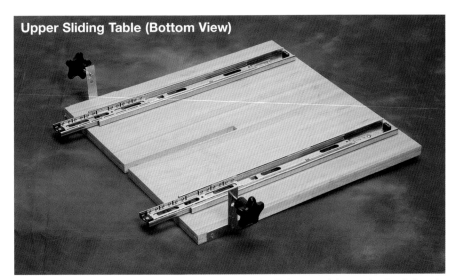

Upper Sliding Table (Bottom View)

Figure 1: *The upper sliding table gets half of the slide, the T-plates, and the star knobs. Drill and tap a hole to accommodate the threads on the star knob.*

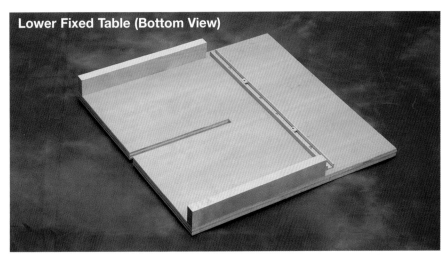

Lower Fixed Table (Bottom View)

Figure 2: *The lower fixed table gets the sides and the adjustable miter bar. Both of these pieces must be custom-fit to ensure that they fit your band saw perfectly.*

Figure 3: *In practice, a small nail is driven up through the bottom of the sliding table. That pivot point and the sliding nature of this jig will allow you to create surprisingly large circles.*

As you can see from Figures 1 through 3, there's nothing too tricky about the construction of this jig. I used quality ¾" material for the fixed and sliding tables (pieces 1) and clear stock for the sides (pieces 2). Using the dimensions in the Material List on page 136 will keep you in pretty good shape with most of the band saws out there, but I suggest you measure yours carefully to determine if any minor adjustments are necessary. After cutting the tables to overall size, use your dado set to make the slot down the middle of each one, and then clean up the cuts with a chisel.

Now, screw the sides in place on the bottom table, testing the fit on your band saw to make sure it's snug. Install the slides (pieces 3) and the mending plates (pieces 4), as shown in the elevation drawings on page 136. With those pieces put together, place the jig on your band saw, and slide it into position to find the exact location for the adjustable miter bar (piece 5) on the bottom of the base.

I drilled and tapped threaded holes in each of my mending plates to accept the star knobs (pieces 6). Before assembling your jig, drive a 1" brad up through the bottom of the upper table to serve as your pivot point, as shown in the exploded view on page 136. The brad needs to be aligned to the front of the saw blade. When you're ready to make your first circle, the radius will be the distance from the blade to the pivot point. This jig can produce circles of surprisingly large diameters. When fully extended, it is sometimes necessary to use clamps to fasten the back of the fixed table to the band saw table to prevent tilting.

Magnetic Drill Press Vise

Every now and then, it's necessary
to clamp odd-shaped or small parts
to a drill press table to drill them
safely and accurately. If your
only option is a metalworking
vise, you've probably discovered
that the jaws aren't really shaped
correctly for woodworking. It's
virtually impossible to clamp a
wooden dowel or molding securely
between them without doing damage
to the wood. No one likes to sacrifice
a carefully made part! If you cringe
each time you tighten the screw, here's
a more gentle option. Build this wood-
jawed vise, and put your other one
out to pasture.

by Dick Dorn

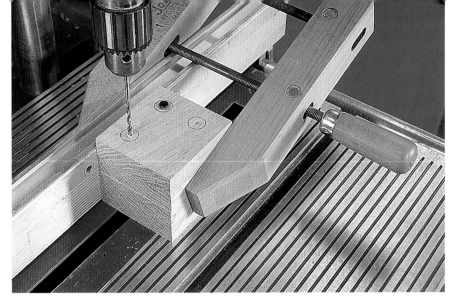

Figure 1: *Make the laminated-oak sliding jaws first. Stack the jaw parts, and machine them while they are still rectangular in shape.*

Every vise is built around a screw or spindle mechanism. If only one jaw moves, this is a single threaded spindle, and it's the common configuration for metalworking vises. In designing this project, I wanted a vise with both jaws controlled from a single handle, eventually meeting in the center of the fixture. Two moving wooden jaws would make the vise easier to operate, as well as provide a more forgiving clamping surface.

Starting with the Jaws

I built this vise out of oak because it's easy to work with and plenty strong. To take maximum advantage of that strength, face glue and screw eight pieces of stock together to create the laminated jaws (pieces 1), referring to the Material List on page 141 for dimensions. Predrill for the 12 screws (pieces 2) at the locations shown in the elevation drawings on page 141, and counterbore the screw holes for walnut plugs (pieces 3). The screws add extra strength to the finished jaws and work as clamps during the glue-up process.

After the glue dries, use the jaw subassembly drawings on page 141 and Figure 1 to locate and drill holes for the ring magnets (pieces 4) in the front face of each jaw. This is easier to do while the jaws are still rectangular. I used ¾"-diameter magnets, but to drill accurately, you should have yours in hand before drilling any

holes. You want the magnets to drop into their shallow bores with a snug friction fit. Use a Forstner bit on the drill press to bore these holes cleanly.

Now, cut each jaw to shape on your band saw (see the jaw subassembly drawings and Figure 2 on page 142). Glue and plug the screw bores, and after the glue dries, trim the plugs flush with a sharp chisel. Then, sand the jaws, and set them aside.

Building Removable Liners

Not everything a woodworker needs to clamp is nice and square, and the removable jaw liners on this vise are designed to handle a diverse assortment of shapes. By inserting just one liner, you can clamp irregular stock, such as triangular or decorative moldings that only have one flat surface. With both liners installed, dowels and other round stock are a breeze to clamp firmly either vertically or horizontally (see Figure 3 on page 142).

After cutting the liners (pieces 5) to size, set your table saw blade to 45°, and use a combination of the saw's miter gauge and rip fence to create the angled grooves in their faces. You'll find all the dimensions for setting up these angled cuts in the drawings on pages 140–141.

Set the saw back to 90° to clean out the squared-off bottom of each groove,

and head for the drill press to bore holes for the magnets that hold the liners to the vise jaws (but don't install the magnets yet).

Making the Frame

The jaws of this vise slide along a frame composed of two sides (pieces 6) and a couple of endcaps with removable wedges (pieces 7 and 8). The sides are rectangular stock with a rabbet cut on one edge (see the side detail drawing on page 140). Cut these rabbets on your table saw. Then, adjust the height of the blade, and use your miter gauge to nibble out the notches on the ends of each frame side. You could do this on your band saw, but it might be difficult to get an absolutely square cut.

See the frame endcap with wedge drawing on page 141 to locate the ½"-diameter hole for the threaded spindle in each endcap, and drill these holes. To make assembling the vise easier, a wedge-shaped part of each endcap must lift off. With your drill press, predrill and countersink holes for the two screws (pieces 9) used to reattach the wedges. Then, following the drawings, use your scroll saw to remove each wedge.

To complete the frame assembly, predrill and counterbore holes for the screws to hold the assembly together (pieces 10) and the plugs to cap them (pieces 11). Now, bore 10 holes in the frame sides for the magnets (see the

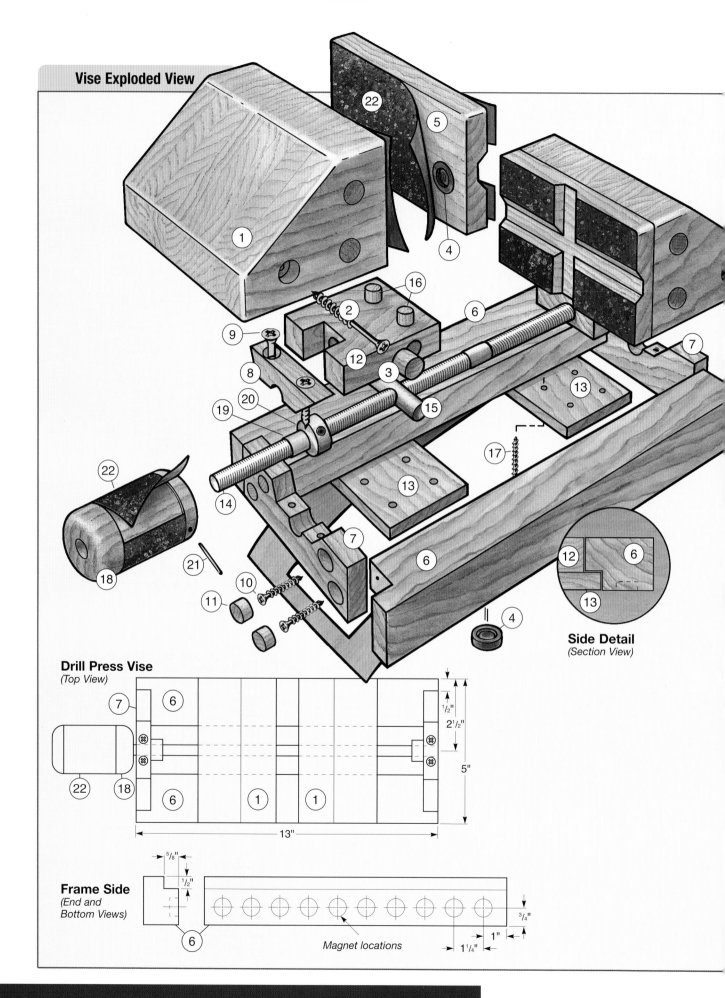

Vise Exploded View

1

22

5

4

16

2

9

12

6

8

3

7

19 20

15

13

22

14

17

13

21

18

11

10

6

7

12   6

4

13

Side Detail
(Section View)

Drill Press Vise
(Top View)

7

6

6   6

1   1

22   18

¹/₂"

2¹/₂"

5"

13"

Frame Side
*(End and
Bottom Views)*

⁵/₈"

¹/₂"

6

³/₄"

1"

1¹/₄"

Magnet locations

Material List

	T x W x L			T x W x L
1 Laminated Jaws (2)	3" x 6" x 3⅜"		**12** Drive Blocks (2)	⅞" x 2" x 2⅜"
2 Jaw Screws (12)	2½" x #10, Square-X		**13** Lock Plates (2)	⁹⁄₁₆" x 2¾" x 2⅞"
3 Jaw Plugs (12)	⅝" Dia. x ⅜"		**14** Double Threaded Spindle (1)	⁷⁄₁₆" Dia. x 14¼"
4 Ring Magnets (32)	¾" O.D.		**15** Spindle Nuts (2)	⅝" Dia. x 1¾"
5 Liners (2)	¾" x 3" x 6"		**16** Drive Block Dowels (4)	½" Dia. x 1½"
6 Frame Sides (2)	1½" x 2" x 13"		**17** Drive Block Screws (8)	1" x #6, Square-X
7 Frame Endcaps (2)	⅝" x 1½" x 5"		**18** Handle (1)	2" Dia. x 3½"
8 Wedges (2)	⅝" x ½" x 2⅜"		**19** Brass Sleeves (4)	½" OD x ⅝"
9 Endcap Wedge Screws (4)	1¼" x #6, Brass		**20** Spindle Collars (2)	½" ID
10 Frame Screws (8)	1½" x #8, Square-X		**21** Retaining Pin (1)	⅛" Dia. x 1⅞"
11 Frame Screw Plugs (8)	⅝" Dia. x ¼"		**22** Nonskid Tape (1)	3" x 60"

Jaw and Drive Block Subassembly
(Face and End Views)

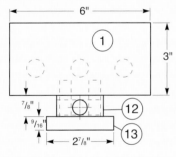
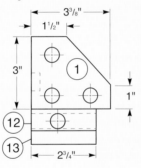

Drill Press Vise
(Side View)

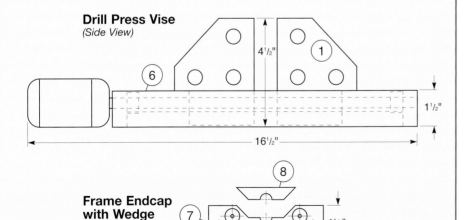

Frame Endcap with Wedge
(End View)

drawings for the hole locations). Magnets will help in setups, but don't rely on their holding strength alone; the vise should always be clamped securely to the drill press table during use. Complete the frame by gluing and screwing it together, and then install and sand the plugs.

Adding Drive Blocks and Lock Plates

An oak drive block (piece 12) is attached to the bottom of each jaw; these ride between the frame sides to keep the jaws in line. A simple rectangular lock plate (piece 13) is attached to the bottom of each drive block (one of the final assembly steps). These plates ride in the rabbets on the frame sides and prevent the jaws from lifting off the frame during clamping.

After cutting the drive blocks to size, use your miter gauge to nibble a rectangular notch in one end of each (see the exploded view on page 140). Then, move to your drill press, and using your old steel vise one last time, bore a ½"-diameter hole through the middle of each block. This allows the threaded spindle (piece 14) to pass through (see Figure 4 on page 142).

Switch to a ⅝"-diameter bit to bore a large hole across the grain in each drive

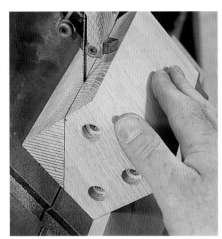

Figure 2: *Use your band saw to complete the laminated jaw's shape. See the elevation drawings for all the dimension details.*

Figure 3: *Use a single liner or both liners at once to effectively grip and secure a wide variety of moldings or other shaped pieces. Difficult end-grain drilling is made easy with this vise fixture.*

block (see the drawings for location). These holes are for the cylindrical spindle nuts (pieces 15) that thread onto the spindle and allow the blocks to move when the spindle is turned. Predrill for the dowels (pieces 16) and screws (pieces 17) to lock the blocks to the jaws (again, see the drawiings for the locations).

Use dowel centers to lay out the dowel drilling locations in the bottom of each jaw, and drill these holes. When everything lines up, glue the dowels in place and the blocks to the jaws, but leave the lock plates aside until final assembly.

Turning the Handle

The cylindrical handle (piece 18) on this vise is large enough to grasp and twist tightly, yet its shape allows for delicate adjustments equally well.

If you don't own a lathe, you should be able to locate 2" oak handrail stock at your local lumberyard. If you decide to turn the handle, use glued-up stock, rather than a single piece of wood, to prevent splitting. Either way, bore out the center (for the spindle) on your drill press before rounding over the ends. Make this boring $7/16$" in diameter. Then, round over the ends of the handle on your router table using a bearing-guided

$3/8$"-radius roundover bit. If you're turning the handle on a lathe, do all your shaping and sanding while the handle is chucked in the machine.

Sand all the wooden parts, dry fit them together, and apply finish. Use a hard finish like varnish; oil is not a good choice, as it tends to soak into clamped parts when they are under pressure.

Time for Final Assembly

Begin the assembly process by sliding the spindle nuts into their borings in the drive blocks and threading the spindle through them. Twirl the drive blocks (and, of course, the jaws) until each is an equal distance from the unthreaded area in the middle of the spindle. Cut a pair of brass sleeves (pieces 19) from a length of rigid brass $1/2$"-O.D. tube. Now, with the wedges removed, spread epoxy on the top half of each of the frame's endcap holes (the halves drilled into the removable wedges), and press the brass sleeves in place.

After the epoxy sets, slip a couple more brass sleeves onto the spindle, and slide the spindle collars (pieces 20) over these. Pass the spindle ends through the brass sleeves in the frame endcaps, line up the spindle/drive block assembly on the frame, and screw the wedges in

place. Secure the lock plates with screws driven into their predrilled holes (don't epoxy them in—you may need to remove them in the future). Then, center the jaws along the frame, and secure them there by tightening the Allen bolts in the spindle collars.

Slide the handle onto the long end of the spindle, and drill a $1/8$"-diameter hole through it (see the drawings) so it pierces the handle and the spindle. Then, remove the handle, apply epoxy in the handle cavity, and remount the handle on the spindle, capping its end with a plug. While the epoxy is still liquid, secure the retaining pin (piece 21) in the handle with more epoxy dabbed in the $1/8$" hole you just drilled.

Continue using epoxy to secure all the magnets in place, keeping in mind that the ones in the jaws and liners should be installed so they attract rather than repel (a matter of flipping them to the correct side). To finish up, apply nonskid tape (piece 22) to the jaw and liner faces, the frame bottom, and the handle, as shown in the exploded view. All that's left to do is to find some round or strangely shaped parts to lock into your new drill press vise, such as those shown in Figures 5 and 6—because you're ready to make some shavings!

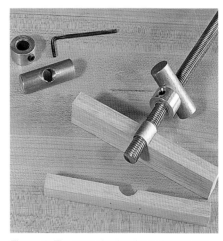

Figure 4: *The operating hardware for this drill press vise is a double threaded spindle (allowing both jaws to be driven by a single handle), teamed up with spindle nuts and collars.*

Figure 5: *With magnets to hold this drill press vise in place and a variety of clamping options available, drilling dowels and circular-shaped objects is a breeze.*

Figure 6: *Drilling odd-shaped stock is easy with this drill press fixture. The double threaded spindle allows for single-handed adjustability, and the overall stability adds a level of safety to drilling operations.*

*Quick*Tip

A steel fractional drill gauge clearly indicates the size of each drill bit, and the wooden block holds bits vertically for easy access.

Drill Bit Holder

If you have only a few twist drill bits, finding the one you need usually isn't a problem—but it's a bigger hassle if you own a full fractional set. Here's a clever way to keep them all organized next to your drill press: Buy a fractional gauge from a metalworking mail-order catalog. This is a 3" x 6" metal plate with holes ranging from ⅟₁₆" to ½", in ⅟₆₄" increments. Screw the plate to two wood blocks glued to a wooden base. Use your drill press to drill down into the base through each of the fractional gauge holes with the correct-diameter bit. Make a ½"- or ⅜"-deep hole for each bit. That way, the holes in the base will hold the bits securely and straight up. Then, load the holder with bits. Now, your bits are visibly numbered and neatly organized. Store them with the cutting end down for added safety.

Adjustable Dado Jig

How do you rout dadoes to match plywood that is a hair under ¾" or lumber that is ¹⁄₃₂" too thick? What you need is an adjustable auxiliary router base that will form one edge of a dado at a time. Two passes will equal the perfect dimension, every time!

by Ralph Bagnall

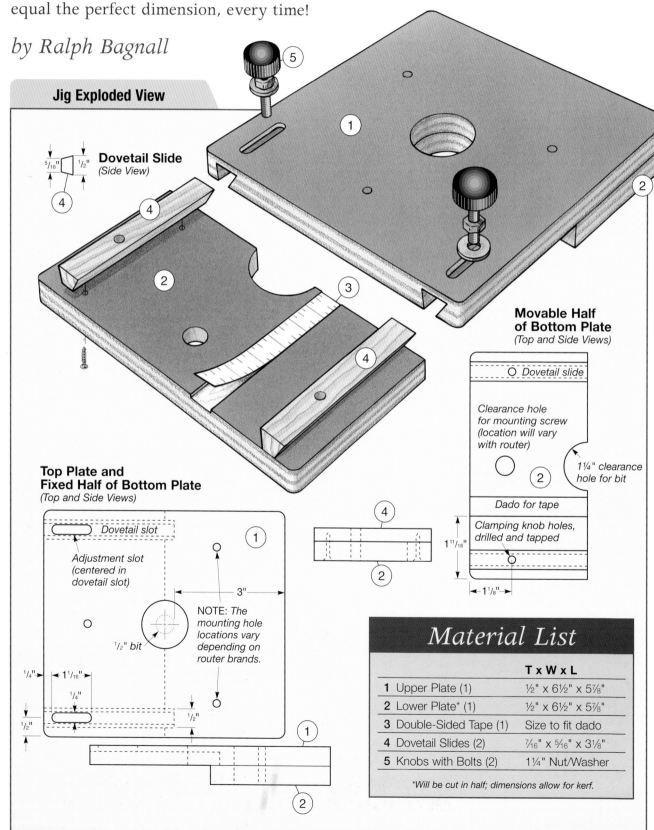

Jig Exploded View

Dovetail Slide (Side View)
⁵⁄₁₆" ½"

Movable Half of Bottom Plate (Top and Side Views)

Dovetail slide

Clearance hole for mounting screw (location will vary with router)

1¼" clearance hole for bit

Dado for tape

Clamping knob holes, drilled and tapped

1¹¹⁄₁₆"

1¹⁄₈"

Top Plate and Fixed Half of Bottom Plate (Top and Side Views)

Dovetail slot

Adjustment slot (centered in dovetail slot)

3"

½" bit

NOTE: The mounting hole locations vary depending on router brands.

¼"   1¹⁄₁₆"
¼"
½"   ½"

Material List

	T x W x L
1 Upper Plate (1)	½" x 6½" x 5⅞"
2 Lower Plate* (1)	½" x 6½" x 5⅞"
3 Double-Sided Tape (1)	Size to fit dado
4 Dovetail Slides (2)	⁷⁄₁₆" x ⁵⁄₁₆" x 3⅛"
5 Knobs with Bolts (2)	1¼" Nut/Washer

Will be cut in half; dimensions allow for kerf.

Every woodworker knows that ¾" is not really three-quarters of an inch and that virtually no two boards are exactly the same thickness. This makes milling snug-fitting dadoes difficult indeed, and it was the impetus for creating this adjustable dado jig.

While there are a number of tried-and-true methods for cutting perfectly sized dadoes, I wanted to be able to set a single straightedge and mill most any size dado needed—in just two passes. My solution involved running two of the auxiliary base's edges along the straightedge. One edge is a fixed distance from the cutting edge of the bit, and the second can easily move in and out to adjust the final dado width.

Milling the Base Pieces

Review the Material List on page 144. Then, begin by cutting ½" material to form the two plates (pieces 1 and 2) of the auxiliary base. It is important that the next step is exactly matched top to bottom, so stick the two parts together with double-sided tape. Lay out the mounting hole locations for your router on the face of the top plate so the cutting edge of your ½" straight bit will be exactly 3" from the fixed edge of the jig (see the elevation drawing of the top plate on page 144). Drill the mounting holes and the clearance hole for the bit through both layers. Separate the two parts, and turn the top plate over to countersink the mounting holes and mill the dovetail slots, as shown in the drawings. Next, mill the ¼" adjustment slots through the top plate, along the centerlines of the dovetail slots.

The lower plate is now cut in half, and the mounting holes are bored out to ½" to provide clearance for the mounting screws. The front half is glued to the top plate to create the fixed edge of the jig. A shallow ½"-wide dado is milled in the movable base for a stick-on ruler (piece 3). For safety, the hardwood dovetail slides (pieces 4) are milled along one edge of a wider ½" board to fit the slots. Once they slide smoothly in the slots, trim them off on the table saw. To attach them, slip them into the slots, clamp the second half of the bottom plate to the rest, and screw (but don't glue) the half plate to the slides. Finally, with the movable base set flush, drill and tap the holes for the clamping knobs (pieces 5).

Using the Jig

Let's say you need a tight-fitting ¹⁹⁄₃₂" dado, and you have a ½" bit chucked in your router. To use the jig, first clamp your straightedge 3" from the desired edge of the dado. Use the tape measure to set the movable edge to ³⁄₃₂" (the difference between the bit and the desired width

of the dado). Tighten your knobs, and make the first pass with the movable edge riding along the straightedge. Spin the router around so the fixed edge is along the straightedge, and form the other wall of your dado—exactly ¹⁹⁄₃₂" wide! Perfect dadoes every time.

The second pass with this jig widens the dado for a perfectly snug fit.

Veneer Jointing Jig

You can use this jointer jig to create dramatic book-matched panel doors and veneered tabletops.

by Bruce Kieffer

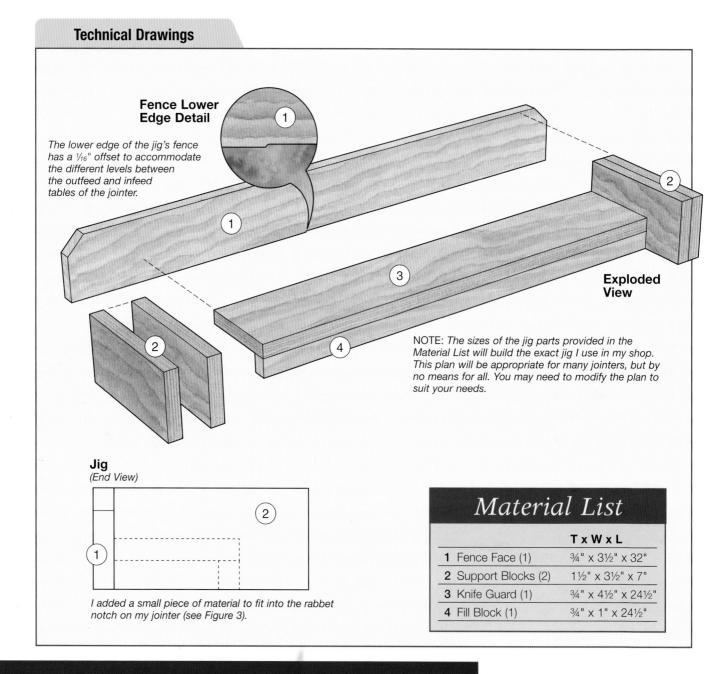

Fence Lower Edge Detail

The lower edge of the jig's fence has a 1/16" offset to accommodate the different levels between the outfeed and infeed tables of the jointer.

Exploded View

NOTE: *The sizes of the jig parts provided in the Material List will build the exact jig I use in my shop. This plan will be appropriate for many jointers, but by no means for all. You may need to modify the plan to suit your needs.*

Jig
(End View)

I added a small piece of material to fit into the rabbet notch on my jointer (see Figure 3).

Material List

		T x W x L
1	Fence Face (1)	¾" x 3½" x 32"
2	Support Blocks (2)	1½" x 3½" x 7"
3	Knife Guard (1)	¾" x 4½" x 24½"
4	Fill Block (1)	¾" x 1" x 24½"

Figure 1: *To achieve a tight joint on bookmatched veneer, you need to get a perfectly straight edge on the two flitch pieces.*

Figure 3: *Once the edges are straight, tape them together. Then, glue the joint, as shown here, and lay them flat until the glue cures.*

I've been veneering for many years, and I've tried nearly every imaginable method to quickly and accurately joint the edges of the veneers I want to join together (see Figure 1). I've tried router jigs, table saw jigs, and hand planes. I didn't like any of those ways, so I settled on using the common method of sandwiching my veneer sheets between two pieces of solid wood, clamping that all together, and passing the entire mess over my jointer. That method works okay, but it's really slow, and you have to deal with clamp heads interfering with the jointer's fence and other problems.

Channeling Inventiveness

So, there I was some years ago, using the sandwich method, when it hit me—why not make an auxiliary fence that creates a narrow channel next to the jointer's fence and just pass the sheets through the channel? I quickly whipped together a prototype jig, tested it, and found it worked better than I had imagined.

As you can see, this jig is simple to make. I used Baltic birch plywood for mine, although MDF (medium-density fiberboard) would work fine, too. The outfeed side of the jig is stepped up 1/16"

to accommodate the different heights of the infeed and outfeed tables. I added some material to the bottom of the left support block to fill in where my jointer's rabbeting notch is cut in the outfeed table. You'll need to modify your jig to work best with your jointer.

To use the jig, turn off and unplug the jointer, make sure the jointer's knife head is not spinning, set the cutting depth to 1/16", and remove the jointer's guard. Clamp the auxiliary fence over the knives and to the jointer's tables (see Figure 2). Adjust the jointer's fence so there's a narrow channel between the fence and the auxiliary fence. To do this, I place two sheets of veneer between the fences, pull them together tightly, and then snug down the jointer's fence. The gap is then large enough for jointing one piece of veneer at a time.

I think you will find this is a great way to joint the edges of your veneers. So, give it a try, get those edges straight, and move on to creating your veneers (see Figure 3).

Figure 2: *Use an auxiliary fence to support the veneer sheets while jointing their edges. Just like when jointing solid wood, it's important to orient the grain direction correctly to avoid edge tearout.*

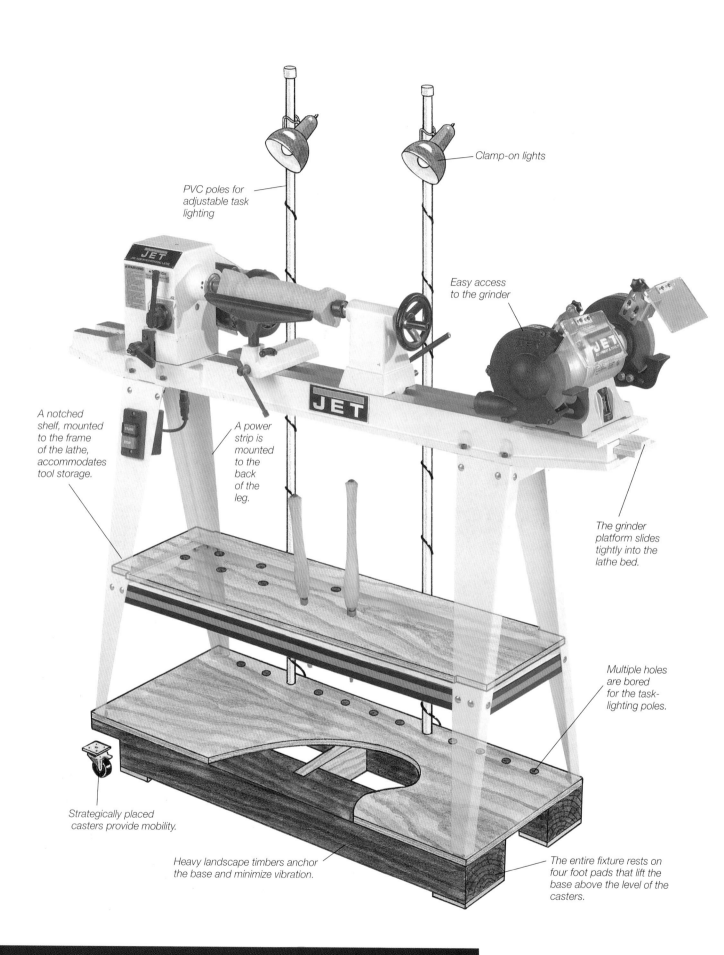

PVC poles for adjustable task lighting

Clamp-on lights

Easy access to the grinder

A notched shelf, mounted to the frame of the lathe, accommodates tool storage.

A power strip is mounted to the back of the leg.

The grinder platform slides tightly into the lathe bed.

Multiple holes are bored for the task-lighting poles.

Strategically placed casters provide mobility.

Heavy landscape timbers anchor the base and minimize vibration.

The entire fixture rests on four foot pads that lift the base above the level of the casters.

Customized Portable Lathe Station

Lathes are one category of shop machinery that is easy to soup up for improved performance and convenience. This lathe station will add portability, tool storage, sharpening capability, and task lighting to your machine for about $75.

by Peter Walsh

Most home-shop floor-standing lathes are well designed machines right out of the shipping carton. But a good machine can usually be made even better with a few enhancements. My lathe station will set you back about $75 and take about a day to construct, but it will add storage, mass, and better lighting right where you need it most. Although the design you see here was intended for my Jet lathe, the concepts can be adapted to virtually any midsize lathe brand or base style.

The first order of business is to add enough weight to ensure that your lathe stays put under duress. My heavy-duty base adds significant mass and rigidity to the stand, and it helps to reduce vibration while turning large or eccentric stock. Portability results from casters strategically positioned in notches cut into the base timbers.

To provide a four-point stance, add ¾" plywood pads below the notched landscape timbers. When you're ready to move the station, simply pick up the tailstock end until the casters clear the pads (about 20°). Center the lathe on the bottom subassembly, and bolt it in place. Drill a series of deep holes on the back edge of the base so you can reposition a lamp pole wherever you need the light as you work (see Figure 1).

I added other custom features, including handy tool storage and a bed-mounted grinder platform for touching up chisel edges without having to move

away from the lathe (see Figure 2). The grinder jig's T-shaped base is sized to fit into the slot in the lathe bed. Use a couple of long carriage bolts and wing nuts to bolt the base to a second filler piece that fits underneath the bed rail and clamps the jig securely.

I drilled a series of different-size holes in the top shelf for accommodating chisel and related tool storage.

Power for the grinder and other auxiliary items (lights, sander, and so forth) comes from a power strip mounted vertically on the stand leg under the lathe motor. This location facilitates access and yet is out of the way of any turning operation. (Note: Don't use this power strip to provide primary power to the lathe

motor, because the amperage won't be sufficient for the load.)

The lamp pole concept is better than clamping task lights directly to your lathe—it keeps them clear of turning tools or spinning blanks and prolongs the bulb life by reducing extra vibration. The holes also allow you to reposition the light for both grinding and turning operations. Use ordinary clamp-on lamps to simplify height adjustment.

You may also want to add a couple of boxes to store the multitude of chucks, faceplates, centers, and other turning and finishing materials that you're sure to add to your collection.

With a customized stand like this, turning will never be sweeter.

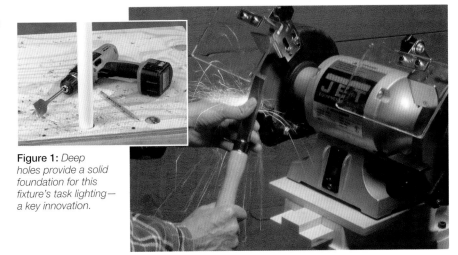

Figure 1: *Deep holes provide a solid foundation for this fixture's task lighting—a key innovation.*

Figure 2: *Quick access to your grinder is another of the custom features that make this lathe station a winner.*

Lathe Attachment for Sanding

Lathe turning and sanding go hand in hand. Many items that come off the lathe need a little touch-up sanding before they're complete. Here's a way to turn your motorized belt sanding/grinding station into a quick and versatile lathe-powered accessory that mounts directly to the outboard side of the lathe.

by Dick Dorn

When the loud motor on my sander/grinder stopped working, I didn't even think about getting a new one. I simply tossed the motor, made a few quick modifications, and then mounted the sander/grinder on the outboard side of my woodturning lathe (see Figure 1).

As a result, the tool actually works better now than when it was brand-new. The loud noise is gone, the sander has variable speed and more power, and it runs more smoothly because it's now a stationary tool.

Most of the sander/grinders available these days are designed to use 1" x 30" or 1" x 42" sanding belts that travel over three flat pulleys arranged in a triangular pattern. The lower pulley is attached directly to the motor and serves to drive the sanding belt. The top pulley, which is kept under spring tension to keep the sanding belt tight, is vertically aligned with the lower pulley and generally features a simple mechanism to change the angle of the pulley axle so the belt tracks straight. A third idler pulley is located at the rear of the vertical frame to allow adequate clearance around the sander table. The table is small, and a curved or flat metal platen is positioned behind the sanding belt to absorb the pressure of the work during sanding operations.

Stripping the Parts

When I decided to mount the sander/ grinder on the outboard side of my lathe, I started by removing the motor housing and the motor. Next, the attached lower pulley, table, and platen arrangement were removed so all that remained was a vertical and horizontal frame, the top pulley, and the idler pulley. The all-important spring-loaded belt-tightening mechanism also remained intact, along with the belt-tracking system. If you were to build such a jig from scratch, these two parts would prove to be the most difficult to duplicate. Both are essential for smooth operation.

To replace and duplicate the size of the original lower drive pulley, laminate some hardwood together, screw it to the outboard faceplate, and turn it in place (see Figure 2). Then, complete your

Figure 2: *The new lower drive pulley is turned right in place on the outboard faceplate, which serves as the power source for the salvaged belt sander.*

new pulley with a few coats of varnish. Cover it with antiskid tape to prevent the sanding belt from slipping.

At this point, you'll need to fabricate your sanding attachment using a little trial and error. When putting a jig like this together, much depends on the particular lathe to which it is being attached. In my case, a piece of plywood was placed against the outboard end of the lathe and secured with bolts and wing nuts for easy removal. A flat plywood surface was attached to that piece at a right angle and carefully braced so it would support the vertical frame of the sander, as well as its two vertical table supports (see Figure 3). You may be able to increase the table size slightly (a nice benefit!) and position it just above the headstock of the lathe.

Construct a new platen from 1"-thick wood, and fasten it to the table top from underneath. I found that my shop-made platen is much more stable than the original metal platen as pressure is applied during sanding tasks. This arrangement does eliminate the possibility of tilting the table, but that may not be a concern for the work you typically do, and it simplifies the construction process. If you want the table to tilt, you could easily incorporate an adjustable lid support and come up with another way to attach the platen. I recommend adding a small

shield at the top of the sander to deflect any material that the sanding belt carries over the top pulley.

When I'm ready to use the lathe, it only takes a moment to remove the sanding belt to prevent needless wear on the pulley bearings.

As mentioned earlier, there are many models and sizes of woodturning lathes and sander/grinders. If you're willing to undertake a little trial and error construction, I think you'll find that any combination, with the right modifications, will make an ideal belt sander lathe attachment.

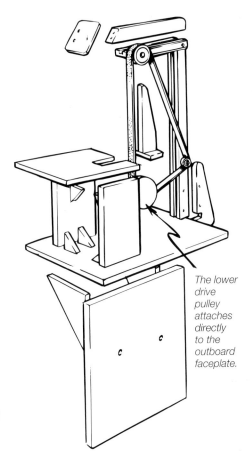

The lower drive pulley attaches directly to the outboard faceplate.

Figure 3: *This exploded view illustrates how simple it is to expand a lathe's capabilities by using the outboard faceplate as a power source.*

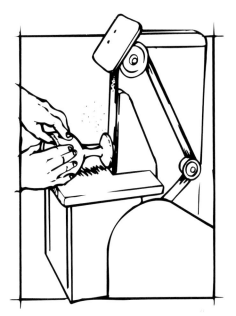

Figure 1: *The sander/grinder was given new life after the original motor blew. With a few modifications, the unit now runs off the outboard faceplate of the lathe. With an alternative platen arrangement and a piano hinge, the top could easily be tilted to hone turning tools for even more functionality.*

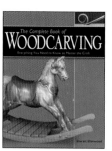

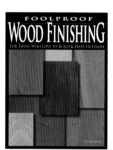